STUDIES ON THE GHANIAN ECONOMY
Volume 3

The Industrial Sector

Amoah Baah-Nuakoh
Associate Professor of Economics
University of Ghana, Legon

D1387227

WOELI PUBLISHING SERVICES
ACCRA
2003

Published by
WOELI PUBLISHING SERVICES
P. O. Box NT 601
Accra New Town
Ghana

Tel. (233-21) 227182
Fax. (223-21) 229294
Email. woeli@libr.ug.edu.gh

© A. Baah-Nuakoh, 2003
ISBN 9964-978-94-4
ALL RIGHTS RESERVED

This publication was funded by African Economic
Research Consortium (AERC), Nairobi, Kenya

Cover Design by George Siaw

PRODUCED IN GHANA

Typeset by GertMash, Accra
Printed by Paragon Printing Press, Accra New Town

For
MY MOTHER
Akua Benewa
as well as
Beatrice, Kwame, Kofi
Kwaku and Afua

Contents

Preface

This is the third of a three-volume series on the Ghanaian economy and devoted solely to the Industrial Sector. The first volume concentrated on the period before 1981 and covered several issues. The second volume was devoted to the environment, the informal sector and factor markets. The papers in this volume, with the exception of the chapters on Obstacles to Growth and Expansion of the Manufacturing Sector; Inter-Firm Linkages; and Demand for Carbonated Soft Drinks, are a collection of the works of the author. The other three have been written jointly with Kwame Baah-Nuako, Dr. Kwadwo Tutu and William Baah-Boateng respectively.

The book will be useful to economists and those interested in issues on the industry and also for the course on Industrial Economics taught at the African Economic Research Consortium (AERC) Joint Facility for Electives in Nairobi, Kenya and other graduate economics programmes.

The works have been supported by various organizations during their initial preparations. The conversion of the various works into this book was made possible more recently by the African Economic Research Consortium based in Nairobi which generously funded the revisions of the papers and the publication of the book.

I am grateful to a number of people, the Executive Director of the AERC, Professor William Lyakurwa who is the Training Director and Deputy Executive Director of AERC. A number of people have provided peer reviews of the studies in this volume. My thanks also go to Dr M. Utton and Mr. M. Mcqueen of Reading University who commented on earlier versions of the chapters on factor use.

I am grateful to my wife Beatrice and the children Kwame, Kofi, Kwaku and Afua for their support and sacrifices.

CHAPTER ONE

Introduction and Overview

This book examines the performance of the industrial sector, emphasizing that manufacturing which constitutes about 60% of sector and the policy and institutional framework within which the sector has functioned, the constraints facing the sector especially since the beginnings of the Economic Recovery Programme. It also examines some of the issues of factor use discussed in Volume 2 empirically, examining the issues of factor intensity, factor substitution, x-efficiency, and technology choice within an imperfectly competitive environment within the Ghanaian context.

Industrial Statistics in Ghana

Industrial Statistics in Ghana are defined to cover the following sectors: mining and quarrying, manufacturing, utilities (water, gas, electricity) and construction. This book will concentrate on the manufacturing sector which is the most important sector in terms of value added and employment.

The agencies involved in the collection and publication of industrial statistics in Ghana are Statistical Service (GSS) (formerly the Central Bureau of Statistics) and the Ministry of Trade and Industry. The most important publication which has over the years provided statistics on industry was the annual "Industrial Statistics" published by the Statistical Service, the last issue of which was for the year 1982.

The Economic Survey also published by the Statistical Service also provided information and statistical data on industry. Just like the Industrial Statistics the last issue was for 1982. Other sources of industrial statistics include the *Quarterly Digest of Statistics* published by the Statistical Service, the Input-Output Table of Ghana: 1968 prepared by M.S. Singal for the Statistical Service in 1973. In 1986/87, the Statistical Service conducted an Industrial Survey.

Since the publication of the 1986/87 Industrial Census, statistical data on industry are usually obtained from survey conducted by researchers.

Ghana Standard Industrial Classification

The industries within the industrial sector of Ghana have been classified following the International Standard Industrial Classification (ISIC). The major divisions at the one-digit, 2-digit and 3-digit levels of classification are:

Division 2 *Mining and Quarrying*
22 Crude petroleum and natural gas production
23 Metal ore mining — iron ore, non-ferrous ore mining, gold mining and dredging, bauxite mining, manganese mining
29 Other mining — stone quarrying, clay etc., salt mining, diamond mining.

Division 3 *Manufacturing*
31 Food, Beverages and Tobacco
32 Textile, wearing apparel and leather
32 Manufacture of wood and wood products, including furniture
33 Manufacture of paper and paper products, printing and publishing
34 Chemicals, petroleum and coal products, rubber, plastics
35 Non-metallic mineral products
36 Iron and steel and non-ferrous metal products
37 Fabricated metals and machinery and transport equipment
38 Other manufacturing not elsewhere classified

Division 4 *Electricity and Water*
41 Electricity, gas and steam
42 Water Works and supply

Division 5 *Construction*
3 digit level classification of manufacturing:

311/12 Food processing
313 Beverages
314 Tobacco

321 Textiles
322 Garments
323 Leather and products
324 Tobacco
331 Sawmilling and wood products
332 Furniture
341 Paper and products
342 Printing and publishing
351 Industrial chemicals
352 Other chemicals
353 Petroleum products
355 Rubber products
356 Plastics
361 Pottery, china and earthenware
362 Glass and products
369 Other mineral products
371 Iron and steel
372 Non ferrous metals
381 Fabricated metals
382 Machinery and equipment
383 Electrical machinery
384 Transport equipment
385 Professional and scientific equipment
390 Other manufacturing

Chapter 1 is an introduction and overview of the Chapters. Chapter 2, Constraints to the Growth and Expansion of the Manufacturing Sector examines the evidence on the importance of constraints on the growth of the manufacturing sector in Ghana. In particular we examine how firms in Ghana perceive the impact of the problems of finance, human capital and technology, regulatory and administrative constraints, infrastructure, labour which have constrained the performance of the firms in the sector.

It has been hypothesized that a more vigorous response of the manufacturing sector to the economic reforms have been impeded by a number of institutional, structural and financial constraints inherent in the present stage of Ghana's economic development. The economy has moved from one of government intervention to liberalisation. Removal of these constraints through various policy mechanisms could increase the manufacturing sector's capacity for expansion, investment, labour absorption and exports. Thus there is the need to identify the type and severity of restrictions and which sectors are vulnerable, in order to be able to devise appropriate policies for the manufacturing sector.

Chapter 3, Inter-Firm Linkages Input-output linkages among micro, small, medium and large scale industries are very essential for the development of industrialization in any country. This is more so in the case of a less industrialized country like Ghana whose industrialization must initially be based on local resources such as agriculture, forestry and minerals. Unfortunately, the early attempt at modernization and industrialization in the early 1960s was non-selective. With a philosophy of import substitution, the state-led industrialization focused on all industrial sectors, irrespective of availability of local raw materials

In our analysis, we identify input-output linkages in terms of forward and backward linkages and subcontracting among firms. We used three different surveys for our analysis. The first was the World Bank Regional Programme for Enterprise Development survey conducted by the Department of Economics, University of Ghana and Oxford Centre for the Study of African Economies which focused on 200 firms in four sectors namely garments and textiles, wood and furniture, metals and food. We also made use of key enterprise survey of 20 firms in the three sectors of food processing, textiles and wood processing. Our last method was to interview nine key firms and institutions about policies and other institutional framework to improve linkages among firms.

Chapter 4, Production Capacity of Agro-Metals examines the production capacity of the agro-metals subsector to produce the equipment needed by the agricultural and food processing sectors of the economy. Ghana is an agricultural country losing about 30 percent of its output through post harvest losses. With the failure of the import dependent IS strategy, attention is now being focused on local-resource based industrial strategy. Ghana may have a comparative advantage in processing local raw materials into products for the local market. The increased processing of the produce of the agricultural sector then becomes the focus of a new industrial strategy. The successful development of the agro-metal sector to supply the requisite equipment should be of immense concern to government.

(i) We make use of existing data and literature;

(ii)　A limited "key enterprise survey" was carried out for 10 micro, 10 small enterprises and 5 medium scale enterprises, all engaged in metal working and producing farm implements and food processing equipment.

(iii)　Additional information was obtained through interviews with a few "key informants."

Chapter 5, analyzes the Demand for Carbonated Soft Drinks. Chapter 6 studies Factor Intensities in Manufacturing Establishments. The chapter has three main objectives. Firstly it examines observed factor intensities as a guide to studying inter-industry differences in technology; secondly it tests whether Ghana's exports of manufactures are relatively more labour-intensive than her importables, and thirdly it examines the relationship between factor intensities and nationality of ownership and scale.

Chapter 7, Factor Substitution Possibilities in a Multi-Input and Non-Competitive Environment examines the pattern of technology in use in Ghanaian manufacturing using establishment data to study the range of technologies available. This is done by comparing capital-labour ratio estimates in various establishments and by quantifying the relationship between factor cost and choice of technologies using rank correlation and the estimation of elasticity of substitution. The framework used to estimate elasticity of substitution incorporates imperfection in both the product and factor markets and the possibilities of non-constant returns, and uses a three input production function. The study reveals some possibilities of substitution between capital and labour, unskilled labour and skilled labour, and elasticity of substitution different from unity in Ghanaian manufacturing.

Attempts have been made to quantify the magnitude of x- or technical efficiency among firms and farms in both the developed and developing economies. Leibenstein (1966) has argued that losses from x-inefficiency may be more important than losses from allocative inefficiency. In Chapter 8, Departures from the Frontier: An Analysis of Firm Level X-Inefficiency, x-efficiency levels are measured for establishments of 16 manufacturing industries as departures from efficiency frontiers based on Farell's (1957) seminal paper on the measurement of productive efficiency. The estimates permit measurements of relative performance of establishments within an industry and thereby give a picture of the structure of industry.

Chapter 9, Choice of Technology in an Imperfectly Competitive

Framework: A Micro Cross-Section Analysis of Manufacturing Firms seeks to analyse inter-establishment differences in technology in Ghanaian manufacturing, specifically the role of the non-competitive product market environment. It is argued that the lack of competitive pressures creates inefficiency and one of the forms of inefficiency in LDCs in the choice of capital-intensive technologies. The analysis is conducted through the specification and testing of a generalized model which incorporates various indicators of market imperfection, and other important determinants of technology choice. In spite of the limitations of the analysis due to economic difficulties, some of the variables proposed to capture product market imperfection proved significant.

REFERENCES

Statistical Service, Quarterly Digest of Statistics, various issues.
Statistical Service, The 1986 Industrial Census.

CHAPTER TWO

Obstacles to the Growth and Expansion of the Manufacturing Sector: A Firm Level Study

(with Kwame Baah-Nuakoh)

Introduction

It has been argued that a more vigorous response of the manufacturing sector to the economic reforms have been impeded by a number of institutional, structural and financial constraints inherent in the present stage of Ghana's economic development. The economy has moved from one of government intervention to liberalization. In previous chapters, the evidence from the RPED survey regarding how firms form and grow were discussed. An important objective of the survey was to investigate the constraints on the structure, conduct and performance of firms. The effects of constraints are transmitted through several variables and their interaction. Removal of these constraints through various policy mechanisms could increase the manufacturing sector's capacity for expansion, investment, labour absorption and exports. Thus, there is the need to identify the type and severity of restrictions and which sectors are vulnerable, in order to be able to devise appropriate policies for the manufacturing sector.

Several studies (Webster and Steel 1991), Sowa *et al.* (1992), Osei *et al.* (1993), Baah-Nuakoh (1993), Baah-Nuakoh and Steel (1993), Thomi and Yankson (1985), Anheir and Seibel (1987) have been conducted to find out the major constraints to their operation and expansion of manufacturing in Ghana. These studies have concentrated on small and medium scale enterprises in Ghana and have found a high proportion of firms citing lack of access to credit as a major constraint. Other important constraints which most of these studies do not bring out is the capability needed to set up and efficiently manage an enterprise — i.e. management, skills and technology (Melford 1986). Although, management could be considered a serious constraint especially within small and medium scale firms, as evidenced by the establishment of training institutions such as the National Board for Small Scale Industries (NBSSI) Entrepreneurship Development Programme and (EMPRETEC), entrepreneurs themselves do not perceive management as a problem. Baah-Nuakoh and Steel (1993) found out that only 0.8 percent of the 133 firms interviewed in 1991 indicated that management was a problem.

This chapter examines the evidence on the importance of constraints on the growth of the manufacturing sector in Ghana based on a firm level survey conducted in 1992 by the World Bank, Oxford Centre for the Study of African Economies, and the Department of Economics, University of Ghana as part of the World Bank Regional Programme for Enterprise Development (RPED) study which began in 1991. In particular, we examine how firms in Ghana perceive the impact of the problems of finance, human capital and technology, regulatory and administrative constraints, infrastructure, labour and other problems which have constrained the performance of firms in the manufacturing sector. Performance of the firms in the sector is measured using three variables: (a) employment since start-up and since 1988, (b) capacity utilization and (c) exports.

Issues

Several hypotheses have been advanced to explain the poor growth record of manufacturing. The performance of firms is related to several determinants.

(i)   The hypothesis is that capital is in short supply and there does not exist an efficiently operating capital market. The inadequate supply of capital and the poor quality of financial intermediation have effects on firm growth and survival; finance and transaction costs to firms are high and this can constrain output in diverse ways; for example, a firm which cannot get bank credit might be forced to use inferior technology by purchasing second hand and discarded technology. The cost of enterprise financing is negatively related to firm size.

(ii) In the area of human capital, the background of the entre-preneur and the labour force in the form of education, training and skill, experience and age influences productivity.

(iii) An important factor is the acquisition and use of new technology. It is argued that given the present age of machines and equipment used by firms, it is now impossible to increase capacity utilization levels and there is a need to replace the outdated technology.

(iv) Government regulations can affect the conditions of entry, growth of firms as well as the exit of firms. The extent and effects of transaction and regulatory costs can prevent the expansion of investment and the growth of firms; there is an asymmetrical incidence of regulation among different size groups and sectors. For example, firms have differential access to government programmes and policies such as investment benefits from Investment Code.

(v) Labour market regulations include minimum wages, hiring and firing restrictions, safety regulations, required payments of benefits and allowances. These regulations tend to raise costs and decrease revenues. Labour regulations are binding at larger firm sizes.

(vi) There is also the problem of lack of investment in infrastructure; the deficiencies affect firms costs, the choice of techniques; they also generate barriers to entry to particular product lines and at scales which are infrastructure intensive; if the firms themselves provide the infrastructure, this will entail large fixed costs which act to limit firms growth; the cost of infrastructure services is negatively related to size.

(vii) Different firms facing different prices because of Government policies of controlling foreign exchange and other prices have been seen as retarding growth of small, more efficient, labour intensive firms. The differences in the supply prices to firms are related to the size of the enterprise.

(viii) Public ownership has been identified as a factor mitigating against efficient operation. This raises the issue of efficiency of private versus public firms.

(ix) The lack of adequate business support services may mean increases in transactions costs for the firm; entrepreneurs must spend time and energy to overcome these problems. The costs reduce productivity and international competitiveness of firms. It also creates barriers to entry and expansion.

METHODOLOGY AND SOURCES OF DATA[1]

This chapter is based on a survey of manufacturing firms in Ghana carried out in the summer of 1992 as part of the World Bank's Regional Programme for Enterprise Development (RPED). The objective of the survey was to investigate the constraints on the growth of firms with a view to understanding the policy mechanisms necessary to promote profitable investment, employment and exports. To meet that objective, the survey was designed to cover all the major areas that have been identified by past research as constraints on the firm. Firm level interviews were conducted with 200 manufacturing firms in Accra/Tema, Kumasi, Cape Coast and Takoradi.

Entrepreneurs' perceptions of how these constraints affect their expansion and productivity are examined in this chapter. We are aware of the problems of the use of perceptions in such an analysis. It can give exaggerated view (negatively or positively) of the effects of policies depending on whether the respondent opposes or supports the policies. Perceptions are also influenced by individual differences and personal judgements and may not reflect actual situations. Inspite of these limitations the survey provides a good indication of the obstacles facing the manufacturing sector.

We hypothesize that size is an important determinant of the degree and effectiveness of constraints; while for some of the constraints large firm size becomes an advantage, the magnitude and severity of other constraints increases with size. The data was thus disaggregated according to four size groups, measured by the number of employees: micro, small, medium and large.

We again hypothesized that the type and magnitude of the constraint will vary by sector; the liberalization and rapid and sustained exchange rate depreciations will tend to affect the sectors differently favouring export-oriented industries and negatively affecting the import-dependent sectors.

Age is an important factor; new firms because they lack a track record and experience, will find it more difficult to obtain loans to ease their financial constraint. Thus, the analysis is done in terms of discussing the relationship between the constraints on firm expansion and improvement in productivity and:

(i)   the size of firms (four main size groups: less than 5 (micro), 5–29 (small), 30–99, (medium) and 100 and above (large);

(ii) the age of the firm (5 years or less (baby), 6 to 10 years (young), 11 to 20 years (mature) and above 20 years (old);

(iii) sector (food, textiles, garment, wood, furniture and metals;

(iv) We also investigate the relationship between performance indicators and the constraints, that is whether firms which performed badly were also the firms facing the constraints. Performance is measured by growth in employment, capacity utilization and exports.

Table 2.1: The Structure of the Final Sample by Sector and Size

	Micro	*Small*	*Medium*	*Large*	*Total*
Sector					
Food Processing	18	1	10	7	50
Textiles	1	1	3	1	6
Garments	11	23	8	1	43
Wood Products	3	2	1	5	11
Furniture	5	22	8	5	40
Metal Working	6	27	10	7	50
Location					
Accra	18	48	29	19	114
Cape Coast	1	5	1	1	8
Kumasi	23	34	8	2	67
Takoradi	2	3	2	4	11
Age					
Aged	6	14	13	11	44
Mature	14	32	15	8	69
Young	23	34	8	2	67
New	16	29	6	2	53
Total	44	90	40	26	200

The distribution of firms in the final sample is given in Table 2.1. Small firms constituted 45% of the sample, micro firms 22%. The medium and large firms constituted 20% and 13% of the sample respectively.

MANUFACTURING PERFORMANCE

The Economic Recovery Programme (ERP) which was introduced in 1983 involved among other things the encouragement of private investment and the shifting of relative prices in favour of production, particularly for export and efficient import substitution industry. While emphasis in the pre-ERP era had been on import substitution, i.e. industrial development under high protection rates, reliance on administrative controls and dependence on large public sector investments, in the ERP period, the emphasis was expected to be shifted to the private sector as the prime mover of industrialization.

The economy responded well to the policies of the ERP in the early years reflected in growth in output averaging 5.7% between 1984 and 1989. After 1989, the initial momentum subsided with the economy averaging a growth rate of 4.4% between 1990 and 1999 (Table 2.2). The output growth pattern which was broadbased was particularly strong in the industrial sector leading to a partial reversal of the share of industrial sector in total output, the dynamism shown by the industrial sector being attributed, *inter alia*, to increased availability of imported inputs, realignment of relative prices, improvement in real producer prices which boosted expansion in the mining and manufacturing sub-sectors.

Growth of the Industrial Sector

One of the fastest growing sectors during the initial years of the ERP was the industrial sector achieving rates of 11.9% and 17.6% in 1984 and 1985 respectively, and averaging 11.2% between 1984 and 1988. Since 1989, growth of the sector has been disappointing, recording rates of 2.6% in 1989 and 1.3% in 1994. During the decade of 1989 to 1999 the sector averaged a growth of 4.4%.

The growth in output of all the four sub-sectors in the industrial sector especially manufacturing has not been consistent but has been fluctuating. The manufacturing sub-sector, has remained the dominant sub-sector, contributing about 60% of total value of industrial production over the years Industrial sector in the early years of the ERP was manufacturing-led with the sector recording rates of 12.9% and 24.3% in 1984 and 1985 respectively (Table 2.3).

Table 2.2: Developments in Output 1984–1999

Year	Growth Rates (%)			(%) of GDP	
	GDP	Industry	Manufacture	Industry	Manufacture
1984	8.6	11.9	12.9	11.62	7.18
1985	5.1	17.6	24.3	13.00	8.49
1986	5.2	7.6	11.0	13.30	8.95
1987	4.8	11.5	10.0	14.14	9.40
1988	5.6	7.3	5.1	14.36	9.35
1989	5.1	2.6	0.6	14.03	8.95
1990	3.1	6.9	5.9	14.52	9.17
1991	5.3	3.7	1.1	14.29	8.80
1992	3.9	5.8	2.7	14.55	8.70
1993	5.0	4.3	2.2	14.46	8.49
1994	3.8	1.3	1.5	14.30	8.30
1995	4.5	3.3	1.8	14.30	8.30
1996	5.2	4.2	3.0	14.20	8.10
1997	4.2	6.4	5.4	14.80	8.40
1998	4.6	3.2	4.0	14.50	8.30
1999	4.4	4.9	4.8	14.60	8.30
Average Annual Growth Rates					
1984–88	11.2	12.7			
1989–99	4.4	3.2			

Source: Calculated from National Accounts Data

The dominance of the manufacturing sub-sector is evident in the behaviour of the trend in the growth rate of industry and manufacturing as shown in Figure 2.1. The rise or fall in manufacturing growth rate to a greater extent determines the overall growth in industrial output.

The initial benefit which accrued to the manufacturing sub-sector was basically due *inter alia* to the improved utilization of installed capacity on the account of the minimization of foreign exchange pressure as a direct consequence of foreign exchange reforms pursued

Table 2.3: Share of Sub-Sectors in Total Industrial Output 1981–1999

Year	Manufacturing %	Mining & Quarrying %	Electricity & Water %	Construction %
1981	71.6	8.1	6.6	13.8
1982	59.7	9.7	7.1	24.1
1983	61.2	9.7	5.0	24.0
1984	61.8	9.8	6.4	22.0
1985	65.3	8.9	6.6	19.2
1986	67.3	8.0	7.3	17.4
1987	66.5	7.8	7.7	18.1
1988	65.1	8.5	8.1	18.3
1989	63.8	9.1	8.5	18.5
1990	63.2	9.1	9.2	18.6
1991	61.9	9.4	9.5	19.3
1992	59.8	9.8	10.1	20.4
1993	58.6	10.2	10.5	20.8
1994	57.6	10.4	10.7	20.8
1995	57.0	10.6	10.6	21.1
1996	56.9	10.5	11.1	21.5
1997	56.8	10.8	11.5	20.9
1998	57.2	11.0	10.3	21.5
1999	56.8	11.0	10.3	21.9

Source: Compiled from National Account Data; *Quarterly Digest of Statistics,* Various Issues. The computaiton adopted 1977 as the base year.

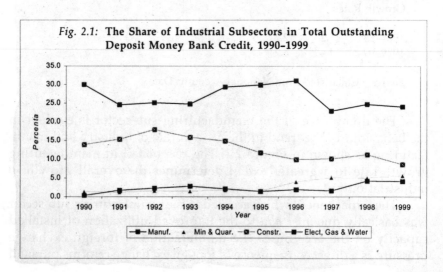

Fig. 2.1: **The Share of Industrial Subsectors in Total Outstanding Deposit Money Bank Credit, 1990–1999**

as part of the ERP. The reduced foreign exchange pressure made available and accessible foreign exchange for the importation of raw materials, spare parts, and equipment as well as other needed inputs necessary for efficient and effective utilisation of installed capacity of existing plants and machinery.

Nonetheless, the declining growth rate of the manufacturing sub-sector is an obvious manifestation of the problems, which accompanied the rapid liberalization of trade and exchange rate coupled with financial reform and its attendant high interest rate and hence high cost of credit. The rapid depreciation of the cedi and high cost of credit compelled many import dependent industries to battle with high cost of production.

Competition arising from the policy reforms came from two sources: (i) local firms which were able to adjust to the reforms; and (ii) increased imports due to removal of import controls such as import licence in 1988 and general trade liberalization — they compete for the limited market for industrial goods. Competitive pressures were intensified for firms whose products could easily be imported; firms which benefited were those that had 'natural' protection from imports — than those with local resource advantages. Several enterprises that had been sheltered from domestic and foreign competition were forced to rationalize their operations or go out of business.

The problems were further compounded by the inefficiency of the import substitution manufacturing sub-sector and the lack of effective linkages between manufacturing and other major sectors, especially agriculture. Thus, the initial benefit of the ERP was fast eroded by the unfavourable macroeconomic environment, which to a significant extent crippled the domestic manufacturing sub-sector of the industrial sector.

Although the other sub-sectors of the industrial sector did not experience any remarkable and consistent output growth between 1989 and 1999, they performed better overall than the dominant manufacturing sub-sector. This sub-sector continues to reign as the dominant sub-sector contributing a little over half of total industry output although other sub-sectors have been making some marginal gains in terms of shares in the industrial sector's real output since 1990. As shown in Table 2.4 the manufacturing sub-sector maintained its position as the leading contributor to real GDP among other sub-sectors in the industrial sector. Its share in real GDP has ranged between 7.2% and 10.9% for the period 1981–1999.

Table 2.4: Share of Industry and Sub-Sectors in Real GDP, 1981–1999

Year	Industry	Manufacturing	Mining & Quarring	Electricity & Water	Construction
1981	15.2	10.9	1.0	1.0	2.1
1982	12.6	7.4	1.2	0.9	3.0
1983	11.3	6.9	1.1	0.6	2.7
1984	11.6	7.2	1.1	0.8	2.6
1985	13.0	8.5	1.2	0.9	2.5
1986	13.3	9.0	1.1	1.0	2.3
1987	14.1	9.4	1.1	1.1	2.6
1988	14.4	9.4	1.2	1.2	2.6
1989	14.0	9.0	1.3	1.2	2.6
1990	14.5	9.2	1.3	1.3	2.7
1991	14.3	8.8	1.3	1.4	2.8
1992	14.6	8.7	1.4	1.5	3.0
1993	14.5	8.5	1.5	1.5	3.0
1994	14.3	8.3	1.5	1.5	3.0
1995	14.2	8.3	1.5	1.6	2.9
1996	14.2	8.1	1.5	1.6	3.1
1997	14.8	8.4	1.6	1.7	3.1
1998	14.5	8.3	1.6	1.5	3.1
1999	14.6	8.3	1.6	1.5	3.2

Source: Calculated from National Accounts Data with 1977 as the base year.

Within the manufacturing sector the various industries have experienced differential responses to the ERP. Table 2.5 gives the index of manufacturing production for the period 1985 to 1998 for 15 subsectors with 1977 as the base year. The more dynamic sectors have been saw milling, cement and non-metallic mineral products, beverages and petroleum refinery. The industries which have not performed well are those that face foreign competition and depend on imported inputs such as textiles, wearing apparel and electrical.

Table 2.6 presents evidence on capacity utilization estimated by the Statistical Service for medium and large manufacturing establishments for the ERP periods. Capacity utilization in manufacturing increased from a low of 18% in 1984 to 45.7% in 1993. Certain subsectors recorded increased capacity utilization rates of over 50% with metals reaching 80%, tobacco and beverages 76.3%, non-metallic minerals 72.8% and wood processing 65%.

Table 2.5:   Index Numbers for Manufacturing Production 1985–1998

	Weight	1985	1986	1987	1988	1989	1990	1991	1992	1993	1994	1995	1996	1997	1998
Food	15.62	41.8	40.6	50.5	53.6	48	57.5	59.3	62.8	90.3	90.8	99.6	102.5	109.3	110.3
Beverage	8.11	59.3	75.1	85.2	89	98	94	93	112.2	116.4	109.4	109	116.2	123.9	124
Tobacco	7.75	61.3	57.6	54.9	58	51	57.1	49.6	47.1	52.2	53	52	53.1	53.1	53.6
Textiles, wearing apparel and leather goods	13.71	19.2	22.9	26.1	28.7	24	37.7	39.1	23.7	60.2	48	54.8	56.1	55.5	55.9
Saw milling and wood	7.22	75.4	79.5	79.3	98.3	80	74.2	133.6	120.2	91.9	98.2	100.2	105.3	105	
Paper products, printing	1.94	65.1	70.5	59.7	52.8	48	53.5	49.3	54.6	33.7	47.1	45.1	49.3	54.1	54.5
Petroleum Refinery	19	80.6	76.6	62.7	67.7	87.2	70.5	92.2	65	65.8	94.4	101.4	103.5		56.6
Chemical products	6.56	31.8	38	51.9	67.5	62	57.6	44.7	56.7	38.4	129.8	140	148.2	159.8	159.8
Cement and non-metallic	2.98	63.6	47.4	49.7	73.4	100	117.3	125.6	177	206.2	217	258.1	258.9	241.8	240.8
Iron and steel	3.25	46.2	38.8	42.9	18.3	12.1	5.2	na	356	392.8	541.1	581.6	584.5	590.5	413.4
Non ferrous metals	9.62	28.4	72.5	90.3	97.3	100.5	103.8	104.6	115.8	109.9	88.8	119.8	125.6	149.9	138.1
Cutlery & other non-ferrous	0.49	34.6	55.2	51.9	46.2	47.9	55.2	63.2	83.3	99.9	124	102.4	116.4	116.4	116.8
Electrical equipment	1.34	28.4	51	31.5	47.1	13.5	25.5	40	46.3	52.6	29.8	42.9	67.8	67.8	61.5
Transport equipment	3.03	Na	na	na	Na	na	na	11							
All manufacturing	100	39.3	49.3	54.2	56.8	63	63.5	71.3	76.9	87.3	101.2	109.9	115	101	103.6

Source: Statistical Service, *Quarterly Digest of Statistics.*

Table 2.6:   Capacity Utilization in Industry (percentage)

Industry	1983	1984	1985	1986	1987	1988	1989	1990	1991	1992	1993
Metals	55	20	16	Na	42	45	47	49	58	68	80
Electricals	44	8	33	30	36	40	11	13	11.7	12	23.9
Plastics	35	30	28	30	39	39	41	40	31	42	45
Vehicle assembly	20	8	20	Na	10	24	Na	25	22	22	16.4
Tobacco& beverages	65	20	40	40	45	58	60	65	68	75	76.3
Food processing	25	23	31	36	42	60	51	55	57	49	52.3
Leather	6	12	22	Na	15	20	15	12	7	10	10
Garment	25	20	26	27	25	35	25	22	30	35	53
Pharmaceuticals	35	Na	17	Na	26	33	33	30	28	25	40
Cosmetics	0	Na	Na	25	29	33	30	25	25	24	16.2
Paper	0	17	15	Na	30	42	30	30	30	32	45
Nonmetallic	22	12	35	Na	37	40	44	48	54	65	72.8
Chemicals	20	22	20	25	30	35	33	30	30.2	30	40
Rubber	22	15	16	23	28	38	43	48	51	49	54
Wood processing	26	28	33	Na	43	70	70	70	65	65	65
Textiles	16	17	20	17	24	33	41	35	45	67	41.3
All manufacturing	30	18	25	30	31	40	40.6	39.8	40.5	44.5	45.7

POLICIES, INSTITUTIONS AND REGULATIONS
IN VARIOUS MARKETS

Industrial sector growth has been influenced by the macroeconomic trade and industrial policies pursued by government. The objectives of government policy during the Economic Recovery period and as restated in *Industrial Policy Statement of January 1992* (pp. 4-5) is as follows:

In the long term . . . to create a balanced industrial structure. In the medium term . . . to create a solid base for increasing the production of manufactured goods with increased local content for national consumption and for export by increasing the exploitation and in-situ processing of the nation's raw materials . . .

In the short term . . . to improve general industrial performance and overcome the problems associated with heavy dependence on imported goods and under-utilization of production capacity."

To achieve these objectives, emphasis was to be placed on,

"(i)   Restructuring the industrial sector and rehabilitating major industries, including the expansion, diversification and modernization of existing viable enterprises and enhancement of their competitiveness;
(ii)   Promoting the establishment of new industrial capacities and environmentally sound industrial operations, including increased investment and development and acquisition of appropriate technologies.
(iii) Promoting the local indigenous private sector and involving both local and foreign private enterprises to a greater degree in the industrial development of the country."

Macroeconomic Policies

During the period of the Economic Reform Programme, government macroeconomic policies and strategies were geared towards ensuring macroeconomic stability especially price and exchange rate stability through the pursuance of tight monetary and to some extent fiscal discipline. The government's flexible exchange rate policy pursued over more than a decade was aimed at providing incentives for increased production of exportable goods as well as enhancing the country's competitiveness on the international market. The government's major policy on trade has been:

(a) the rationalization of tariff regimes in the economy; for example the policy to reduce import tariff on goods to be used for export production was implemented while some categories of imports which compete with domestically produced goods were subject to specific duties as alternative to import duties;

(b) monetary policy was geared towards reinforcing the declining trend in inflation through tight monetary policy; there has been rapid depreciation of the domestic currency and the crowding out of the private sector by government through its domestic bank financing.

Availability and Cost of Finance

There was a decline in the percentage of commercial banks' loans and advances to the manufacturing sector declining from around 70% in 1989 to about 56.7% in 1999 (Table 2.7).

An important factor explaining the resource flow from the banks to the industrial sector, especially to the manufacturing sector is the trend in the interest rates. Firms have complained about the high interest rates.

This declining trend in the bank rate impacted to some extent on the lending rates of the commercial banks.

The Ghana Stock Exchange

The Ghana Stock Exchange, which was incorporated in July 1989 as a private limited company, has helped a number of companies to raise long-term capital through the floating of shares on the Exchange. Companies which raise capital from the issue of shares or stocks, are able to expand their services, replace equipment and develop new products, which invariably results in an increase in employment and incomes both directly and indirectly. Large businesses with cash needs for expansion have their best prospects when they turn to the stock exchange.

As at December 1999, the total number of companies listed on the Exchange for floatation of shares stood at 22, as compared to 21 in 1998. A total number of 15 companies out of the 22 were operating in the industrial sector. Three out of the 15 were operating in the brewery sector, one each in tobacco and mining, two in housing, and the rest engaged in other forms of manufacturing.

Table 2.7: Outstanding Credit by Deposit Money Banks to the Industrial Sector 1990–1999 (billion cedis)

End of	Manufacturing	Mining & Quarrying	Const-ruction	Electricity, water & Gas	Industry Total of	Mfg as % Industry
1988						69.2
1989						70.7
1990	22.88	1.03	10.59	0.29	34.79	65.8
1991	23.02	1.16	14.39	1.58	40.16	57.3
1992	37.94	2.46	27.04	3.42	70.86	53.5
1993	51.19	3.17	32.78	5.83	92.97	55.1
1994	86.55	5.37	43.58	6.16	141.66	61.1
1995	129.30	6.50	50.80	6.30	192.90	67.0
1996	230.40	31.40	76.60	14.28	352.68	65.3
1997	295.84	66.32	130.96	20.82	513.94	57.6
1998	Q1 310.78	66.81	155.50	51.43	584.52	
	Q2 401.39	64.72	164.74	57.74	688.59	
	Q3 460.93	73.97	176.38	66.40	777.68	
	Q4 445.13	90.68	202.31	75.53	813.65	54.7
1999	Q1 454.59	102.80	209.79	71.51	838.69	
	Q2 536.42	127.30	219.07	81.42	964.21	
	Q3 572.43	127.83	212.04	136.05	1048.35	
	Q4 717.11	166.96	257.23	122.03	1263.33	56.7

Source: Bank of Ghana Annual Reports & Quarterly Bulletin, Various Issues.

The floating of shares on the Ghana Stock Exchange by these firms has afforded them the opportunity to tap the savings of many people in the country to obtain long-term capital that may not be available from their own resources or their bankers.

Business Assistance Fund (BASF)

This Fund was a Government of Ghana Credit line of ¢10bn to support distressed but potentially viable industries. It was launched in 1993 and disbursements began in 1995. For a company to qualify as a beneficiary of the fund, a number of characteristics of the company was taken into consideration: the current performance of the company, the calibre of staff and whether the company has the capability of continuing with production.

Table 2: 8: Lending Rates of Commercial Banks (Minimum and Maximum) to the Industrial Sector, 1990–1999

Year	Export	Manufacturing	Mining & Quarrying	Construction
1990	20.00–30.25	22.50–30.25	24.00–27.00	26.00–29.00
1991	22.50–31.50	18.25–31.50	23.20–27.20	23.20–29.20
1992	19.75–26.00	21.50–26.50	24.00–26.50	23.25–29.00
1993	23.00–39.00	26.00–39.00	28.00–39.00	28.00–39.00
1994	20.38–35.50	26.00–35.00	29.00–37.50	29.00–37.50
1995	34.25–47.00	33.00–47.00	30.00–47.50	39.00–47.50
1996	30.00–47.00	39.00–47.00	35.00–47.50	41.00–47.50
1997				
March	35.00–47.00	39.00–47.00	35.00–47.50	41.50–47.50
June	35.00–47.00	39.00–47.00	35.00–48.00	41.50–47.50
September	35.00–49.00	35.00–49.00	35.00–49.00	41.50–47.50
December	35.00–49.00	35.00–49.00	35.00–49.00	41.50–49.00
1998				
March	35.00–49.00	39.00–49.00	35.00–49.00	41.50–49.00
June	35.00–48.50	39.00–48.50	35.00–48.50	39.00–48.50
September	35.00–48.50	36.00–46.00	36.00–46.00	36.00–46.00
December	31.00–45.00	32.00–45.00	33.00–45.00	32.50–45.00
1999				
March	33.00–41.50	33.00–41.50	33.00–41.50	33.00–41.00
June	31.00–36.50	31.00–36.50	31.00–36.50	31.00–36.50
September	27.00–44.00	27.00–44.00	27.00–44.00	27.00–44.00
December	31.00–39.75	32.50–40.00	32.00–39.75	32.00–40.00

Note: Interest Rate figures from 1990 to 1996 represent December Rates.
Source: Bank of Ghana Annual Reports & Quarterly Bulletin, Various Issues.

Table 2.9 summarizes the progress of disbursements. This Fund has been widely welcomed and highly patronised by the private sector. It is estimated that, the Fund has been over-subscribed by ¢5bn. Over the relatively short period of existence the Fund has enabled a number of beneficiaries to be in operation. Some of the problems faced by participants of the Fund include the difficulty in raising collateral to

Table 2.9: BASF Approval and Disbursement Data

Year	No. of Beneficiaries	Amount Approved ¢	Amount Disbursed ¢
1995	310	4.87bn	2.83bn
1996	242	5.32bn	5.73bn
Total	552	10.19bn	8.56bn

secure loans, the time it takes to prepare the supporting legal documents, the high cost of accessing the Fund by micro and small enterprises outside the Greater Accra Region and poor loan recovery. The private sector has also been agitating for the Fund level to be increased since the real value of the ¢10bn had been eroded by the inflationary pressures. In a bid to make the Fund more accessible, it was decentralised in the latter part of 1996, with each region being capitalised to the tune of ¢50.0m.

Funds for Small and Medium Enterprises Development (FUSMED)

Under the private Small and Medium Enterprise Development project, the International Development Association (IDA) of the World Bank has since 1990 made available $30m for the development of private small and medium enterprises in the productive sectors of the Ghanaian economy. The credit facility was to be used for the following general purposes:

(i)   rehabilitation of existing enterprises
(ii) expansion of existing enterprises
(iii) establishment of new enterprises
(iv) leasing of industrial and business equipment

Table 2.10 summarises the progress of work as at the end of 1999. This credit facility is administered by the Fund for Small and Medium Enterprises Development (FUSMED) located in the Development Finance Department of the Bank of Ghana. Beside offering credit facilities to these enterprises it also provides leasing facilities. The maximum size of FUSMED loan is $750,000 and the fund finances up to 70% of the cost of new investment projects and 100% of the cost of investment projects in the case of expansion and/or rehabilitation. A breakdown of Loan Disbursed by FUSMED is given in Table 2.11.

Table 2.10: Breakdown of Loan Disbursed by FUSMED

PERCENTAGE FINANCING BY SECTOR			
Sector	*No.*	*U$m*	*% of Total*
Manufacturing	75	19.9	69.4
Service	40	5.6	19.8
Transport	6	3.1	10.8
DISTRIBUTION BY SIZE			
Micro	10	0.13	8.3
Small	32	3.22	26.4
Medium	79	25.28	65.3
LEASING BY SECTOR			
Manufacturing	10	0.74	41.4
Service	16	1.1	58.6

Source: Development Finance Department, Bank of Ghana.

Table 2.11: Breakdown of Loan Disbursed by FUSMED, 1990–95

Year	*1990*	*1991*	*1992*	*1993*	*1994*	*1995*
Medium	16	8	22	8	6	16
Small	2	6	4	1	0	3
Micro	4	7	9	3	2	1
Total	22	21	35	12	8	20
Total ($m)	7.1	2.9	8.3	2.4	1.7	5.1

Source: Statistical Service, *Quarterly Digest of Statistics*, various issues.

Private Enterprise and Export Development (PEED)

This, like the FUSMED was also a credit line of $41m from IDA to the government of Ghana, aimed at promoting and encouraging the private sector to produce and export non-traditional products.

The two main schemes involved in this development project were:

(i) An Export Re-Finance scheme which was to enable banks to refinance short term credit. The maximum loanable amount under the scheme was $500,000 or its equivalent and the maximum term of any such loan was 360 days.

(ii) The Export Credit Guarantee Scheme where the Export Finance Office guarantees up to 75% of pre-shipment credits extended to Non-Traditional Exporters (NTEs) by participating banks.

PEED started in January 1994. At the end of 1996, $34m had been allocated to export credit. Total commitments were, however, $12m and 68 companies had benefited from it. Thirty-five companies have also benefited from the $2.5m commitments. Notwithstanding all these developments the lack of export finance continues to be the main problem of exporters.

Trade and Investment Programme (TIP)

The Trade and Investment Programme is a USAID, sponsored programme aimed at increasing the total export earnings of the Ghanaian economy. This is being accomplished through the relaxing of official policies that hinder exports, providing technical assistance capability to exporters through state agencies and non-governmental organizations. The programme was slated to end in 1997. Some of the successes achieved include:

(a) *Changes in Government Policy*
 (i) The removal of the foreign exchange control regulations that requires non-traditional exporters to surrender most of their foreign exchange earnings to the monetary authorities. Consequently exporters have access to their foreign exchange earnings;

(ii) The introduction of the new export form for non-traditional exports which replaces the cumbersome and lengthy "Single Administrative Document";

(iii) The elimination of the price control and price guidelines for exporters;

(iv) The enactment of a new Export and Import Act (Act 503) which allows anyone the right to export any product for commercial purposes.

(b) *Provision of Infrastructure*
(i) The construction of a brand new air freight terminal in October 1993;

(ii) The rehabilitation of shed 9 at Tema port to serve as a one stop centre for exports by sea.

(c) *Technical Assistance*
The TIP Secretariat has been working with the Ghana Export Promotion Council, Amex International, Africa Project Development Facility, International Executive Service Corps, Aids to Artisans and Technoserve to provide various Consultancy Services to exporters.

Divestiture Implementation Programme

Divestiture involves the transfer of state-owned enterprises (SOEs) to either foreign or Ghanaian private investors. SOEs are divested either as whole entities or in fragmented divisions. The mode of divestiture is typically through the sale of assets to private investors by competitive tender. Thus investors enter bids to purchase the SOE with the winner being selected on the basis of, among other things, the evaluation of management skills, financial resources as well as business plans. The new investor with the winning bid pays a negotiated price to become the new owner and assumes management responsibilities for the company. Other options include the sale of shares, joint venture agreement between the state and private sector and long term leasing of assets.

The Divestiture Programme was launched in 1988 by the Government in response to the need to reduce the managerial and financial burden that SOEs put on the public sector as a direct consequence of their poor performance. The Divestiture Implementation Committee (DIC) was subsequently established as the implementing agency to implement and execute all government policies in respect of the divestiture programme.

At the outset of the programme, SOEs dominated the economy with 300 SOEs operating in all sectors. Whilst a large number of them were operating in manufacturing and agriculture (including cocoa and coffee plantations, poultry and fishing), others were in the mining, hotel and timber sectors. The SOEs were characterised by poor financial performance and low productivity and accumulated huge debts.

The divestiture programme has since its implementation registered some successes in the field of manufacturing, mining and finance. As at December 31, 1998, the divestiture of 212 SOEs (or parts thereof) had been authorized by the President's Office. The breakdown on an annual basis highlighting the mode of divestiture is reported in Table 2.12. Out of the total number, Government's share in eight listed companies was off-loaded on the Ghana Stock Exchange.

Since its inception in 1989/1990 to December 1998, proceeds from the divestiture programme amounted to about ¢909.617 billion with a significant amount of about US$400 million coming from the divestiture of AGC Ltd. alone.

Many problems have been encountered, including:

(a) the lack of clear title to property, which causes major delay in divestiture;

Table 2.12: Progress on Divestiture Programme, 1991–1998

Mode	1991	1992	1993	1994	1995	1996	1997	1998	Total
Sale of Assets	16	4	3	30	19	18	15	7	12
Sale of Shares	11	5	2	2	6	1	2	2	31
Joint Venture	6	3	1	4	0	4	1	2	21
Lease	3	1	0	1	0	0	1	0	6
Liquid	24	2	5	5	6	0	0	0	42
Total	60	15	11	42	31	23	19	11	212

Source: Divestiture Implementation Committee.

(b) the settlement of liabilities of SOEs has also been a major
     hurdle in the implementation of the programme as in some
     cases liabilities exceed proceeds. Many critics of the pro-
     gramme were concerned about the speed with which the
     programme was carried out as well as the use of divesti-
     ture proceeds to finance recurrent expenditure.

Industrial Supporting Institutions

These include the Ghana Investment Promotion Centre, the NBSSI
which offers both Advisory and Credit Support, the CSIR which
undertakes research into industrial problems and technology transfer
units such as GRATIS.

Ghana Investment Promotion Centre (GIPC)

The Ghana Investment Promotion Centre was set up under the GIPC
Act of 1994 to replace the Investment Code 116 with the main objective of attracting financing capital from investors at home and especially from abroad. Prior to its inception, net foreign direct investment averaged a mere US$15.6 million. In 1994 however, it reached
its new peak of US$233 million, thanks to intensive foreign invest-
ment in gold mining, export and manufacturing. In 1997, foreign flows
rose to US$270 million.

The GIPC Act aims at ensuring the liberalization of imports and
foreign exchange transactions, as well as easy remittance of divi-
dends, profits and fees. The GIPC also implements a comprehensive
array of income tax incentives, customs import duty exemptions and
investment guarantees, all designed to improve corporate profitability. Under the Act, plant machinery, equipment and spare parts are
zero rated which means that no custom duties are paid on them.

To encourage industries to locate in the hinterlands and enable
economic activity and development to spread evenly around the country, industries that locate in the regional capitals other than Accra
and Tema are entitled to a 25% tax rebate while industries located
outside regional capitals receive 50% rebate.

Since the implementation of the GIPC Act, the Centre has registered a total of 972 projects. Out of this, a total of 251 projects representing 25.8% are registered to operate in the manufacturing sector
compared with 83 (8.5%) operating in the building and construction

sub-sector while the rest are found in the service, tourism and agriculture sector.

The pattern of regional distribution of projects since 1994 continues to be skewed in favour of Greater Accra Region with 766 projects out of 972, representing 78.81%, followed by Ashanti Region with 77 projects (7.92%). A total of 45 projects are located in the Western Region with Central and Eastern regions accounting for 28 and 27 projects respectively, while Upper East and Upper West Regions have 2 and 1 projects respectively.

National Board for Small Scale Industries (NBSSI)

The NBSSI was established by Act 434 in 1985 to oversee the growth of micro and small-scale industries in Ghana. This was in response to the realization of the essential role played by Micro and Small Enterprises (MSEs) in the economy in fulfilment of the mandate in Act 434.

The Ghana Trade and Investment Gateway Project

In the context of the Ghana Vision 2020, the programme was designed as a strategic thrust to mobilize foreign and domestic private sector investment. The programme was to promote Ghana as the Trade and Investment Gateway to the West Africa region, using Export Processing Zones (EPZ), industrial parks, free ports and liberalised skies policies. The programme focused on the processing of local and imported raw materials and goods for export and re-export and creation of service industries.

By the end of the project which was scheduled to last for six years, it was expected that Ghana would emerge as the key and preferred investment destination in West Africa with cost of doing business brought to internationally best case levels.

The Ghana Free Zones Board

The Ghana Free Zones Board (GFZB) was established on August 31, 1995 by the Free Zones Act of 1995. The Act affords free zone enterprises the right to produce goods and services which are not hazardous to the environment, for export. The Board has nine members with the Minister of Trade and Industry as the Chairman. Four of the other members are from the public sector whilst the other four are from the private sector. The functions of the Board are to:

- Grant licences to applicants under the free zones act Assist applicants for licences by providing services for obtaining other relevant licences, permits and facilities,
- Examine and recommend for approval, agreements and treaties relating to the development and activities of the free zones
- Monitor the activities and performance of free zones developers and enterprises
- Ensure compliance by free zone developers of laws relevant to free zone activities;
- Register and keep records and data of programmes and developers, operators and enterprises in the free zone.

By the end of 1997 the Ghana Free Zones Board had approved 46 projects of which three (3) were enclave developers while the other 43 were to operate single enterprises. The privileges that industries in the Free Zones enjoy include:

(a)   total exemption from payment of direct, indirect duties and levies on all imports for production and sale of export products manufactured in the free zones, including Value Added Tax (VAT). This applies to plant and equipment, raw materials and intermediate goods, significantly reducing business cost.

(b)   There is also total exemption from payment of income tax on profits for the first ten years. Upon expiration of the ten year holiday, developers and enterprises are only liable to tax at a rate not exceeding 8% percent as long as they operate in the free zone. In return, companies with free zones status must export at least 70% of their production although the rest can be sold on Ghana's domestic market.

EMPRETEC

This is a comprehensive technical cooperation programme executed by the Transnational Corporations and Management Division of the United Nations. EMPRETEC has embarked on numerous training and workshop programmes geared at catalysing private sector participation in national development by helping and supporting small and medium scale entrepreneurs.

Regulating Institutions

The institutions that directly or indirectly regulate the industrial sector mainly by way of policy are the Ministry of Trade and Industry, Internal Revenue Service, Ghana Export Promotion Council and Ghana Investment Promotion Centre for the manufacturing sector.

Although the thrust of policy being pursued by government has been towards liberalization and de-regulation, the laws and administrative requirements are not normally consistent with the enunciated direction of policy.

To strengthen the response of the private sector to the economic reforms especially with respect to promoting domestic and foreign private investment, the government established in 1991, a Private Sector Advisory Group (PSAG) to review the laws relating to the regulation of private investment.

Labour Regulations

The Ministry of Mobilization and Social Welfare through its Labour Department implements the regulations and legislation regarding the general conditions under which labour is employed in Ghana. The function of the Department are described by the Labour Decree 1967, NLCD 157 with respect to the contracts and agreements, termination of agreements, provisions relating to severance pay, and minimum wage regulation. There are already eight labour laws which in theory apply to both the formal and informal sector although in practice they do not. For example, the Minimum Wage Law (L.I. 1495 of 1990) expects that no worker should be paid below the stipulated wage rate. Firms have to go to the Labour Office Public Employment Centres to hire workers; notices and consultations are needed to initiate redunduncies. These regulations add to the firms' costs and operational flexibility and will be more felt by medium and large scale firms than the micro and small enterprises.

Legal Environment

The legal environment which has been carried over from the early sixties can be described as complex and unclear. Registration procedures are cumbersome. These include the Foreign Exchange Control Act (1961), the Industrial Relations Act (1965), the Labour Decree

(1967), the Manufacturing Industries Act (1971), and the Investment Code (1985).

Stemming from the recommendations of Private Sector Advisory Group, the government in 1992 made the following changes in the administrative and regulatory environment to address the problems of the private sector:

(a) abolition of the Manufacturing Industries Act, 1971 (Act 356) which removed a bottleneck in the investment establishment process.

(b) repeal of a number of Price Control laws which did not permit manufacturers to price their goods according to the dictates of market forces.

(c) amendment of Investment Code, 1985, PNDCL 116, which among other things seeks to promote joint ventures between foreign and local industries.

(d) enactment of a Legislative Instrument on Immigrant Quota which grants automatic immigration quota for investors.

(e) introduction of Technology Transfer Regulations which has brought about transparency in the technology transfer approach process and makes it permissible for an entrepreneur to decide freely on the type of technology it requires. But the environment still does not reflect the new attitude to investment. Lack of transparency in the "rules of the game" is another problem.

ENTREPRENEURS' PERCEPTION OF CONSTRAINTS

The problem of the impact of regulation can be analyzed by using time series observations covering periods before and after regulation. We do not have that type of data. We depended on information provided by entrepreneurs to determine how binding the various constraints are to firm growth.

The survey approached the question of constraints from three angles by asking the entrepreneurs to identify the main constraints to the expansion of their firms' development. Firstly, the entrepreneurs were asked to rank the three most serious problems which affect expansion of their firms. These problems relate to growth potential of firms. Secondly, the entrepreneurs were to rank the severity of each constraint on a scale of 1 (not important) to 5 (very important). Thirdly, they were to indicate whether their firms were subject to certain laws and regulations, or whether those regulations affected their operations.

Overview of the Constraints on Firm Expansion

Entrepreneurs were asked to indicate the foremost obstacles that constrain expansion of their business and then list up to two others. Tables 2.13 and 2.14 summarize the constraints by size, sector and age, under ownership regulations, taxes, gaining investment benefits, government restrictions on activities, labour regulations, difficulty in obtaining licences, price controls, foreign exchange controls, lack of business support services, lack of infrastructure, utility prices, lack of credit demand and location regulations, competition from imports. One weakness inherent in the list is that, like the structural adjustment programme being implemented in Ghana, the list focuses on incentive factors; human capital and technology factors are excluded.

Irrespective of the size, sector or the age of the firm, lack of credit is overwhelmingly perceived by entrepreneurs/firms to be the single most serious constraint facing manufacturing firms in Ghana. The problem of credit was cited more frequently by micro (55%) and small firms (57%) than medium (29%) and large firms (32%).

When the problems (up to three) mentioned by the firms are aggregated, credit still remains the commonly cited problem. The problem is more serious for micro firms and declines with size with 71% of micro firms compared with 60% and 58% of medium and large firms respectively citing this as a constraint. Lack of access to credit emerges as the most serious constraint for all sectors but more significant for textiles and garments. It seems it is easier for the older firms with better track record, experience and better contacts to get access to credit than the younger ones.

The second most important constraint to the expansion of firms is demand. This problem declines with size with 16% of micro firms citing demand as the most serious constraint. Although, none of the large firms considered demand as the most important constraint, about 12% cited it as a problem while 42% of the micro firms, about

a third of the small and a quarter of the medium firms considered it
as a problem. The importance of demand supports the finding by
Webster and Steel (1991).

The older firms are more concerned with demand related
problems, such as lack of domestic demand, competing imports and
competition from local firms. The new incentive structure offers little
protection to local firms. The problem for the younger firms are taxes,
infrastructure and utility prices, in addition to credit. The very new
ones trying to break into the market also cite demand as a problem.
At the industry level, entrepreneurs in garment and textiles perceived
demand as a serious problem.

**Table 2.13: Constraints on Firm Expansiuon by Size of Firm
(Percentage of Respondents in each Category)**

Ranking[a]	First ranking				Aggregate			
	micro	small	medium	large	micro	small	medium	large
Owner Regulations	0.0	0.0	0.0	0.0	0.0	0.0	0.0	0.0
Taxes	5.3	2.3	0.0	4.0	0.0	10.0	15.0	7.7
Government Restrictions	0.0	0.0	2.4	0.0	0.0	0.0	2.5	0.0
Investment Benefit	0.0	0.0	0.0	0.0	0.0	1.0	2.5	0.0
Labour Regulations	0.0	0.0	0.0	0.0	0.0	0.0	2.5	7.7
Licences	0.0	0.0	0.0	0.0	0.0	0.0	0.0	0.0
Price Control	0.0	0.0	0.0	0.0	4.2	0.0	0.0	0.0
Business Support	0.0	0.0	0.0	0.0	0.0	6.0	5.0	3.8
Infrastructure	2.6	1.2	0.0	4.0	8.3	14.0	2.5	7.7
Utility Prices	5.3	0.0	2.4	0.0	4.2	17.0	15.0	11.5
Credit	55.3	57.0	29.3	32.0	70.8	77.0	60.0	57.7
Demand	15.8	14.0	7.3	0.0	41.7	33.0	22.5	11.5
Foreign Exchange	0.0	0.0	2.4	0.0	0.0	3.0	7.5	3.8
Imports	2.6	2.3	12.2	12.0	0.0	6.0	17.5	15.4
Local Firms	0.0	0.0	4.9	0.0	0.0	1.0	12.5	0.0
Uncertainty	0.0	0.0	0.0	0.0	0.0	0.0	2.5	0.0
Skill Labour	2.6	1.2	2.4	0.0	4.2	7.0	7.5	3.8
Other	7.9	16.3	17.1	40.0	45.8	45.0	32.5	57.7
Total no. of Firms	38	100	41	25				

[a] Firms could list up to 3 problems, hence the percentages can add to more than
100%. Constraints which were never mentioned by any firm are shown: owner
regulations, licences.

Table 2.14: Constraints on Firm Expansion by Sector (Percentage of Respondents in Each Category)

	First ranking					Aggregate ranking				
	Garment	Food	Wood	Furniture	Metal	Garment	Food	Wood	Furniture	Metal
Owner Regulations	0.0	0.0	0.0	0.0	0.0	0.0	0.0	0.0	0.0	0.0
Taxes	2.3	0.3	0.0	5.0	2.0	11.6	8.0	9.1	15.0	12.0
Government Restrictions	0.0	0.0	2.4	0.0	0.0	0.0	2.0	0.0	0.0	0.0
Investment Benefit	0.0	0.0	0.0	0.0	0.0	0.0	0.0	0.0	5.0	0.0
Labour Regulations	0.0	0.0	0.0	0.0	0.0	0.0	2.0	9.1	0.0	0.0
Licences	0.0	0.0	0.0	0.0	0.0	0.0	0.0	0.0	0.0	0.0
Price Controls	0.0	0.0	0.0	0.0	0.0	0.0	0.0	9.1	0.0	0.0
Business Support	0.0	0.0	0.0	0.0	0.0	2.3	2.0	0.0	7.5	8.0
Infractructure	2.6	0.0	0.0	2.5	4.0	11.6	14.0	0.0	10.0	14.0
Utility Prices	2.3	6.0	0.0	0.0	0.0	18.6	16.0	27.3	5.0	10.0
Credit	60.5	40.0	45.5	52.5	48.0	72.1	72.0	72.7	75.0	64.0
Demand	7.0	14.0	18.2	10.0	8.0	32.6	40.0	18.2	30.0	16.0
Foreign Exchange	0.0	0.0	27.3	2.5	4.7	2.0	0.0	2.5	4.0	0.0
Imports	9.3	4.0	0.0	0.0	6.0	11.6	6.0	0.0	0.0	12.0
Local Firms	2.3	0.0	0.0	0.0	2.0	2.3	2.0	0.0	0.0	8.0
Uncertainty	0.0	0.0	0.0	0.0	0.0	0.0	0.0	0.0	2.5	0.0
Skill Labour	2.3	0.0	0.0	5.0	0.0	4.7	2.0	9.1	10.0	8.0
Other	9.3	24.0	0.0	12.5	20.0	44.2	38.0	45.5	50.0	46.0
Total no. of Firms	43	50	11	40	50					

Source: RPED Survey data.

Other serious problems include taxes which are more serious for micro and large firms, infrastructure (micro and large), utility prices(micro and medium), imports which is a demand related problem(medium and large), skilled labour(micro and medium).

Problems which were more binding in the controlled pre-ERP era have now been somewhat eased with liberalization. Price controls do not appear to be a problem; only 4% of the micro firms mentioned this as problem; foreign exchange is also not a problem, 2.4% of medium firms ranked this as the most serious problem. In the pre-liberalization period of foreign exchange controls, large firms and state-owned firms found it easier to get foreign exchange allocations than the smaller ones. The sample firms do not perceive this as a problem.

Table 2.15: Constraints on Firm Expansion by Age of Firm

	First ranking				Aggregate ranking			
	Baby	Young	Mature	Old	Baby	Young	Mature	Old
Owner Regulations	0.0	0.0	0.0	0.0	0.0	0.0	0.0	0.0
Taxes	1.9	2.9	4.3	0.0	15.1	11.8	7.2	11.4
Government Restriction	0.0	0.0	1.4	0.0	–	0.0	1.4	–
Investment Benefit	0.0	0.0	0.0	0.0	–	2.9	1.4	–
Labour Regulations	0.0	0.0	0.0	0.0	–	2.9	0.0	4.5
Licences	0.0	0.0	0.0	0.0	–	–	–	–
Price Controls	0.0	0.0	0.0	0.0	0.0	2.9	–	–
Business Support	0.0	0.0	0.0	0.0	3.8	8.0	4.3	2.3
Infrastructure	1.9	2.9	1.4	0.0	20.8	5.9	10.1	6.8
Utility Prices	3.8	2.9	1.4	0.0	9.4	20.6	13.0	15.9
Credit	56.6	52.9	56.5	25.0	75.5	79.4	75.4	50.0
Demand	18.9	2.9	4.3	22.7	37.7	26.5	24.6	25.0
Foreign Exchange	0.0	0.0	0.0	2.3	2.9	2.9	9.1	–
Imports	1.9	2.9	5.8	11.4	3.8	5.9	7.2	18.2
Local Firms	0.0	0.0	0.0	4.5	3.8	0.0	2.9	4.5
Uncertainty	0.0	0.0	0.0	0.0	1.9	–	2.5	–
Skill Labour	1.9	0.0	1.4	2.3	5.7	5.9	7.2	4.5
Other	9.4	32.4	13.0	22.7	43.4	55.9	39.1	40.9
Total firms	53	34	69	44				

Index of Severity of Constraints

We then tried to find out quantitatively, how important are these constraints inhibiting satisfactory firm performance. This was achieved by examining the firms' perception of the severity of the constraints on expansion by asking the entrepreneurs on a scale of 1 (not important) to 5 (very important) to measure the extent of the severity. For each constraint the score was averaged for each size, age and sector group to derive a rough index of severity. Tables 2.16, 2.17, 2.18 provide information on the firms' perception of the severity of the individual constraints.

Lack of access to credit is the most important constraint for all firms in all size, sector and age categories; but it is more severe for smaller firms than larger ones, more severe for wood firms accounting for a score of 4.40 out a maximum of 5.0, followed by garment

Table 2.16: Severity of Constraints to Firm Expansion

	All firms	Micro	Small	Medium	Large
Ownership regulations	1.08	1.13	1.06	1.03	1.18
Taxes	1.94	1.88	1.87	2.20	1.91
Government restrictions on activities	1.13	1.13	1.07	1.20	1.35
Investment benefits	1.26	1.13	1.22	1.49	1.26
Labour regulations	1.13	1.04	1.03	1.20	1.57
Difficulty in obtaining licences	1.08	1.04	1.11	1.00	1.13
Price controls	1.04	1.67	1.00	1.00	1.17
Foreign exchange controls	1.10	1.00	1.03	1.29	1.26
Lack of business support services	1.55	1.33	1.66	1.44	1.64
Lack of infrastructure	1.77	1.42	1.71	1.80	2.04
Utility prices	2.24	1.38	2.06	2.66	3.13
Lack of credit	3.80	3.71	4.08	3.49	3.21
No demand	2.57	2.96	2.53	3.09	1.74
Location regulations	1.34	1.33	1.33	1.46	1.23
Competition from imports	1.82	1.21	1.72	2.65	2.07
Other	2.86	2.50	2.83	2.00	4.09

Note: Survey scores range from 1 to 5. Figures are averages for firms surveyed in each category.

Table 2.17: Severity of Expansion Constraints by Sector

	Food	Textile	Garment	Wood	Furniture	Metal
Owner Regulations	1.19	1.00	1.00	1.33	1.00	1.0
Taxes	1.78	2.00	1.88	1.90	2.19	1.9
Government Restrictions	1.26	1.67	1.00	1.50	1.19	1.0
Investment Benefits	1.23	1.00	1.02	1.40	1.34	1.4
Labour Regulations	1.02	1.50	1.00	2.20	1.08	1.1
Licences	1.11	1.00	1.02	1.20	1.14	1.0
Price Controls	1.00	1.33	1.00	1.60	1.00	1.0
Forex Control	1.00	1.00	1.12	1.00	1.17	1.2
Business Support	1.45	1.00	1.34	1.50	1.89	1.7
Infrastructure	1.70	1.00	1.71	1.70	1.69	2.1
Utility Prices	2.47	3.17	2.19	2.50	2.08	2.0
Credit	3.61	3.33	3.95	4.40	3.94	3.7
Demand	2.91	3.00	2.55	2.30	2.75	2.1
Locality Regulations	1.36	1.00	1.66	1.00	1.40	1.1
Imports	1.50	3.00	1.96	1.83	1.80	1.9
Other	2.61	5.00	2.82	4.00	2.50	2.9

Table 2.18: Severity of Expansion Constraints by Age of Firm

	Baby	Young	Mature	Old
Owner Regulations	1.00	1.09	1.08	1.16
Taxes	1.88	2.15	1.76	2.10
Government Restrictions	1.1	1.18	1.08	1.18
Investment Benefit	1.17	1.41	1.28	1.21
Labour Regulations	1.06	1.21	1.05	1.28
Licences	1.11	1.18	1.03	1.03
Price Controls	1.00	1.12	1.00	1.10
Forex Control	1.02	1.18	1.06	1.21
Business Support	1.42	1.97	1.51	1.42
Infrastructure	1.75	1.88	1.74	1.74
Utility Prices	2.12	2.06	2.39	2.31
Credit	4.00	3.74	4.03	3.23
Demand	2.42	2.68	2.64	2.54
Locality Regulations	1.31	1.58	1.31	1.22
Imports	1.41	1.47	1.10	2.16
Other	2.30	3.50	2.60	3.60

Note: Survey scores range from 1 to 5. Figures are averages for firms
surveyed in each category

(3.95) and furniture (3.94), and is very severe for baby (4.00) and
mature (4.03) firms. The ranking is almost identical for various size,
ages, and sectors, credit being the principal constraint, followed by
demand and then utility prices. Taxes ranked fourth followed by
competition from imports, the latter being more binding on medium
and large, textiles and garments and the older firms.

Financial Constraints

From the previous section it emerged that finance is the most important constraint impeding expansion and growth of firms of all sizes,
ages and sectors in Ghana. The incidence of the constraint is asymmetrical with very high severity index for baby (4.00), mature (4.03),
wood (4.40), garment (3.95), furniture (3.94) and small firms (4.08).

What is the source of finance for investments in the manufacturing sector? Why does finance constrain the operation of small firms?
How much external source is used by firms? In most countries an
important distinguishing characteristics of the source of financing
for small firms is its self-financing capacity. The capital originates
from the entrepreneur himself, whether it is for starting a new business or for subsequent development. The survey revealed that over
78% of the entrepreneurs irrespective of size used their own savings
to establish their firms. Friends were important for the micro and
small firms. Local commercial banks provided none of the micro firms
with start funds but 28.6% of large firms benefited from bank funds.
The table also gives an indication of the relative magnitudes of the
funds from various sources. About 76% of the funds came from own
savings, and 25% was borrowed from friends (Table 2.19).

This dependence on internal sources for funding the establishment of new enterprises and expansion means that the manufacturing sector faces the problem of size and quality of capital which can
reduce the potential of the sector to employ a greater number of
persons. The havoc done to employment growth and the provision
of skills by the problem of inadequate capital is not fully highlighted
by the survey results, for there are those entrepreneurs who were
denied entry into the sector by their inability to mobilise enough
funds to start the business, and there are those whose enterprises
collapsed due to the problem.

The problem of credit is more severe for small enterprise than
the larger ones. Credit rationing in the pre-ERP era discriminated
against small firms. The discrimination should have eased in a period

Table 2.19: Sources of Start-Up Capital

Size

	All firms A	Micro A	B	Small A	B	Medium A	B	Large A	B
Own savings	76.3	78.0	80.0	74.9	84.3	83.6	79.7	69.7	78.9
Friends	25.1	36.7	41.6	30.6	41.2	1.3	6.7	3.8	7.7
Foreign Banks	1.0	-	-	-	-	5.5	7.1	-	-
Local banks	6.6	-	-	6.6	11.6	10.0	12.4	8.9	28.6
Money lenders	0.6	-	-	1.2	2.4	-	-	-	-
Suppliers	2.9	-	-	4.4	6.9	3.3	6.7	-	-
Other	34.4	27.3	27.3	30.2	32.0	39.0	45.0	50.0	50.0

Age

	Baby A	B	Young A	B	Mature A	B	Old A	B
Own savings	70.9	82.6	75.0	80.0	78.0	86.5	68.0	73.2
Friends	40.3	58.6	21.4	33.3	22.4	24.1	26.1	33.3
Foreign Banks	3.3	4.3	-	-	5.5	-	-	-
Local Banks	2.6	4.3	5.9	18.8	10.2	27.9	7.5	10.7
Money Lenders	2.2	4.3	-	-	-	-	-	-
Suppliers	-	-	4.7	6.7	2.6	7.4	1.0	3.8
Other	23.6	28.0	29.4	35.3	43.0	44.4	35.0	39.2

Sector

	Food A	B	Textile A	B	Garment A	B	Wood A	B	Furniture A	B	Metals A	B
Own savings	68.0	73.2	100.0	100.0	71.2	86.7	75.1	90.0	79.	83.9	83.2	0.5
Friends	26.1	33.3	0	0	49.6	55.6	3.0	20.0	28.0	33.3	11.6	24.0
Foreign Banks	-	-	0	0	0	- ·	-	0	0	0	3.7	4.8
Local banks	7.5	10.7	0	0	10.0	15.4	13.0	60.0	8.3	13.3	1.8	4.5
Money lenders	-	-	0	0	3.8	7.7	-	0	0	0	0	0
Suppliers	1.0	3.8	0	0	10.7	14.2	14.0	20.0	0	0	0	
Other	35.0	39.2	25.0	25.0	37.5	40.0	19.8	20.0	38.9	38.9	32.4	36.0

Notes: A — percentage of total funds from particular source.
       B — percentage of respondents using particular source.

of liberalization, but the credit stringency help the small firms. There are also reasons of greater information problems and transactions costs biasing credit delivery to small firms. For the small firms loan sizes are small, and the track record and reputation all add to the processing cost. The informal sources are used by the smaller and the starting firms. The food, metals and textiles sectors and the older firms were more successful than other sectors in accessing external finance.

The lending programmes in the country have not been successful; the banks are generally reluctant to lend, because there are secure government bonds. The rudimentary state of the capital market makes it difficult for firms to find other means of financing investment other than reliance on credit.

Table 2.20: Sources of Equipment Financing by Size

	0–9	10–29	30–49	50–99	100+	Total
Profits	63.0	66.7	57.1	58.3	72.2	63.8
Personal savings	27.7	28.6	28.6	0.0	0.0	23.2
Borrowed from friends	12.8	9.5	0.0	0.0	5.9	9.5
Borrowed from bank	4.3	45.8	14.3	36.4	25.0	10.4
Supplier	2.2	0.0	7.1	9.1	11.8	3.7
Money lender	0.0	0.0	0.0	0.0	0.0	0.0

General Regulations

Does the regulatory environment continue to constrain firms after a decade of stabilization and structural adjustment programmes? Many entrepreneurs complain about the complexity and limited transparency of the legal and administrative framework. Tables 2.22 and 2.23 provide the information on the responses of firms on relevance of general regulations. The regulations whether beneficial or costly is positively related to size, that is, they have greater impact on larger firms than on small firms. Firms which are concerned with regulations are concentrated in the wood sector. On the severity of general regulations it seems, based on our index of severity, these constraints are not binding.

Table 2.21: Access to Formal and Informal Finance (percentages and means of respondents in each category)

Size

	All	Micro	Small	Medium	Large
Received overdraft facilities last year	8.3	13.0	45.0	61.5	
Received loan last year	0	6.1	21.1	7.7	
Latest loan — maturity (days)	603	–	479	603	1095
— interest rate (%)	23.3	–	22.0	24.0	20.0
— collateral asked	75.0	75.0	50.0		
Applied for loan last year	8.3	23.5	18.8	12.0	
Ever applied for loan	10.0	35.9	61.5	81.0	
Informal borrowing from friends relatives, money lenders, informal groups	30.4	37.9	23.1	12.5	

Age

	Baby	Young	Mature	Old
Received overdraft facilities last year	7.5	26.5	27.5	28.0
Received loan last year	7.7	8.8	9.0	12.2
Latest loan — maturity (days)	455	517	314	364
— interest rate (%)	24.5	19.0	25.0	23.0
— collateral asked	75.0	66.7	80.0	100.0
Applied for loan last year	12.2	11.8	23.8	17.4
Ever applied for loan	20.0	46.4	48.1	37.5
Informal borrowing from friends relatives, money lenders informal groups	39.6	31.3	33.8	28.0

Sector

	Food	Text	Garmt	Wood	Furn.	Metals
Received overdraft facilities last year	28.0	50.0	11.6	18.2	15.0	38.0
Received loan last year	12.2	0	7.0	0	5.3	10.2
Latest loan — maturity (days)	364	0	405	–	638	1095
— interest rate (%)	23.0	0	26.0	–	22.5	23.3
— collateral asked	100.0	0	33.3	–	100	75.0
Applied for loan last year	17.4	33.3	23.3	18.2	10.8	17.4
Ever applied for loan	37.5	100.0	25.7	50.0	53.1	41.7
Informal borrowing from friends relatives, money lenders informal groups	28.0	16.7	58.1	0	28.2	22.4

Table 2.22: The Effects of General Regulations by Sector (percentage of respondents)

	Sector						Size			
	Food	Textiles	Garments	Wood	Furniture	Metal	Micro	Small	Medium	Large
Affected by government regulations concerning ownership	6.4	40.0	0	0	0	8.7	0	3.5	8.6	13.0
Received a capital allowance for tax purposes	23.4	40.0	5.2	35.7	15.8	30.4	4.4	11.7	48.6	47.8
Receiving a tax rebate	6.4	0	0	14.2	0	2.20	1.2	5.7	13.0	
Subject to the Selective Alien Employment Tax	6.4	20.0	0	28.6	2.6	19.6	0	4.7	22.9	26.0
Who have applied for benefits under the Investment Code	23.4	40.0	5.2	42.9	10.5	30.4	2.2	5.9	48.6	69.6
Who have received benefits under the Investment Code	19.1	40.0	5.2	42.9	10.5	23.9	2.2	2.4	42.9	69.6
Who have received exemptions from duty on imported machinery	17.0	20.0	+ 5.3	35.7	10.5	19.6	2.2	2.4	34.2	60.9
Who have received reductions in company tax rates	6.4	20.0	0	21.4	10.5	4.3	2.2	1.1	17.1	21.7
Who have received rebates on tax due	4.3	20.0	0	0	0	4.3	0	1.2	8.6	4.3
Who have received deferrals and/or reductions in income tax	2.1	0	0	0	0	4.3	0	1.2	5.7	0

Table 22 (cont'd.)

	Sector						Size			
	Food	Textiles	Garments	Wood	Furniture	Metal	Micro	Small	Medium	Large
Accelerated depreciation	8.5	0	0	7.1	5.3	6.5	0	2.4	14.3	13.0
Regional tax reductions	2.1	0	0	7.1	0	2.2	0	1.2	0	8.7
Percentage of Respondents who regard the following Regulations as constraints:										
Restrictions on activities in which they can participate	4.3	0	2.6	21.4	2.6	2.2	0	3.5	5.7	13.0
Capital requirements	2.1	0	2.6	21.4	5.3	6.5	0	3.5	11.4	13.0
Joint venture restrictions	2.1	0	5.2	7.1	2.6	8.7	0	5.9	2.9	13.0
Restrictions on access to domestic capital	2.1	20.0	2.6	14.2	10.5	6.5	0	5.9	11.4	13.0
Restrictions on repatriation of profits	4.2	0	2.6	7.1	5.2	4.3	0	2.4	8.6	13.0

Table 2.23: The Severity of General Regulations

	Sector							Size				Age			
	All firms	Food	Textiles	Garments	Wood	Furniture	Metal	Micro	Small	Medium	Large	Baby	Young	Mature	Old
Restrictions on activities in which they can participate	1.11	1.23	1.20	1.00	1.55	1.05	1.0	1.17	1.07	1.05	1.31	1.09	1.25	1.03	1.15
Capital requirements	1.10	1.05	1.20	1.00	1.55	1.08	1.2	1.09	1.07	1.13	1.23	1.02	1.28	1.10	1.08
Joint venture restrictions	1.11	1.09	1.20	1.05	1.09	1.05	1.2	1.00	1.14	1.03	1.27	1.00	1.0	1.05	1.38
Restrictions on access to domestic capital	1.12	1.09	1.40	1.00	1.36	1.16	1.1	1.13	1.08	1.18	1.15	1.11	1.19	1.06	1.15
Restrictions on repatriation of profits	1.08	1.13	1.20	1.00	1.09	1.08	1.1	1.00	1.02	1.18	1.19	1.02	1.06	1.13	1.08

Labour Regulations

Labour regulations as hypothesised are more binding for larger firms than smaller firms, increasing the cost to firms. Unlike general regulations which do not matter much, the labour regulations based on the severity index are more constraining (Tables 2.24 and 2.25). Layoff restrictions are more severe than other labour regulations. Their incidence differ between sectors and newer and older firms. Minimum wage regulation is more severe for textile and wood firms and mature firms; hiring restrictions are more important for baby firms; layoff restrictions and layoff benefits were cited by wood and textiles firms, mature and old firms, and the micro and large firms.

Infrastructure

Another important problem is the lack of adequate infrastructure. Services considered included electricity, water, public transport, roads, telephone, the ports and waste disposal (Table 2.26). Electricity and telephone were the most binding constraints for the responding firms. How did the manufacturers respond to the infrastructure deficiencies?

Price Controls

With the liberalization of the economy, the problems of price and foreign exchange controls have been reduced or completely eliminated. Only the wood sector consider output price control as important. Large firms and the wood sector perceive controls on access to foreign exchange as problem.

Ownership — State versus Private

Public ownership is seen as a factor mitigating against efficient operation and use of capital intensive production methods. The private sector perceives credit, demand and taxes as more serious constraints than the state enterprises. Imports and labour regulations especially minimum wage legislations, layoff restrictions and benefits are more binding on the state firms.

Human Capital and Acquisition of Technology

The availability of credit stands out clearly as the major constraint on growth. Capital has three dimensions: the human capital stock in the form of skilled labour used by the firm, the working capital

Table 2.24: The Effects of Labour Regulations by Size, Sector and Age of Firm

	Sector						Size				Age		
	Food	Textiles	Garments	Wood	Furniture	Metal	Micro	Small	Medium	Large	Baby	Young	Mature	Old
(Percentage of respondents subject to regulation)														
Minimum wage legislation	40.4	20.0	15.8	57.1	31.6	43.4	8.9	21.0	74.2	86.9				
Hiring Restrictions	6.4	20.0	5.3	7.1	2.6	15.2	0.0	4.7	20.0	17.4				
Limits on temporary hiring	12.7	0.0	2.6	21.4	5.3	13.0	4.4	2.4	17.1	34.8				
Layoff restrictions	23.4	60.0	13.1	57.1	15.8	26.1	4.4	11.8	51.4	65.2				
Layoff benefit requirements	31.9	40.0	13.2	50.0	15.8	32.6	6.7	14.1	60.0	60.9				
(Percentage of respondents for which the regulations matter)														
Minimum wage legislation	6.4	20.0	0.0	35.7	7.9	19.5	0.0	5.9	22.9	34.8				
Hiring Restrictions	2.1	0.0	0.0	0.0	0.0	8.6	0.0	2.4	2.9	8.7				
Limits on temporary hiring	0.0	0.0	0.0	14.	5.3	2.2	0.0	1.2	0.0	17.4				
Layoff restrictions	8.5	40.0	2.6	42.9	7.9	17.4	0.0	8.2	20.0	43.5				
Layoff benefit requirements	6.4	20.0	2.6	42.9	7.9	17.4	0.0	5.	14.3	52.2				

Table 2.25: Severity of Labour Constraints

		Sector						Size				Age			
	All Firms	Food	Textiles	Garments	Wood	Furniture	Metal	Micro	Small	Medium	Large	Baby	Young	Mature	Old
Minimum wage legislation	1.66	1.41	2.33	1.00	2.83	1.64	2.0	1.33	1.75	1.59	1.73	1.25	1.73	1.96	1.56
Hiring restrictions	1.38	1.50	1.00	1.00	1.00.	1.00.	1.6	1.00	1.70	1.11	1.33	2.33	1.20	1.25	1.33
Limits on temporary hiring	1.17	1.00	–	–	1.67	1.33	1.1	1.00	1.14	1.00	1.36	1.00	1.43	1.11	1.10
Layoff restrictions	2.04	1.79	2.67	1.5	2.86	1.88	2.0	3.00	2.07	1.70	2.35	1.00	2.09	2.47	1.95
Layoff benefit requirements	1.87	1.50	3.00	1.5	3.14	1.50	1.9	2.00	1.79	1.52	2.44	1.00	2.17	2.13	1.85

Table 2.26: The Effects of Infrastructure

	All Firms	Sector						Size				Age			
		Food	Textiles	Garments	Wood	Furniture	Metal	Micro	Small	Medium	Large	Baby	Young	Mature	Old
Electricity	2.63	2.34	2.33	2.72	2.64	2.59	2.9	2.04	2.76	2.63	2.56	2.62	2.23	2.81	2.66
Water	1.49	1.80	2.50	1.19	1.73	1.41	1.3	1.33	1.49	1.40	1.68	1.32	1.26	1.60	1.68
Public transport	1.49	1.39	1.00	1.58	1.09	1.41	1.7	1.30	1.41	1.53	1.72	1.53	1.41	1.56	1.40
Roads	1.42	1.38	1.33	1.40	2.09	1.36	1.4	1.25	1.29	1.48	2.08	1.30	1.21	1.59	1.45
Telephone	2.21	2.14	3.00	1.57	2.55	2.10	2.8	1.21	2.04	2.83	3.24	1.68	2.18	2.42	2.58
Air and sea ports	1.39	1.50	1.00	1.07	1.45	1.18	1.7	1.00	1.21	1.85	1.88	1.36	1.29	1.49	1.34
Waste disposal	1.38	1.34	1.67	1.09	2.45	1.34	1.4	1.08	1.28	1.38	2.12	1.26	1.26	1.48	1.45

requirements, and the physical capital stock. Although, entrepreneurs emphasize finance as their problem, when pressed further it was revealed that the problem lies with availability of working capital, and the costs are too high relative to entrepreneurs' desired levels. (Baah-Nuakoh and Steel 1993). In this section, we take up the question of the third dimension of capital and consider human capital and technology.

The problem of human capital and acquisition of technology was examined from two angles: (a) the entrepreneurs were asked to rank the three most important constraint to improvement in productivity. (b) we also relate several selected constraints (general regulations, labour regulations, infrastructure, to the educational background of entrepreneurs.

Constraints on Improvement in Productivity

The list of constraints considered in addition to finance and demand variables included human capital and technology variables: availability of information on technology, availability of engineering manpower, availability of technicians and skilled manpower, availability of imports of technology, availability of external training facilities, availability of local consultants, support from science and technology

Table 2.27: The Effects of Price and Foreign Exchange Controls

Size	Price Control on Inputs	Price Control on Output	Controls on Access to Foreign
Micro	0	0	0
Small	0	0	0
Medium	0	2.9	0
Large	4.3	21.7	4.3
Sector			
Food	0	0	0
Textiles	0	0	0
Garments	2.6	2.6	0
Wood	0	35.7	7.1
Furniture	0	0	0
Metals	0	0	0

Table 2.28: Severity of Constraints: State Versus Private

	Private Firms	*State Firms*
A. Constraints on Firm Expansion		
Owner Regulations	1.1	1.3
Taxes	2.0	1.4
Government Restrictions	1.1	1.4
Investment Benefit	1.3	1.2
Labour Regulations	1.1	1.2
Licences	1.1	1.0
Price Controls	1.0	1.1
Foreign Exchange Control	1.1	1.1
Business Support Services	1.6	1.4
Infrastructure	1.8	1.8
Utility Prices	2.2	3.0
Credit	3.9	3.0
Demand	2.6	2.4
Locality Regulations	1.3	1.3
Imports	1.8	2.1
Other	2.7	4.2
B. General Regulations		
Restrictions on activities in which they can participate	1.1	1.4
Capital requirements	1.1	1.1
Joint venture restrictions	1.1	1.1
Restrictions on access to domestic capital	1.1	1.1
Restrictions on repatriation of profits	1.1	1.1
C. Labour Regulations		
Minimum wage legislation	1.6	2.0
Hiring restrictions	1.4	1.0
Limits on temporary hiring	1.2	1.2
Layoff restrictions	1.9	2.8
Layoff benefit requirements	1.8	2.3
D. Infrastructural Constraints		
Electricity	2.7	2.2
Water	1.5	1.8
Public transport	1.5	1.9
Roads	1.4	1.1
Telephone	2.1	3.1
Air and sea ports	1.4	1.0
Waste disposal	1.4	1.5

institutions, and support from standards institutions. "An increase in technological capability would seem to be a prerequisite for further, fast-paced industrial growth".[2] The results are presented in Table 2.29.

Entrepreneurs ranked finance and demand above human capital and technology variables; they considered technology factors not important constraints to improvement in productivity, the only relevant one being the problem of import of technology. It seems then that demand for investment finance is the desire of the firms to upgrade their technology through imports.

An important constraint to the improvement in productivity in manufacturing is the lack of technicians and skilled workers. This problem affects mostly the large firms and mainly the wood, furniture and metals firms.

Educational Background and Experience of Entrepreneurs

The skill problem can also be attributed to the educational background of both entrepreneurs and apprentices. About 10% of entrepreneurs are illiterate, 6% have had a taste of primary education, 38% have been to middle school, 21% have attended secondary school; About 8% have been to university, 5% have professional qualification and 12% have gone to polytechnics. This means a majority of them are capable of absorbing basic management skills. Smaller firms make use of apprentices whose training programme is devoid of any instructions in management techniques and bookkeeping.

We related severity of constraints measured on the scale of 1 (not important) to 5 (very important) to the level of education of the entrepreneurs. Apart from the major constraint of credit which is negatively related to the level of education with a larger porportion of the less educated citing this as a problem, for most of the other constraints listed, it seems the larger proportion of the more educated perceived the constraints as negatively affecting their businesses. This could mean that the more educated were operating larger sized firms.

Relationship Between Perceived Contraints and Performance of Firms

This section examines the relationship between perceived constraints and indicators of performance. We expect the more successful firms

Table 2.29: Principal Constraints on Improvement of Productivity (Percentage of Respondents in Each Category)

	Micro	Small	Medium	Large	Garment	Food	Wood	Furniture	Metal	Baby	Young	Mature	Old
Availability of Finance	4.0	10.0	15.4	–	4.0	27.3	5.0	5.0	3.8	2.9	7.2	11.4	
Availability of Technicians & Skilled workers	1.0	2.5	3.8	–	–	9.1	5.0	5.0	–	2.9	2.9	–	
Availability of Imports of Technology	1.0	–	–	–	–	–	–	–	–	2.9	–	–	
Availability of external Training facilities	–	2.5	–	–	2.0	–	–	–	–	2.9	–	–	
Level of Demand (Size)	3.0	5.	–	2.3	2.0	–	–	1.9	1.9	2.9	–	6.8	

Table 2.30: Aggregate Constraints on Improvement of Productivity by Size, Sector and Age (Percentage of Respondents in Each Category)

	Micro	Small	Medium	Large	Garment	Food	Wood	Furniture	Metal	Baby	Young	Mature	Old
Availability of Finance	–	8.0	15.0	19.2		4.0	45.5	12.5	12.0	3.8	11.8	11.6	3.6
Availability of Technicians and Skilled workers	–	4.0	2.5	7.7	2.3		18.2	5.0	5.0	1.9	2.9	4.3	4.5
Availability of Imports of Technology	–	2.0	–	–	–	–	–	2.5	2.0	–	5.9	–	–
Availability of external Training facilities	–	–	2.5	3.8	–	2.0	–	2.5	–	–	2.9	1.4	–
Level of Demand (Size)	–	5.0	15.0	3.8	4.7	4.0	9.1	5.0	8.0	1.9	5.9	2.9	5.9

Note: Constraints which were never mentioned by any of the firms are not shown: availability of information on technology, availability of engineering manpower, availability of local consultants, support from standards institutions, support science and technology institutions.

Table 2.31: Severity of Constraints and Entrepreneur's Education Background and Experience

	None	Primary	Middle	Secondary	University	Profession	Polytechnic	Experience	Inexperience
Experience in years	13.8	8.5	6.6	7.7	9.8	10.5	7.8	2.7	8.0
A. Constraints on Firm expansion									
Owner Regulations	1.0	1.0	1.0	1.2	1.1	1.0	1.2	1.0	1.1
Taxes	1.3	1.7	2.0	1.8	2.6	2.7	1.8	1.7	2.0
Government Restrictions	1.0	1.0	1.0	1.2	1.6	1.6	1.1	1.0	1.1
Investment Benefit	1.0	1.0	1.2	1.4	1.6	2.4	1.5	1.3	1.3
Labour Regulations	1.0	1.0	1.0	1.2	1.1	1.2	1.1	1.0	1.1
Licences	1.0	1.0	1.0	1.1	1.4	2.0	1.0	1.0	1.1
Price Controls	1.0	1.0	1.0	1.1	1.0	1.0	1.2	1.0	1.0
Foreign Exchange Control	1.1	1.0	1.0	1.3	1.1	1.2	1.3	1.0	1.1
Business Support Services	1.3	1.0	1.6	1.8	1.9	2.8	1.7	2.3	1.5
Infrastructure	1.5	1.0	1.7	1.8	2.4	2.5	2.1	1.0	1.8
Utility Prices	1.5	1.5	2.0	2.5	2.6	2.7	2.5	1.0	2.3
Credit	4.2	3.6	4.2	3.8	3.1	3.1	3.8	4.3	3.8
Demand	2.5	2.5	2.6	2.6	2.7	2.4	2.3	3.3	2.6
Locality Regulations	1.6	1.0	1.4	1.2	1.6	1.5	1.2	1.0	1.3
Imports	1.4	1.4	1.7	2.0	1.9	1.7	1.9	2.5	1.8
Other	3.0	4.0	2.4	2.6	2.7	4.3	2.2	–	2.9

Table 2.31 (Cont'd.)

	None	Primary	Middle	Secondary	University	Profession	Polytechnic	Experience	Inexperience
B. General Regulations									
Restrictions on activities in in which they can participate	1.0	1.0	1.1	1.4	1.4	1.2	1.0	1.1	
Capital requirements	1.0	1.0	1.0	1.2	1.3	1.0	1.3	1.0	1.1
Joint venture restrictions	1.0	1.2	1.1	1.2	1.1	1.0	1.2	1.0	1.1
Restrictions on access to domestic capital	1.0	1.0	1.0	1.2	1.4	1.0	1.3	1.0	1.1
Restrictions on repatriation of profits	1.0	1.0	1.0	1.1	1.4	1.0	1.1	1.0	1.1
C. Labour regulations									
Minimum wage legislation	1.0	1.5	1.4	1.8	1.3	1.1	2.0	1.3	1.7
Hiring restrictions	1.0	1.2	1.0	1.3	2.0	5.0	1.2	1.0	1.4
Limits on temporary hiring	1.0	-	1.0	1.1	1.3	1.0	1.0	1.0	1.2
Layoff restrictions	2.0	1.3	1.0	2.2	1.6	1.0	2.4	1.5	2.1
Layoff benefit requirements	1.0	1.0	1.7	2.1	1.2	1.6	1.8	2.5	1.9
D. Infrastructural Constraints									
Electricity	1.9	3.1	2.9	2.6	1.5	1.4	2.8	2.4	2.6
Water	1.8	1.7	1.3	1.3	1.3	1.5	1.3	1.4	1.5
Public transport	1.1	1.0	1.4	1.5	1.9	1.5	1.6	1.6	1.5
Roads	1.2	1.0	1.3	1.4	1.6	2.0	1.5	1.6	1.4
Telephone	1.4	1.7	1.8	2.3	3.9	3.0	2.2	2.6	2.2
Air and sea ports	1.0	1.0	1.2	1.4	2.8	2.0	1.4	1.4	1.4
Waste disposal	1.0	1.3	1.3	1.4	1.5	2.0	1.6	1.8	1.4

to have been subjected to less severe constraints; that is, because of less binding constraints these firms were able to succeed. Thus the index of severity for the successful firms is expected to be lower for successful than for the unsuccessful firms. Performance here is measured by employment growth, capacity utilization and exports. Each indicator is analysed in terms of the constraints.

Employment Growth

Two measures of employment growth were used: (a) growth between start-up and 1991, (b) growth between 1988 and 1991. These firms were then categorised into 3: (a) those that experienced positive growth, (b) those that stagnated, (c) those that experienced decline. Table 2.32 presents the results. Credit is regarded as the most serious constraint regardless of growth performance. Using the severity index, declining and stagnant firms are more concerned with credit than growing firms. Demand is the second most important problem, with the unsuccessful firms blaming demand as constraint to growth. Limiting ourselves to the 1988–91 period while declining firms were very concerned with the problem of imports, the successful firms complained more about the problem of infrastructure, utilities and taxes.

Capacity Utilization and Manufactured Exports

The firms were grouped into four categories with respect to their utilization levels: (a) 0–25%, (b) 26–50%, (c) 51–75% and (d) 76–100% and these were related to various constraints (Table 2.34). Credit was a problem for all categories, but demand was less a severe problem for firms operating at high utilization levels than low utilization firms. Utility prices were also a problem but more severe for high utilization firms; this is expected because operating at high utilization levels will involve more consumption of electricity and other services.

Manufactured exports are not very significant in Ghana, although government pronouncement point towards the promotion of manu-factured exports. The exporting firms complain of high utility prices, taxes and labour regulations, while the non-exporting firms are con-strained in addition to credit by demand, layoff restrictions and taxes.

Table 2.32: Relationship Between Constraints and Firm Performance (Employment Growth)

| | *(Percentage of Respondents in Each Category)* | | | | | |
| | *Principal Constraint* | | | *Aggregate Constraint* | | |
	Growth	*Stagnant*	*Decline*	*Growth*	*Stagnant*	*Decline*
(A) (Start-up to 1991) Firms						
Taxes	2.3	6.2	2.0	12.0	12.5	7.8
Government Rest	0.8	0	0	0.8	0	0
Investment Benefit	0	0	0	1.5	0	0
Labour Regulation	0	0	0	1.5	0	2.0
Price Control	0	0	0	0	0	2.0
Business Support	0	0	0	5.3	6.2	2.0
Infrastructure	2.3	0	0	11.3	12.5	11.8
Utility Prices	·1.5	6.2	2.0	16.5	12.5	7.8
Credit1	41.4	62.5	64.7	69.2	75.0	72.5
Demand1	9.8	12.5	11.8	23.3	31.3	41.2
Forex1	0.8	0	0	3.0	0	5.9
Imports1	6.8	3.9	9.0	0	9.8	
Local Firms1	1.5	0	0	3.8	0	0
Certificate	0	0	0	0.8	0	0
Skill Labour1	2.3	0	0	8.3	· 6.2	0
Other1	21.1	6.2	11.8	43.6	37.5	45.1
No. of firms	133	16	51			
(B) (1988–1991) Firms						
Taxes1	3.4	4.8	0	12.9	4.8	9.5
Government Restrictions1	0.9	0	0	0.9	0	0
Investment Benefit	0	0	0	0.9	0	1.6
Labour Regulation	0	0	0	1.7	0	1.6
Price Control	0 0	0	0	0	1.6	
Business Support	0	0	0	4.3	9.5	3.2
Infrastructure1	2.6	0	0	12.1	9.5	11.1
Utility1	2.6	0	1.6	18.1	19.0	4.8
Credit1	45.7	61.9	50.0	71.6	71.4	68.3
Demand1	10.3	23.8	6.3	25.9	33.3	31.7
Forex1	0.9	0	0	3.4	4.8	3.2
Imports1	4.3	0	9.5	6.0	9.5	12.7
Local Firms1	0.9	0	1.6	2.6	0	0
Certificate	0	0	0	0.9	0	3.2
Skill Labour1	1.7	0	1.6	8.6	0	0
Other1	19.0	0	20.6	47.4	33.3	39.7
No. of firms	116	21	63			

Table 2.33: Severity of Constraints (Measured by Employment)

	Growth	*Stagnant*	*Decline*	*Growth*	*Stagnant*	*Decline*
A. Constraints on Firm expansion						
Owner Regulation	1.07	1.00	1.10	1.04	1.10	1.14
Taxes	2.02	1.69	1.82	2.12	1.70	1.67
Government Restriction	1.15	1.00	1.14	1.17	1.00	1.12
Investment Benefit	1.27	1.13	1.26	1.26	1.35	1.22
Labour Regulation	1.18	1.00	1.04	1.18	1.05	1.07
Licences	1.07	1.00	1.12	1.11	1.00	1.05
Price Controls	1.03	1.00	1.08	1.04	1.00	1.07
Forex Control	1.10	1.00	1.14	1.10	1.15	1.08
Business Support	1.57	1.63	1.48	1.67	1.35	1.40
Infrastructure	1.87	1.31	1.68	1.89	1.40	1.68
Utility Prices	2.34	2.56	1.88	2.46	1.90	1.93
Credit	3.77	4.12	3.78	3.94	3.50	3.66
Demand	2.44	2.13	3.02	2.45	3.05	2.61
Locality Regulation	1.33	1.75	1.22	1.33	1.30	1.36
Imports	1.91	1.40	1.72	1.61	1.54	2.28
Other	2.69	2.60	3.72	2.70	2.00	3.62
B. General Regulations						
Restrictions on activities in which they can participate	1.09	1.00	1.21	1.12	1.00	1.13
Capital requirements	1.13	1.00	1.07	1.13	1.00	1.09
Joint venture restrictions	1.12	1.00	1.17	1.09	1.19	1.11
Restrictions on access to domestic capital	1.07	1.40	1.14	1.11	1.19	1.09
Restrictions on repatriation of profits	1.10	1.00	1.02	1.08	1.00	1.09
C. Labour regulations						
Minimum wage legislation	1.63	1.00	2.00	1.55	2.20	1.77
Hiring restrictions	1.29	1.00	1.71	1.47	1.00	1.30
Limits on temporary hiring	1.18	–	1.14	1.25	1.00	1.10
Layoff restrictions	1.93	–	2.50	1.74	4.00	2.32
Layoff benefit requirements	1.82	1.00	2.22	1.68	1.75	2.29

Table 2.33 (*Cont'd.*)

	Growth	Stagnant	Decline	Growth	Stagnant	Decline
D. Infrastructural Constraints						
Electricity	2.83	2.31	2.18	2.87	2.14	2.33
Water	1.50	1.31	1.50	1.58	1.33	1.37
Public transport	1.57	1.31	1.34	1.49	1.38	1.52
Roads	1.53	1.69	1.26	1.45	1.19	1.43
Telephone	2.42	1.25	1.84	2.33	1.52	2.23
Air and sea ports	1.47	1.25	1.20	1.46	1.29	1.29
Waste disposal	1.45	1.34	1.24	1.39	1.25	1.40

Table 2.34: Severity of Constraints, Capacity Utilization and Manufactured Exports

Capacity Utilization(%)

	0–25	26–50	51–75	76–100	Export Firms	Non-export Firms
A. Constraints on Firm Expansion						
Owner Regulations	1.3	1.0	1.0	1.1	1.5	1.0
Taxes	1.6	2.1	1.9	2.1	2.4	1.9
Government Restrictions	1.1	1.1	1.2	1.2	1.6	1.1
Investment Benefit	1.0	1.3	1.4	1.1	1.6	1.2
Labour Regulation	1.1	1.1	1.1	1.1	1.8	1.1
Licences	1.0	1.1	1.1	1.0	1.2	1.1
Price Controls	1.0	1.0	1.0	1.1	1.4	1.0
Foreign Exchange Control	1.2	1.1	1.0	1.0	1.1	1.1
Business Support	1.3	1.7	1.5	1.7	1.9	1.5
Infrastructure	1.8	1.7	1.9	1.8	2.1	1.7
Utility Prices	2.0	2.2	2.1	2.8	3.3	2.1
Credit	3.6	3.9	3.9	3.7	3.6	3.8
Demand	2.8	2.7	2.7	2.0	1.7	2.6
Localiity Regulation	1.5	1.4	1.5	1.1	1.3	1.3
Imports	2.3	2.0	1.6	1.0	1.5	1.8
Other	2.8	2.6	2.7	4.0	5.0	2.7

Table 2.34 (*Cont'd.*)

	0–25	26–50	51–75	76–100	Export Firms	Non-export Firms
B. General Regulations						
Restrictions on activities in which they can participate	1.0	1.1	1.1	1.1	1.3	1.1
Capital requirements	1.0	1.1	1.1	1.2	1.2	1.1
Joint venture restrictions	1.3	1.1	1.1	1.1	1.1	1.1
Restrictions on access to domestic capital	1.2	1.1	1.1	1.1	1.2	1.1
Restrictions on repatriation of profits	1.0	1.0	1.2	1.1	1.1	1.1
C. Labour Regulations						
Minimum wage legislation	1.8	1.2	1.5	2.0	1.9	1.6
Hiring restrictions	1.5	1.4	1.4	1.0	1.0	1.5
Limits on temporary hiring	1.0	1.0	1.4	1.3	1.2	1.2
Layoff restrictions	2.5	1.8	1.6	2.7	1.9	2.0
Layoff benefit requirements	2.2	1.5	1.6	2.5	2.4	1.8
D. Infrastructural Constraints						
Electricity	2.8	2.5	2.7	2.5	3.1	2.6
Water	1.5	1.6	1.4	1.2	1.5	1.5
Public transport	1.7	1.4	1.4	1.4	1.8	1.5
Roads	1.4	1.4	1.4	1.6	2.2	1.3
Telephone	2.5	1.9	2.4	2.3	3.3	2.1
Air and sea ports	1.4	1.3	1.5	1.5	1.6	1.4
Waste disposal	1.3	1.3	1.5	1.4	2.3	1.3

Conclusion

This chapter has examined the major obstacles constraining firm growth in the Ghanaian manufacturing sector using the 200-firm RPED survey. The problem of credit has been identified as the majoɪ constraint facing all firms irrespective of size, age, and sector, but it is more severe for smaller firms, wood firms and newer firms. Although, firms also complained about general regulations, labour regulations and infrastructure, these were not binding factors. Thus, although the liberalization policy of the ERP period with differential responses by different firms has gradually removed some of these regulations, finance problems have not yet been fully addressed. It must be noted that the paper has concentrated on the problems of existing firms. It did not touch on the problems of firms which had to exit due to problems generated by the structural adjustment programme.

NOTES

1. For a fuller discussion of the choice of the sample and methodology see Baah-Nuakoh and Teal (1993).
2. World Bank (1994) p.152.

REFERENCES

Anheir H. K. and D. Seibel (1987). Small-Scale Industries and Economic Development in Ghana Business Behaviour Strategies in Informal Sector Economies. Cologne Development Studies. Cologne. Verlag Breitenbach Publishers.

Aryeetey, E., A. Baah-Nuakoh, T. Duggleby, H. Hettige and W. F. Steel (1993). Meeting the Financing Needs of Small- and Medium-Sized Enterprises in Ghana. Report of a Study Commissioned by the National Board for Small Scale Industries,Accra. October

Baah-Nuakoh, A. (1982). "Elements of Ghanaian Industrial Market Structure," *Legon Economic Studies* No. 8201, Department of Economics, University of Ghana, Legon.

—— (1993). *Development Policies and Institutional Environment for Employment Promotion in the Informal Sector in Ghana* ILO/JASPA, Addis Ababa.

—— and W. Steel (1993). Background Paper on SME Demand for Finance for the Study on Meeting the Financial Needs of Ghana's Small- and Medium-Scale Enterprises, March 1993.

Baah-Nuakoh, A. (1993). The Economy of Ghana in 1992: The Industrial Sector. Paper prepared for ISSER, University of Ghana Project on the Ghanaian Economy. June.

—— and F. Teal, "The Design of the Survey and Sample Characteritics" in F. Teal and A. Baah-Nuakoh (ed) Economic Reform and the Manufacturing Sector, The Africa Regional Programme on Enterprise Development., December.

Department of Economics, University of Ghana, Legon and Centre for the Study of African Economies, University of Oxford (1992). Economic Reform and the Manufacturing Sector, Country Background Paper,

Levy, B.(1993). "Obstacles to Developing Indigenous Small and Medium Enterprises:An Empirical Assessment," *The World Bank Economic Review*, Vol.7 No. 1. January, pp. 65–83.

ISSER, *The State of the Ghanaian Economy, 1992 to 2001* issues, chapters on the Industrial Sector.

Little, I. M. D., D. Mazumdar, and J.M. Page, Jr. (1987). *Small Manufacturing Enterprise: A Comparative Analysis of India and Other Economies.* New York. Oxford University Press for the World Bank.

Meier, G. and W. Steel (1989). *Industrial Adjustment in SubSaharan Africa.* Oxford University Press. Published for the World Bank. EDI Series in Economic Development.

Melford, R. N. (1986) "Introducing Management into the Production Function." *Review of Economics and Statistics.*

Osei B. A. Baah-Nuakoh, N. Sowa and K. Tutu (1993). "Impact of Structural Adjustment on Small Scale Industries in Ghana" in A. H. J. Helmsing and Th. Kolstee (ed), *Small Enterprises and Changing Policies: Structural Adjustment, Financial Policy and Assistance Programmes in Africa.* Intermediate Technology Publications, London.

Sowa, N., A. Baah-Nuakoh, K. A. Tutu, B. Osei (1992). *Small Enterprises and Adjustment: The Impact of Ghana's Economic Recovery Programme.* Overses Development Institute and University of Ghana, Accra.

Steel, W. and Leila Webster (1991). *Small Enterprises under Adjustment in Ghana.* World Bank Technical Paper No.138. Industry and Finance Series.

Thomi and Yankson (1985). Small Scale Industries and Decentralization in Ghana: A Preliminary Report on Small Scale Industries in Small and Medium Sized Towns in Ghana. Frankfurt/Accra.

World Bank (1994). *Adjustment and Growth.*

World Bank, *The Dynamics of Enterprise Development in Africa: Concept.*

CHAPTER 3

Inter-Firm Linkages

(with Dr Kwadwo Tutu)

Introduction

At independence, Ghana assigned to the industrial sector the central role for the achievement of economic development. This was consistent with the contemporary thinking in development economics which equated development with industrialization. The nation launched an industrialization drive based on import substitution strategy. The strategy was emphasized to reduce the economic dependence, by manufacturing locally what was previously imported. The vigour with which the industrialization programme was pursued is evidenced by the rapid growth rates experienced in the sector. By 1976, industry accounted for 21.1% of GDP, with manufacturing accounting for 13.8% of GDP. The shares had declined to 11.6% and 7.2% in 1984 respectively. By 1996 there had been slight recoveries of the shares to 14.2% and 8.1% respectively.

The import-substitution strategy coupled with the fiscal and financial incentives (tax holdings, import duty exemptions, subsidized credit, accelerated depreciation etc.) led to the development of an industrial sector highly dependent on imported capital goods and raw materials and very little linkages with the other sectors of the economy. However, a useful part of the import substitution programme was the emphasis on agro-based industrialization. The very size of the agricultural sector, contributing about 50 percent of GDP and the diversity of crops produced, from grains/cereals to roots/tubers, (Table 4.4) made agro-based industry a priority sub-sector in manufacturing.

The garments and textiles sectors have been dependent on imports of raw material, while the food and wood sectors depended in most part on domestic inputs. For the textiles and garments sectors there is some local manufacturing using local raw materials.

It has been argued that there exist possibilities for local industries both small and large to source their input requirements locally. Large firms currently import inputs which could be produced locally by smaller firms. The demand constraint which thwart the growth of small firms could be removed by increased linkages between small and large firms with the latter making increased use of output of the small firms as inputs.

We can define linkages between firms as all possible forms of economic relationships between firms in an economy. In most cases the relationship should be continual with repeated transactions. Linkages among firms are mutually rewarding in several ways. In the present changing economy, an industry's vitality depends on low levels of market friction and a high degree of flexibility. A broad based industrial structure with strong inter-firm linkages achieves these.

Repeated interactions between firms lower transaction costs of obtaining and acting on information as well as standardizing market norms, thus reducing market frictions. Firms also realize higher flexibility as subcontracting relationships are established allowing firms to meet production schedules as they occur without having to maintain high levels of inventory.

For the economy as a whole inter-firm linkages also remove one of the most important constraint to small and medium scale enterprises, that is, low skill levels, by increasing the absorptive capabilities of these enterprises, making it possible for them to upgrade their skills, and thus promote small and medium scale enterprises.

Types of Linkages

There are three stages in the process of linkage creation:

(a) the sourcing of inputs — the choice between import (foreign linkages) and local procurement (the possibility of local linkages); the import substitution industrialization adopted in Ghana was dependent on imported intermediate inputs.

(b) the make/buy choice — for a locally procured input whether it is made by the firm itself (complete market failure leading to internalization) or purchased from an independent supplier (transaction costs lower than internalization costs).

(c) the linkage decision — what form of direct relationships have to be established with the supplier to overcome the deficiencies of pure market relationships.

Categories of Linkages

We can distinguish between two main types of linkages, forward and backward linkages. Forward linkage or "output utilization" relates to a situation where "every activity that does not by its nature enter exclusively to final demand, will induce attempts to utilize its output as inputs in some new activities."[1] For example, the logging industry leads to the establishment of sawmilling industries to utilize the products as inputs. For backward linkage or input provision effects, "every non-primary economic activity will induce attempts to supply through domestic production the inputs needed in that activity,"[2] for example the establishment of textiles industries leads to the production of cotton domestically to feed the industries.

In the empirical estimation of forward and backward linkages, input-output tables have been used for several countries. [Watanabe (1958, Cella (1984), Nugent and Yotopoulos (1982)]. Lall (1980) has categorized linkages as follows:

Inputs (Raw Materials)

(i) Establishment: direct assistance provided by enterprises to prospective suppliers to launch production in order to provide cheaper or more reliable components, or to act as alternative sources so as to avoid excessive dependence on a few suppliers.

(ii) Locational: assistance and/or encouragement to local suppliers to set up facilities near the buyer, and foreign suppliers to invest in the country, again to provide cheaper or alternative sources of inputs.

(iii) Informational: placing of firm orders for specified periods to facilitate current production planning; and communication of long term plans to facilitate investment.

(iv) Procurement: assistance to buy raw materials or the direct provision of raw materials, to overcome uncertainties about their quality and availability.

Technical

(v) Technical: provision of technical assistance or exchange of technical information, to ensure the precise matching of needs with supplies, to provide for adequate quality and to facilitate innovation.

(vi) Financial: grants and concessional loans etc. to ensure that suppliers are able to meet their current and future commitments.

(vii) Managerial: provision of training and other help with management to improve suppliers performance.

(viii) Pricing; setting up a negotiation procedure to determine prices.

(ix) Other distributional: allocation of inventory and product development costs.

(x) Diversification: assisting suppliers to find other customers to increase financial stability.

Subcontracting

Subcontracting is a type of inter firm linkage. It is market transaction between a large firm which is the buyer and a small and medium scale enterprise (SME) supplier.

Why do firms subcontract?

Firstly, the finished products of most items consist of various parts and components. A firm might find it costly to establish separate manufacturing units for each of these components and parts. A firm therefore establishes subcontracting arrangements with other firms to produce the parts and components. It means a firm will subcontract if the transaction costs of the subcontracting arrangements are lower than costs of in-house production of the part. Secondly, a firm may subcontract where the production of these parts do not involve a critical or strategic technology. Thirdly, industries which are involved in subcontracting arrangements are usually modern with relatively well educated entrepreneurs who know how to manage subcontracting arrangements.

An important benefit to SMEs from subcontracting is the increased absorptive capacity of SMEs with these firms receiving skill upgrades. This is also a constraint to the development of subcontracting. The low skills of SMEs labour and management often leads to poor quality of products and late delivery which may discourage further subcontracting.

Methodology

To study interfirm linkages we make use of different surveys: the World Bank Regional Programme for Enterprise Development Ghana (RPED) Survey, a Key Enterprise Survey and a Key Informant Survey.

The chapter concentrates on the input (raw material) output linkages — input-output ratios to find the extent of use of intermediates, the sourcing of inputs, spares and components (domestic/foreign/in house) and subcontracting of inputs, spares and components.

RPED Survey

Data has been collected for a sample of 200 firms in the manufacturing sector for the years 1991, 1992. This data source is used in this study to examine input-output linkages and subcontracting. The survey has been described in Chapter 2.

The survey considered firms in the food processing, textiles and garments, wood and furniture and metal working industries. The sample size was 200 firms in 5 areas — Accra, Tema, Kumasi, Cape Coast and Takoradi.

Key Enterprise Survey

The purpose of this survey was to explore the various types of linkages in the three sectors — food processing, textiles and garments and wood processing. The survey was undertaken by the authors between November 1996 and March 1997. The key enterprise survey covered 20 firms in three major clusters: Accra-Tema, Kumasi, Cape Coast/Sekondi-Takoradi in the three subsectors. The key informants survey covered 9 institutions and firms. Several firms refused to cooperate, arguing that they had been over-interviewed and have not gained anything from previous interviews.

Because of the non-existence of a complete list of all food processing, textiles and garments and wood processing firms in the country, we had to resort to the 1987 Industrial Census list of firms provided by the Statistical Service. The selection of firms was not random but was based on previous knowledge of the firms acquired through earlier surveys and was not meant to achieve statistically representative results.

The use of subcontractors and type of linkages are all related to firm size. Thus we attempted to survey a mix of firms of different sizes. We considered four size categories, micro, small, medium and large. The term "micro-enterprise" is sometimes used to describe firms with fewer than 5 workers.

For the purposes of this study we adopted the following classification of size:

1-9	workers —	"micro-enterprises"
10-29	workers —	"small";
30-99	workers —	"medium".
100+	workers —	"large"

Additional information was obtained through interviews with a 9 "key informants" from the sectors.

SURVEYS AND RESULTS ON LINKAGES

In this section, we set out the results of the surveys and seek to use the results to answer the central question of linkages at the firm level.

Sourcing of Inputs and Linkages

The sourcing of inputs for firms could result in all aspects of linkages including forward, backward and subcontracting. We notice that five of our eight industrial sectors have at least 50% of their output as raw materials. While in 1991, it was textiles, garments and machinery which had an average of 47% raw material-output ratio, the situation in 1992 was a little different. Textiles, wood and garments had less than 50% with the latter two averaging 37% (Table 3.1).

Tables 3.1-3 which have been derived from the 1991 and 1992 RPED surveys do not show any significant difference between firms in their raw material output ratio either in size or age. What this implies is that, generally there is some good proportion of raw material input which could provide a basis for linkages. The issue is whether these inputs are sourced locally and the degree of the processing. Table 3.5 shows that metal, machinery, textiles in 1991 imported at least 50% of their raw materials. The only sector whose imports of raw materials of 49% is counter to expectation is food.

In terms of raw materials, it is expected that with the exception of a few textile and garment firms, all the firms will source these

Table 3.1: Raw Material Output Ratio 1991–1992 By Sector

	1991	1992			
Value Label	Mean		Std Dev	Sum of Sq	Cases
Bakery	.6941	.7128	.2199	.9190	20
Foods	.5272	.5463	.1413	.4394	23
Furniture	.5013	.5036	.161	1.0366	41
Garments	.4508	.3980	.2336	2.1827	41
Machinery	.4909	.5903	.2959	.5254	7
Metal	.5944	1.1533	3.9007	593.4129	40
Textiles	.4836	.4765	.1135	.0515	5
Wood	.5697	.3636	.3134	.7859	9
Within Groups Total		.6436	1.8248	599.4015	189

F = 3.2039   F = .5573
Sig. = .0021   Sig. = .8117

Table 3.2: Raw Material Output Ratio in 1992 by Size

Value Label	Mean	Std Dev	Sum of Sq	Cases
Large	1.5024	5.1642	586.7240	23
Medium	.4804	.1917	1.7275	48
Small	.5194	.2440	5.1797	88
Zmicro	.6106	.1844	.9859	30
Within Groups Total	.6436	1.7928	594.6171	189

Source	Sum of Squares	d.f.	Mean Square	F	Sig.
Between Groups	19.6311	3	6.5437	2.0359	.1104
Within Groups	594.6171	185	3.2141		

Table 3.3: Raw Material Output Ratio 1992 by Age

Value Label	Mean	Std Dev	Sum of Sq	Cases
	.4676	.2288	.5234	11
Old	.4640	.2243	1.7604	36
Mature	.9173	3.0865	600.1519	64
Young	.5221	.2535	1.8637	30
New	.5296	.2346	2.5876	48
Within Groups Total	.6436	1.8161	606.8870	189

Source	Sum of Squares	d.f.	Mean Square	F	Sig.
Between Groups	7.3613	4	1.8403	.5580	.6935
Within Groups	06.8870	184	3.2983		

inputs locally. This must be especially so with the processing of the food sector considering the fact that it is the largest proportion of GDP. The results from our key enterprise survey show that only 13% of firms imported all their raw materials and these are textile and garment firms. There were 27% other firms which sourced some proportion of raw materials from outside Ghana. About half of these firms imported at least 50% of inputs from outside with the other half importing only 20% of materials. For firms that used local raw materials, the problem that most of them (44%) cited was poor quality. The other problems that were mentioned were unreliable supply and high price. Each problem was cited by 33% of the firms. Table 3.3 show significant differences at the level of 96% between sizes of firms indicating that medium, large and small firms have a higher proportion of raw material imports than micro firms. Most of these firms being large and medium tend to be the old stock of the import substitution legacy where the objective was industrialization and modernization irrespective of whether local raw material was available.

We consider sourcing of inputs in terms of backward and forward linkages and subcontracting both generally and sectorally.

Forward linkage

We have indicated from our initial linkage characterization that while cement, blocks and tiles top the list of forward linkage industries, agricultural sectors have generally weak forward linkages. Our recent sample seemed to confirm this finding. Most of the firms (64%) sold most of their output to final demand. Even this outcome is higher because we included in our sample agricultural oil processing firms which were set up to feed soap related firms.

Some firms indicated that they were selling their products to the final consumer even though they can be used by other manufacturers. The fact that there was low forward linkages did not depend on sector or size. This means that there are potential linkages that can be created for existing products.

Wood Processing

We have already surveyed the structure and technology of this sector. The wood sector has a lot of outputs that the furniture sector uses. The major problem here is the waste that takes place in terms of trees that are destroyed during harvesting and the sawn wood that does not meet specifications and are discarded to be used for furniture or for fuel. Secondly, the saw dust that results could be put to several uses including chipboard making but this is not done. They explained that there were no firms producing those lines of product and that there was the need for public policy and support for other firms to enter those lines of production.

The other area of forward linkage that can be developed in the furniture sector is production of furniture parts to be used by other firms. All firms produced final products and few firms only sought the services of others in very limited areas where firms do not have the technology to produce certain parts of the furniture. The strategy of clustering whereby most firms will be brought together so that some firms will produce specific parts for other firms is being mooted. The only problem there is quality of production but this can be solved by bringing in only very noted good firms as a trial basis, upgrading their technology and offering training.

One other shortcoming of the wood sector is poor quality wood. The situation is that most of the quality wood is exported while the local furniture sector mainly depends on offcuts whose quality in terms of dryness and specifications are poor. While a kiln-dried wood would improve quality furniture, the cost is such that dried wood should be used in selected technology-upgraded furniture firms meant for export.

Food Processing

While we noted that the food sector uses about 50% of imported raw materials it is found that there is very low forward linkage for the food firms. We have discussed the fact that it was only the oil processing firms that have forward linkages in that they were set up just for that purpose. It was even found that further processing of by products of palm fruits such as kernels could be done.

As to why firms cannot initiate other lines of production to utilize the by-products, it was learnt that firms were already finding difficulty in maintaining the present lines of production and would not want to increase the difficulty by adding more. An example is one of the by-products from oil processing mills which could be used as feeds for chicken. Although, the feed mills bought these products the market is not handled in joint determination of price as is done in the case with producers and consumers of palm oil. Since feed mills see this input as waste by-products of oil mills, they pay very low price within this oligopolistic market. There is the need for a coordinating institution like the Ministry of Agriculture to help establish an association as is the case with the oil palm.

Textiles and Garments

There is generally a very low forward linkage for the sectors. The garments sector sells to final consumers. Where it is expected that a strong forward linkage will develop is the production of textiles for the garment industry but this is not happening due to quality, price, lack of credit and the dependence on reworking of imported used clothing. Another major obstacle to linkages, mainly low subcontracting is the lack of standardization of production in the garment industry. This problem has been discussed below.

Backward Linkage

We have indicated above that as agriculture forms the largest part of GDP, most of the processing should be based on the agricultural sector. Therefore, we expect significant backward linkage from that sector. Our key enterprise survey showed that only about 25% of our sample had their spares locally produced although 53% admitted that the spares can be produced locally.

Food Processing

The small food processing firms make use of local agricultural raw materials, but the large firms mainly the foreign affiliates do not have local linkages. They rarely use local producers of spares and components since their technology is not up to their requisite standards. All the agricultural oil processing firms had most of their spares and aspects of the machinery produced locally. There is a particular firm that produced 90% of its machines in-house. Firms who stated that their spares could be manufactured locally but are not being done cited lack of capital to start production and inability to obtain licence to do so as the reason. It would seem to imply that the macroeconomic bottleneck of high inflation rate, lending and exchange rates together with inappropriate industrial strategy strongly account for the low linkages.

With the exception of one firm (a multinational) in this sector that set up another firm to supply it with inputs, no firm helped set up another firm neither did they provide technical nor financial assistance to firms supplying inputs. However, in the case of the food sector, some limited amount of financial assistance was found. Some firms gave credits either to farmers supplying palm fruits or soap making firms gave credits to firms supplying oil palm to them. There are a lot of in-house training and other linkages that take place in the multinational firm by utilizing the international linkages.

The foregoing shows the urgent need for support for farmers in terms of finance, technology and its extension and marketing. If the appropriate linkages are developed in the processing area, it will be easy to arrange marketing within such an association as is done in some oil palm, cotton and tobacco sectors.

In terms of pricing, it is instructive to note that where agricultural raw materials are involved, prices for the inputs are set through special negotiations. There is always an association of producers and consumers of the raw materials and negotiation within the association results in the price which is fair to both parties. In setting prices for oil palm fruits and cotton this process is used. In the present case of oil palm, the world price is paid to local mills and a corresponding palm fruit price to assure adequate profit to farmers is reached. This reinforces the need to strengthen the linkages especially in the agricultural sector so that prices to farmers who produce the raw material inputs to the firms will receive prices which take into consideration their cost of production.

Another type of linkage that could be developed especially for the food sector was considered to be the packaging industry. This was seen as important because of the importance of the health effects of preservation, its attractiveness of packaging to the consumer and the environmental effects of disposal and reuse of containers.

Wood Processing

We have already noted that wood and furniture firms source at least 80% of their raw materials from the local source. We have drawn attention of the low quality of wood for the furniture firms and the extreme waste in the wood sector. Another major problem is the sustainability of the industry because the wood is fast depleting with very little replacement being done. (This will be dealt with in the policy section.)

Textiles and Garments

The textile industry now uses the local raw cotton produced. It is during the few times of shortage that cotton is imported. Like the oil palm and tobacco sectors, there is an association of producers of cotton, ginners and users which makes sure that transactions on pricing and distribution run smoothly. However, the garment industry has no linkages with the textile firms; almost all the fabrics are imported. Lall's study also found out that there were no linkages of the garment firms with any official institution for training, technology, standards or design.

Table 3.4: Percentage of Raw Materials Imported by Sector, 1991

Value Label	Mean	Std Dev	Sum of Sq	Cases
Bakery	18.7500	37.5000	4218.7500	4
Foods	49.7375	31.6662	15041.2375	16
Furniture	25.2000	26.2071	4120.8800	7
Garments	34.0000	46.6905	8720.0000	5
Machinery	51.6667	44.8144	4016.6667	3
Metal	61.3222	39.1755	26090.1711	18
Textiles	51.1667	40.3010	8120.8333	6
Wood	16.0000	15.5563	242.0000	2
Within Groups Total	46.1475	36.4900	70570.5386	61

F = 1.4187
Sig. = .2174

Table 3.5: Percentage of Raw Materials Imported 1991 by Size of Firm

Value Label	Mean	Std Dev	Sum of Sq	Cases
large	51.2294	34.5586	19108.7153	17
medium	55.9333	37.7881	24274.9600	18
small	47.9294	37.9778	23076.9553	17
micro	13.6111	26.4313	5588.8889	9
Within Groups Total	46.1475	35.5532	72049.5195	61

F = 3.0971
Sig. = .0338

Table 3.6: Percentage of Raw Materials Imported 1991 by Age of Firm

Value Label	Mean	Std Dev	Sum of Sq	Cases
Old	56.0773	36.5113	27994.5186	22
Mature	38.1333	35.4358	17579.7333	15
Young	40.0000	41.7852	15714.0000	10
new	43.5214	38.1278	18898.4836	14
Within Groups Total	46.1475	37.5071	80186.7355	61

F = .8547
Sig = .4699

Subcontracting

Subcontracting is initiated based on the reputations of subcontractors; there might be a degree of familiarity between the subcontractor and the parent firms or the one could be a former employee of the parent firm. Normally, this is initiated in small quantities for products with simple production process. The parent firm considers the following factors when initiating subcontracts: ability of the subcontractor to meet delivery schedules, quality of the product, price of the product and technological capability of the subcontractor.

To the best of our knowledge there is no organised private sector initiative to formally promote any form of interfirm linkages in Ghana. Subcontracting which creates linkages between firms is not well developed. A survey of small, medium and large manufacturing firms in Ghana found that only a few firms engaged in subcontracting. Table 3.7 shows that only 29 out of a sample of 120 did any form of local subcontracting of spares and components and only 3.5% of spares and components.

Table 3.7: Number of Firms and Percentage of Spares and Components Subcontracted Locally by Sector, Size and Age

	% Sub-contracted				no. of firms	mean % sub-contracting	S.d	cases
	0	1–4	5–50	50+				
Sector								
Bakeries	9	1	3	0	4	4.5	10.1	13
Food	13	2	2	0	4	1.7	4.2	17
Furniture	21	2	3	1	6	4.6	19.2	27
Garments	30	0	3	2	5	6.9	21.7	35
Machines	4	0	2	0	2	1.7	2.6	6
Metals	31	2	2	0	4	1.2	5.3	35
Textiles	5	0	0	0	0	0	0	5
Wood	6	1	1	0	2	2.1	5.2	8
Size								
Micro	26	0	3	1	4	3.7	14.9	30
Small	59	0	7	2	9	5.1	18.3	66
Medium	26	0	2	0	2	0.9	2.6	28
Large	20	0	5	0	5	2.2	4.5	25
Age								
New	30	1	5	1	7	4.1	14.2	37
Young	20	2	4	1	7	5.7	19.5	27
Mature	45	4	2	1	7	2.3	13.9	52
Old	25	2	6	0	8	3.1	7.9	33
Total	120	9	17	3	29	3.5	14.0	149

Source: RPED Survey.

With respect to the type of sectors involved garments formed 6.9%, furniture, (4.6%) and bakeries (4.5%) accounted for the largest share.

In our key firm survey only 17% of firms ever did some form of subcontracting. About 95% of these firms only subcontracted their spares needs locally and for these firms only one of them sub-contracted more than 20% of the spares. Firms who would subcontract would do so in order to reduce costs.

Table 3.8: Percentage of Spares and Components Imported by Sector, Size and Age (No. of firms)

	0	% imported< 50	51–90	100	Mean	Cases
Sector						
Bakeries	1	2	1	6	75.0	10
Food	5	1	1	9	63.8	16
Furniture	3	1	3	12	77.1	19
Garments	15	2	3	17	54.6	37
Machines	1	1	0	3	70.0	5
Metals	7	1	3	19	72.7	30
Textiles	0	0	1	3	97.5	4
Wood	0	0	0	3	87.5	4
Size						
Micro	6	4	0	16	66.9	26
Small	18	4	6	28	61.3	56
Medium	5	0	4	16	77.2	25
Large	3	1	2	13	80.0	19
Age						
New	6	2	5	19	66.4	36
Young	10	3	2	11	63.6	22
Mature	6	3	3	24	68.9	40
Old	10	1	2	19	74.3	28
Total number of firms	3	9	12	73	68.5	126

Source: RPED survey

Firms do not subcontract because they do not find the need to do so. The reason for this is that most of the firms (91%) are already producing below capacity. There are several factors firms will take into consideration in selecting sub-contractors. Most of the firms (75%) would contract firms who can produce quality products, while 50% each would in addition look for firms with technological capability and the ability to meet delivery need.

Push Factors for Subcontracting

There are factors which are internal and others which are external to the firm which could improve subcontracting and hence linkages. The external factors have been grouped under the heading of government policies. For internal adjustments, most firms talked of technology upgrading. Firms conceded that low and old-fashioned technology made it impossible to expand and be competitive. Consequently, they always produce with excess capacity leading to the situation of lack of need for subcontracting. Technology upgrading will also result in improved quality which will make such firms be used for contracting. The garment sector suffers from lack of standardization. There is too much customization of the product. Incentives in terms of credits and tax allowances should be given to shops which will sell standardized clothing. Such standardization will make it easy for large firms supplying such shops to subcontract parts of their products to other firms. Firms recognized the need for skill training and acquisition of adequate technology. Support from such firm adjustment can be given by government institutions, such as NBSSI.

Problems with Subcontracting

We have discussed the fact that there is little subcontracting among firms. Some of the problems cited for its non-existence include poor quality of products, non- and late-delivery of schedules and non- and late payments of credits. These border on contractual relations which are not respected or at best very informal.

Contractual Relations

The literature on contractual relations yields results which show that potential debtors differ on how likely they are to comply with a particular contract. Whenever their characteristics cannot be readily assessed, the wrong type may assume contractual obligations knowing that they are unlikely to satisfy them but cannot be forced to comply. As a result, creditors may refuse to contract even at terms (trade credit, delivery date, promised quality) that appear very favourable because they fear attracting bad types. Business transactions will then be rationed (Stiglitz and Weiss, 1981). Forms of rationing include: certain clients will be turned down for credit, others will not be able to place orders without paying a deposit, certain people will not be allowed to pay by check, etc. These contractual limitations are on the basis of the low linkages and subcontracting in the Ghanaian situation.

However, two types of contract enforcement mechanisms, namely legal enforcement and reputation enable firms to operate within a large group and to rapidly establish business relations with partners (Fafchamps, 1996). In the case of a young business environment as in Ghana, institutions to promote business could establish this confidence to speed up the linkages. They will develop a knowledge of credibility of firms with close contact.

Our survey found that the main problems faced by SMEs in terms of subcontracting were many and included, *inter alia,* the following:

   (i)   low level of technology in Ghana compared with the demands of modern industry;
  (ii)   the poor quality of their products, and the poor appreciation of the need for quality improvement. In Lall's study he found out that most firms did not make use of institutions such as Ghana Standards Board and the Industrial Research Institute.
 (iii)   delay in delivery,
  (iv)   instability in management of SMEs,
   (v)   shortage of qualified SMEs.
  (vi)   undercapitalization with both fixed and working capital
 (vii)   non availability of raw materials with precise specification for certain types of products;
(viii)   imprecise pricing and the large margin demanded by SMEs.
(viii)   most of the parent firms indicated that they had sufficient production capacity to undertake the production of the commodities themselves.

Impact of SAP on Linkages

Ghana's Structural Adjustment Programmes have also had various impacts on certain macroeconomic variables with widespread implications on industrial linkages. Policies which have been undertaken were ranked by firms on the scale of 1–5 in terms of importance, 1 less important and 5 being most important in either helping or hindering linkages. On the positive implication of SAP on linkages only 25% of firms answered those questions while on the negative impacts, 40% of firms responded. The positive-policy impacts included access to working capital, foreign exchange and foreign tools and equipment. They scored an average of 3.5. The negative impacts included increased cost of bank loans receiving the maximum average of 5 followed by increased cost of foreign exchange with an average of 4.2.

Change in tax laws and increased competition from imports averaged 3.5 and 3.0 respectively. It is clear that while access to bank credit and foreign exchange would improve linkages, the lack of access in terms of the cost of obtaining these facilities were paramount and has been discussed above.

In summary, the three most important constraints to the development of linkages among firms were availability of finance, availability of information on technology and lack of support from science and technology institutions. These problems cut across sectors and sizes of firms. Of the three the greatest constraint cited by firms was availability of finance (54% of the firms).

Again 42% of the firms indicated availability of finance as the second most important problem followed by lack of information on technology. Lack of support from science and technology institutions came third as a hindrance to the development of linkages. These constraints are various reasons that have been given for the lack of development of all types of linkages among industries. In the first place, granting financial assistance to other firms is possible within a stable environment where it is easy to borrow money in a non-prohibitive situation.

Also firms which could be set up to produce inputs or process by-products of other firms do not spring up due to financial and technical difficulties. As to the overall linkages of the constraints, 54% of the firms said availability of finance was the single most important constraint.

POLICY INTERVENTION FOR STRENGTHENING LINKAGES

We have identified several factors which influence the development of inter firm linkages-ownership, market arrangements involving buyer-supplier relationship and government policy.

While policy-making during the ERP period has had the objective of promoting the development of internationally competitive manufacturing sector, there is a need for policy intervention which will deepen and strengthen the industrial structure. This can be accomplished through policy initiatives which emphasize the development of linkages between the manufacturing sector and other sectors, particularly the primary sector, including agriculture, forestry and mining. Mutually supportive and profitable inter-industry linkage should be established between large, medium and small enterprises, and within the industrial sector the establishment of linkages between upstream and downstream industries.

In this section we examine government policy intervention and other private sector initiatives to strengthen linkages.

General Economic Policies to Foster General Market Development

Firms discussed government policies which can boost subcontracting and linkages in general. In the first place, government must improve its own major business of maintaining a stable macro economic environment. This they conceded must imply policies to reduce budget deficits, stem growth and employment in agriculture so as to reduce high inflation with its attendant high interest, lending and exchange rates. The next issue is the provision of long term credit facilities for capital goods for either new ventures or for retooling.

In addition to maintaining a stable macroeconomic environment, government must urgently promote the enhancement of infrastructure, especially electricity, telecommunication, water and roads. More importantly, the provision of uninterrupting electricity and telecommunication is a sine-qua-non to advancing a vibrant industrial sector. This stable system will ensure that the rate of inflation and other rates will fall drastically providing the basis for easy access to credit both short term and long term to facilitate entry of firms that can provide linkages as discussed above. It will also give a basis for cost-effective productive system making production of inputs or outputs for further production more attractive because of the likely lower cost.

Government must constantly review its own policies which have negative impacts on industry and indirectly on linkages. An example is the policy of trade liberalization which does not take into account the difficulties of doing business in this environment. The result is a tottering manufacturing sector which is producing far below capacity and hence is not capable of generating any linkages.

Inconsistent government policy has been argued as a major hindrance to the development of linkages, especially in the forestry sector. This creates incredibility among agents who consequently behave perversely. Because of the huge capital intensity of the sector, it is suggested that government maintains a pool of equipments on a cooperative basis to ensure access to efficient technology to reduce the wastes in the sector. Another case with the food sector is tariff. For instance there is a 15% tariff on imported raw soya beans but there is none on soya cake which is processed beans. The policy is contradictory in the sense that although it intends to promote local beans production the fact that there is none on cake will give incentives to process the beans outside. The need to have the inputs of the Association of Ghana Institutes (AGI) and various sectoral production and associations in such policies is important.

In general, it is the consensus that government must have a strategy of industrialization that has the basis in processing what is produced at home. This primarily falls on agriculture and calls for the development of strong linkages. This strategy will put the onerous task on responsible ministries to ensure that constraints are removed in sub-sectors where they are found. It is found out in our survey that linkages in agriculture with raw materials as inputs imply a system of credit, marketing and extension schemes that is well coordinated. That coordination is best achieved when association among producers and consumers is nurtured.

Tax Incentives

Some of the linkages that can be created or strengthened can survive initially at a cost to either of the firm. In some cases, there are no mutual benefits that can be reaped in the initial period but with time mutual benefits will be realized. For such situations, some incentives which will relieve the firm bearing the cost will help such a linkage. Such incentives include tax breaks of all kinds, for example large firms could be given tax rebates for purchasing components and parts from the small enterprises.

Government Contractual Relations

Government is a major customer in the supply of items manufactured both locally and externally. This governmental activity must be used as an incentive to support certain goals such as linkage development. Government may undertake an open policy which does business with large companies which promotes subcontracting or gives some support to smaller firms. If such policy is openly known to all and pursued eagerly, it will serve as an incentive for firms to develop linkages.

Support Institutions

Specific Institutional Arrangements to Increase the Absorptive Capabilities of SMEs

These arrangements include the "umbrella strategy" practised in Malaysia, the "foster father" plan in Indonesiaand the "local industry upgrading programme"in Singapore. The umbrella concept is a means of linking small SMEs to large marketing intermediaries. A large company with financial resources and expertise helps the SMEs in areas such as production, design, quality control and marketing. With the help of the intermediaries the firms are able to participate in government supply contracts; the umbrella firm gets a commission as a marketing agent. Such coordination in the form of arranging subcontracting relationship with bigger firms is being tried by NBSSI. The government can support such a scheme by giving the umbrella firm contracts without competitive bidding.

With the foster father plan the foster father provides management assistance, technical assistance to increase production skills, marketing assistance, and might also advance working capital to small firms. In order for the partnership to be viable and sustainable, certain principles should be recognized — the principle of mutual need, the principle of mutually strengthening each other and the principle of mutual benefits.

The challenge with these approaches is that of being able to sustain forced marriages and partnerships. It has already been indicated that firms do not undertake such arrangements because of the negligible or non-existent benefits. Firms therefore need incentives such as tax breaks. It has also been suggested that individual institutions with the collaboration of the linkage departments can develop these arrangements.

But as an example of a successful institutional arrangement, one can cite the case of Intel (Malaysia) which decided to develop greater linkages between itself and small enterprises. A staff cooperative was established to invest in a company to provide subcontracting services; it also encouraged its engineers to set up their subcontracting businesses. It also developed a long-term supplier partnership with suppliers. In all these cases, the subcontractors obtained management technology transfer from Intel.

Industrial Technical Assistance Fund

This can be established to encourage SMEs to upgrade and modernize their operations. It should provide subsidies for product development, quality improvement, marketing and feasibility studies.

Infrastructure and Industrial Clusters

The government could encourage infrastructure development for small enterprises to facilitate their relocation. For example, the relocation and creation of foundry and engineering parks near urban centres and large industrial estates would strengthen the formation of clusters needed for the development of interfirm linkages. The clustering of complementary enterprises provides technical assistance to SMEs. It also creates incentives to subcontract since the transaction cost of such collaboration is considerably reduced due to proximity. The problems of quality and meeting delivery dead lines will be eliminated or reduced.

Local Content Requirement Requiring Firms to Procure Certain Percentage of Raw Materials and Spares Locally

Our survey revealed that a lot of potentials exist within agriculture for a cluster of industries to be established. In the first place there are infinite processing potentials in that sector. Secondly, we found that all agricultural processing firms depended significantly on locally or in-house built spares and machinery. Baah-Nuakoh (1994) found that local metal firms have the capability to produce agricultural and food processing equipment. These firms which produce agricultural machines and spares must be singled out for support with incentives.

Firms that depend on imports for raw materials should be targeted for encouragement to source a certain percentage of their spares and raw materials locally. This responsibility must fall on the proposed linkage departments in the relevant ministries

Information Provision and Exchange to SMEs

There is lack of information on SMEs about what is being produced in the country. The government could establish within the Ministry of Trade and Industry, a Subcontracting Exchange Scheme to support subcontracting arrangements. The local supporting industries are linked to the large scale manufacturers, linking the buyer's requirements with the vendor's capacity to supply.

The need to establish linkage departments at the various responsible ministries was advocated. For instance the ministries of agriculture and industry could create within its establishment departments of linkages. If oil palm processing is examined, the present uses of all the by-products is identified to see what could be processed and the obstacles to such processing. If it is machinery or finance or market, this is identified and a potential investor identified. Whatever support that is needed is then provided to make sure that such new venture is initiated. This process can be done for almost all agricultural products which have high post-harvest losses or even have very low value added. The linkage departments will liaise with the banks, Ghana Investment Promotion Centre (GIPC), Private Enterprise Foundation (PEF), the Association of Ghana Industries (AGI) to find out what linkages can be strengthened or created. This will help a lot in establishing linkages or strengthening existing ones.

The establishment of AGI is not sufficient for the development of the industrial sector. Individual sectoral associations with strong secretarial and research units to liaise with the linkage departments that is suggested will facilitate the identification of needs and their solutions. A lesson that has been learnt with the existence of institutions such as NBSSI, PEF, EMPRETEC, etc. is that coordination among them is poor. In order to avoid duplication and enhance effectiveness of their activities, there should be regular interaction among institutions that are geared towards the same objectives.

Technology and Training

For any linkages such as subcontracting, quality control is very important. Good quality output can be achieved through skilled personnel and upgraded technology. An enhanced capital market as already discussed could solve the problem of technology. We have discussed the need to support local metal firms which are producing some technologies for local industry. The food sector has been addressed in connection with this. In the wood sector, for instance, one quality-improving process is kiln dried logs. The centre at Ejisu in Ashanti has developed a prototype kiln which reduces cost significantly. The linkage departments to be set up at the ministries will also be responsible for technology.

Constant training needs for skills in the relevant area can improve quality levels in industries. Although, some training is done by NBSSI and other bodies, this should be linked to the technical institutions and should be need-based. The state institutions must identify the urgent training needs of sectors with the strong involvement of AGI and PEF. There is the need for training centres with updated technologies for various sectors as the one set up at Ejisu for the wood sector.

There is a need to stimulate private sector training to support the introduction of new technology or new products. This could target critical areas such as upgrading craft skills, training foremen and supervisors, and providing training in advanced technical skills for professionals, engineers and technicians.

Training is expensive and cannot be obtained for free. A fund could be set up to which trade associations, donors and state institutions can contribute to subsidize firms, especially small and medium scale ones on the cost of training.

Entrepreneurial Development

There is a need to increase the awareness of entrepreneurs of the need for acquisition of technology and the use of technical expertise.

Innovative Financing

We have identified both short- and long-term financing as a problem in existing firms and prospective new ones. Key informant discussions about financing revealed an innovative scheme that is being tried with some measure of success. This is where such investment finance firms search for a firm which supplies inputs to another firm but needs finance. The finance firm acts as an intermediary between the two firms and establishes the credibility of the need. The intermediary then negotiates with the firm that needs the input and works out some credit or financing scheme from the big firm. By so doing, existing linkages have been strengthened and new ones can be created. What is needed is a credible investment firm which can even guarantee the small firm needing support. Incentives in terms of tax allowances can be created for such firms.

NOTES

1.   Hirschman, A. C. The Strategy of Economic Development. Yale University Press, New Haven & London, 1958 p.100.
2.   *Ibid.*, p.100.

REFERENCES

Anheir, Helmut and Hans Seibel (1987). *Small Scale Industries and Economic Development in Ghana: Business Behaviour and Strategies in Informal Sector Economies. Verlag* Breintenbach Publishers, Scarbruken.

Baah-Nuakoh, A. (1992). Skill Acquisition and Shortage in the Informal Sector in Ghana, unpublished, Department of Economics, University of Ghana, Legon.

—— (1993a). Development Policies and Institutional Environment for Employment Promotion in the Informal Sector in Ghana. JASPA, Addis Ababa.

—— (1993b). Industrial Sector in the State of the Ghanaian Economy, 1992.

—— (1993c). "Constraints on the Growth and Expansion of the Manufacturing Sector in Ghana", in Baah-Nuakoh, A. and Francis Teal eds *Economic Reform and the* Manufacturing Sector in Ghana.

—— and W. F. Steel, (1993). Background Paper on SME Demand for Finance. Report prepared for NBSSI. Accra.

—— and Francis Teal (ed.) (1993). Economic Reform and the Manufacturing Sector in Ghana. Report prepared for World Bank. RPED.

Baark, E. (1991). "The Capital Goods Sector in Ghana: Options for Economic and Technological Development," *Industry and Development*, 29, pp. 37–61.

Cella, Guido. "The Input-Output measurement of Inter-Industry Linkages," *Oxford Bulletin of Economics and Statistics*, 46, No. 1 pp. 73–84.

Chenery H. and watanabe T. (1958). "International Comparisons of the Structure," *Econometrica* Vol. 26 October pp. 487–521.

Clark, Colin (1951). *The Conditions of Economic Progress,* Macmillan and Co. London, second edition.

Dawson, Jonathan (1990). "The Wider Context: The Importance of the Macroenvironment for Small Scale Enterprise Development", *Small Enterprise Development, An International Journal*, Vol. 1 No. 3 pp. 39–46.

Fafchamps, M. (1996). *World Development.*

Ghana (1992). *Industrial Policy Statement of January.*

Ghana Statistical Service (1987). Ghana National Industrial Census, Phase I & Phase II Reports, Accra.

Government of Ghana (1985). *Republic of Ghana, Investment Code*, Accra.

Grayson, Leslie (1971). "The Promotion of Indigenous Private Enterprise in Ghana," *Journal of Asian and African Studies*, Vol. 1 No. 9 May.

Hakam, A. N. (1976). Technology Diffusion from Modern to the Informal Sector: Automobile Repair Trades in Ghana. ILO Geneva.

Hart, Keith (1970). "Small Scale Entrepreneurs in Ghana and Development Planning," *Journal of Development Studies*, pp.104–120.

——— (1973). "Informal Income Opportunities and urban Employment in Ghana," *Journal of Modern African Studies*, pp. 61–89.

Hemsling A. H. J. and The Kolstee, *Small Enterprises and Changing Policies – Structural Adjustment and Financial Policy and Assistance Programmes in Africa.*

Hirschman H. (1958). *The Strategy of Economic Development*, Yale University Press, New York and London.

Killick, Tony (1978). *Development Economics in Action: A Study of Economic Policies in Ghana*, Heineman, London.

Klu, F. E. (1985). "Technology Diffusion and Linkage Mechanisms in the Small Scale Auto Repair Industry: A Case Study of Accra," *Legon Geographer*, Vol. 1 No. 1 August, pp. 54–67.

Lall Sanjay, Giorgio Navaretti, Simin Teitel and Ganeshan Wignaraja, (1994) *Technology and Enterprise Development: Ghana Under Structural Adjustment.* Macmillan Press Ltd, London.

Levy, Brian (1993). "Obstacles to Developing Indigenous Small and Medium Enterprises: An Empirical Assessment," *The World Bank Economic Review*, Vol. 7 No. 1 January, pp. 65–83.

Ministry of Agriculture (1987). *Performance of the Agricultural Sector*, compiled by PPME, Accra.

Nugent and Yotopoulos (1982). "Morphology of Growth: The Effect of Country Size, Structural Characteristics and Linkages," *Journal of Development Economics*, Vol. 10, pp. 279–95.

Osei B., A. Baah-Nuakoh, K. Tutu and N. Sowa (1993). "Impact of Adjustment on Small-scale Enterprises in Ghana" in *Small Enterprises and Changing Policies – Structural Adjustment and Financial Policy and Assistance Programmes in Africa.*

RPED (1992) *Economic Reform and the Manufacturing Sector in Ghana.* Prepared for the Regional Programme for Enterprise Development, World Bank, by the Centre for the Study of African Economies, Oxford, and Department of Economics, University of Ghana. December 1992.

Steel W. F. and Leila Webster (1993). *Small Enterprises Under Adjustment in Ghana.* World Bank Technical Paper No. 138 Industry and Finance Series.

Technology Transfer Centre (1989). *Institutions Supporting Scientific and Industrial Development*, Accra. Ghana. UNDP/TTC Doc.1.

——— (1990a). *Report on Food Processing Sector*, CSIR, Accra. UNDP/TTC Doc. 15.

——— (1990b). *Report on Capital Goods Sector Study*, CSIR, Accra, UNDP/TTC Doc.5.

Technology Transfer Centre (1991a). *Technology Profiles on Capital Goods, Energy and Food Processing,* CSIR, Accra.
—— (1991b). R & D Projects on Capital Goods, Energy and Food Processing, CSIR, Accra.
—— (1991c). *Report on Small and Medium Enterprises Study,* CSIR Accra, UNDP/ TTC Doc.16.

CHAPTER 4

Production Capacity of the Agro-Metals Sector

Introduction

The agro-metal subsector producing farm implements and the food processing equipment sector is a small part of the metal sub-sector which in Ghana is at the early stages of development using "easy technologies" with simple processes. Although, there is some local manufacturing of agricultural implements and food processing equipment, using imported second hand machines dependent on scraps and imported raw materials, and manufacturing simple products, the history of the development of Ghana's capital goods sector (of which agricultural and food-processing equipment manufacture firms form a part) indicates an apparent neglect of the sector.

Ghana is an agricultural country losing about 30% of its output through post harvest losses. With the failure of the import dependent IS strategy, attention is now being focused on local-resource based industrial strategy. Ghana "may have a comparative advantage in processing local raw materials into products for the local market. An analysis of the food processing sub-sector reveals that the country does have an advantage in the production of vegetable oil, (particularly palm oil), fruit processing and cassava processing for the domestic market."[1] The increased processing of the produce of the agricultural sector then becomes the focus of the new industrial strategy. The successful development of the agro-metal sector to supply the requisite equipment should be of immense concern to government.

In Ghana, one of the perennial problems militating against the growth of the agricultural and food processing sectors is the low level of technology in use. In fact, technological progress, that is, the increased application of new scientific knowledge in the form of inventions and innovations with regard to capital, both physical and human is very low in the agricultural and food-processing sectors in Ghana. It must be noted that technology is of crucial importance in any manufacturing process. This is because it promotes efficiency and the production of high quality goods. Given the foreign exchange constraints of a typical developing country like Ghana, it is imperative that measures are taken to ensure that the economy's potential to produce high quality agricultural and good-processing equipment is considerably enhanced.

The role of the local capital goods sector in producing the machinery and equipment for the food processing and farm sector would need to be re-examined, with its attendant inter-relationship with capital accumulation indigenous technological capabilities, employment and balance of payments. Although, Ghana abounds in relatively high level of educated manpower and a pool of artisans and apprentices, when it comes to capital goods production, "Ghana does not have any comparative advantage in the local, regional or international markets because of lack of basic raw materials (iron and steel), and lack of expertise in product design and process engineering."[2] The question then is, in the area of agro-metals, does Ghana have the capacity to satisfy local needs? Are imports substitutes to local tools and equipment? What interventions are required to improve the capacity of the sector?

This chapter analyses the present local capacity to produce farm implements and food processing equipment, by distinguishing between production by blacksmiths and micro-metal workshops, small metal working firms, and medium scale enterprises, indicating the constraints which hamper the expansion of production and/or the increase of productivity in the sub-sector, analysing the importation of farming and food processing equipment and the effects of the Economic Recovery Programme on the sector and drawing conclusions on the economic potential for the local production of equipment for farming and food processing under prevailing and foreseeable conditions in Ghana.

Defining the Agro-metals Sector

The metal working industries comprise a broad spectrum of products:

ISIC code	Products
371	Iron and Steel Smelting
372	Non-ferrous Metals
381	Fabricated Metal Products
382	Non-Electrical Machinery
383	Electrical Machinery
384	Transport Equipment

Within the metal sector, we shall in this study concentrate on the industries producing agricultural implements and food processing equipment, which we shall term the "agro-metals sector."

The ISIC codes of the various industries producing agricultural implements and food processing equipment are:

3811 Manufacture of cutlery, hand tools and general hardware: The manufacture of table, kitchen and other cutlery; hand and edge tools such as axes and hatchets, cutlasses, chisels and files, hammers, shovels, rakes, hoes and other agricultural and garden tools, hand saws and plumbers, masons, mechanics and machinists precision hard tools, hardware such as fire place equipment and brackets, locks and other key sets and builders and furniture hardware, coasters, champs and marine luggage vehicle hardware, blacksmith shops, nails, bed hooks.

3819 Manufacture of fabricated metal products except machinery and equipment, not elsewhere classified (nec) which includes baking pans, aluminium pots, cooking utensils

3822 Manufacture of Agricultural Machinery and Equipment: — The manufacture and repair of agricultural machinery and equipment such as ploughs, harrows, stalk butter, milking machines and farm tractors.

3824 Special industrial machinery and equipment except metal and wood working machinery such as food machinery (corn mills, cassava graters, dough kneading machines etc.)

3829 Machinery and equipment n.e.c includes tractors.

3849 Manufacture of transport equipment nec. such as animal drawn or vehicles wagons carts, wheel-barrows

Methodology

To achieve the objectives of the study, the following methodology was adopted:

(i) We made use of existing data and literature; several studies

have been conducted on the industrial sector in general
and on the metal sub-sector. These include among others,
TTC (1989, 1990a, 1990b, 1991a, 1991b, 1991c), Baark (1991),
Aboagye (1981, 1991), Berger (1989), Levy (1993), Damptey
et al. (1989), RPED (1992), Baah-Nuakoh (1993a, 1993b,
1993c), Baah-Nuakoh and Steel (1993), Steel and Webster
(1993), Baah-Nuakoh and Teal (1993), Lall *et al.* (1993).

(ii)   A limited "key enterprise survey" was to be carried out
       for 10 micro, 11 small enterprises and 4 medium enter-
       prises, all engaged in metal working and particularly pro-
       ducing farm implements and food processing equipment.

(iii) Additional information was obtained through interviews
       with 7 "key informants" from relevant organizations.

The chapter is organized as follows. Following the Introduction, the
economic policy and institutional environment within which the agro-
metals sector developed, the effects of recent policy changes and
trends in imports of agricultural machinery and food processing equipment are discussed; a description of the structure of the Food Processing and Farming subsectors, existing technology, the equipment needs
of the sector and the future demand for food processing equipment
and farm implements; an examination of the present local production capacity of the agro-metals sector; a discussion of the structure
of the sub-sector, types of workshops and existing technology, the
raw materials and skills, the type of products presently produced; a
discussion of the constraints on production and productivity growth;
a discussion of the required policy and institutional reforms to promote local manufacture of agro-metals, and possible areas of interventions.

THE STRUCTURE AND EQUIPMENT NEEDS OF THE FOOD
PROCESSING AND AGRICULTURAL SECTORS

The Structure of Food Processing and Agricultural Sectors

The agricultural sector requires tools, implements, machines and
equipment for land development, farm production and crop harvesting and primary processing. The type of farm implements used will
depend upon the type of soil, the size of the farm and vegetation.

We can divide Ghana into 4 ecological zones — pure forest, coastal savanna, transitional zone, and guinea savanna; land preparation for cultivation varies among the zones. These four zones produce various types of crops:

(i)   cereals (maize, rice and guinea corn).
(ii) starchy staples (cassava, cocoyam, yam, plantain).
(iii) pulses and nuts (groundnuts, coconut, oil palm, beans).
(iv) vegetables (tomatoes, pepper, okro and garden eggs)
(v)   others (sugar cane, orange, pineapple, banana).
(vi) export crop cocoa.

Table 4.1 shows the trends in the production of some of these crops between 1970 and 1990. Most of the crops experienced declines in the late seventies and early eighties. A few of them picked up in the second half of the eighties; in 1990 production levels for almost all the crops were below the 1988 levels. The diversity of crops produced in this country and the perishable nature of these products makes food processing a high priority area for the economy.

The industries within Food Processing consist of:

ISIC Code   Products

3111   Slaughtering, preparing and preserving of meat
3112   Manufacture of dairy products
3113   Canning and preserving of fruits and vegetables
3114   Processing of fish, crustaces and similar foods
3115   Manufacture of vegetables and animal oils and fats
3116   Manufacture of grain mill products
3117   Manufacture of bakery products
3118   Sugar factories and refineries
3119   Manufacture of cocoa, chocolate and sugar confectionery
3121   Manufacture of foods n.e.c
3122   Manufacture of prepared animal feeds

The history of food processing dates back to 1955, when the Agricultural Development Corporation established fish and pineapples canneries at Osu in Accra. The Fruit Canning Industry had expanded by 1967 when Ghana Industrial Holding Corporation (GIHOC) took over Government of Ghana-INGRA of Zagreb,

(Yugoslavia) projects aimed at processing excess fruits and vegetables. The fruit and vegetable canning was followed by cereal and grains processing with the introduction of flour milling in 1963. Meat processing and fish processing plants were procured by 1968. Also by the late 1960s the two sugar factories at Asutuare and Komenda were built.

Table 4.1: Production of Important Crops (Thousand tons)

Crop Cereals	1970	1977	1980	1983	1984	1986	1988	1990
Maize	482	312	354	141	574	559	751	554
Rice	49	63	64	27	76	70	84	53
Guinea corn	186	140	156	106	176	128	178	251
Starchy Staples								
Cassava	2388	2119	2896	1375	4065	2876	2788	2717
Cocoyam	1136	633	848	613	2835	1005	907	816
Yam	909	497	525	354	725	1048	902	1060
Plantain	1641	776	931	755	1234	1088	1135	635
Pulses and Nuts								
Groundnuts	102	91	142	91	167	190	230	113
Coconut	302	132	174	339	265	-	-	-
Oil palm	696	446	914	889	768	-	-	-
Beans	11	9	16	12	14	20	15	15
Vegetables								
Tomatoes	93	36	83	57	46	39	79	67
Pepper	95	77	86	62	74	137	124	114
Okro	102	111	99	20	121	146	60	-
Garden Eggs	10	19	32	23	23	8	6	-
Others								
Sugar Cane	112	70	171	86	90	110	-	-
Orange	129	156	154	129	-	-	-	-
Pineapple	29	7	7	6	-	-	-	-
Banana	16	3	3	3	-	-	-	-
Cocoa	258	158	174	228	300	260	-	-

Source: Statistical Service, *Quarterly Digest of Statistics*, various issues.

Table 4.2: Characteristics of the Food processing Industry by Employment Size, 1987

(a) **Number of Establishments**

		Total	Micro 1-4	Small 5-9	Medium 10-29	Large 30-99	100+
311/12	Food processing	1361	675	374	176	86	50
3111	Slaughtering etc. of meat	8	2	1	3	1	1
3112	Dairy products	6	2	1	3	1	2
3113	Canning/pres. fruit/veg.	13	5	2	1	3	2
3114	Canning/pres of fish etc.	198	86	67	23	11	11
3115	Veg. and animal oils & fats	92	28	9	29	19	7
3116	grain mill products	381	315	49	8	3	6
3117	Bakery products	575	270	223	86	33	13
3118	Sugar	5	–	3	–	1	1
3119	Cocoa, chocolate,& sugar confectionery	14	1	2	4	2	5
3121	Food products nec*	43	14	11	12	5	1
3122	Animal feed	26	4	6	8	7	1
	Total Manufacturing	8351	2884	3391	1411	423	242

*nec: not elsewhere classified.

(b) **Number of Establishments for Selected Towns**

		Total	Sekdi T'di	Accra	Tema	Ksi	Other
311/12	Food processing	1361					
3111	Slaughtering etc of meat	8	1	2	2	1	2
3112	Dairy products	6	-	4	1	-	1
3113	Canning/Pres. fruit/veg.	13	2	3	-	1	7
3114	Canning/Pres of fish etc.	198	20	44	61	5	68
3115	Veg. and animal oils & fats	92	3	3	-	13	73
3116	Grain mill products	381	34	71	57	82	137
3117	Bakery products	575	12	229	63	33	238
3118	Sugar	5	-	-	-	-	5
3119	Cocoa, chocolate, etc.	14	3	7	2	1	1
3121	Food products nec.	43	7	6	3	9	18
3122	Animal feed	26	1	7	2	4	12

Table 4. 2 (*cont'd.*)

(c) Persons Engaged by Size Class (Employment)

		Total	1–4	5–9	10–29	30–99	100+
311/12	Food processing	26385	1731	2312	3017	4325	14982
3111	Slaughtering etc of meat	259	8	5	61	57	128
3112	Dairy products	881	–	6	46	77	752
3113	Canning/Pres. fruit/veg.	702	9	12	15	178	488
3114	Canning/Pres of fish etc.	4794	236	436	421	569	3132
3115	Veg. and animal oils	4486	73	57	525	956	2857
3116	Grain mill products	2944	696	293	146	118	1691
3117	Bakery products	8442	669	1362	1312	1745	3354
3118	Sugar	186	-	22	-	30	134
3119	Cocoa, chocolate, & sugar	2144	2	11	96	99	1936
3121	Food products nec.	709	25	67	236	181	200
3122	Animal feed	838	13	41	159	315	310
Total manufacturing		157084	7400	21264	21541	21710	85169

(d) Nationality of Ownership

		Total	Ghanaian	Non-Ghanaian	Mixed
311/12	Food processing	1361	1227	6	27
3111	Slaughtering etc of meat	8	7	–	1
3112	Dairy products	6	1	1	4
3113	Canning/Pres. fruit/veg.	13	12	–	1
3114	Canning/Pres of fish etc.	198	196	–	2
3115	Veg. and animal oils & fats	92	88	1	3
3116	Grain mill products	381	374	1	6
3117	Bakery products	575	571	1	3
3118	Sugar	5	5	–	–
3119	Cocoa, chocolate,& sugar	14	9	2	3
3121	Food products nec.	43	40	–	2
3122	Animal feed	26	24	–	2

Source: Statistical Service, Industrial Census Part I.

Thus, the food processing subsector is just as old as the Ghanaian industrial sector. It forms a significant proportion of the manufacturing subsector. Its share of manufacturing value added rose from 4.9% in 1962 to about 17.5% in 1975, but had declined in 1986. The food processing subsector accounted for 16.8% of manufacturing employment in 1987.

The policies of import substitution industrialization and agro-based industrialization of the Government at Independence made food to stand-out as a beneficiary of government policy. The government effort at collaboration with foreign companies and efforts of expatriate companies like UAC and that of private individuals placed food processing in its own class as far as manufacturing is concerned. The industry at that time was capital intensive using predominantly imported machinery. However, by 1993 problems of capacity utilization due to lack of patronage of products, raw material availability, factory breakdowns and shut downs due to spare part problems led to the near collapse of the industry.

The deterioration in the food processing sector was seen as a reflection of the declining performance of the economy as a whole during the dismal 1970s. It is common knowledge that the severe economic decline affected the manufacturing sector in general, but some believe the food processing sector in particular was severely hit.[3]

To resuscitate the sector, the ERP's industrial sector programme could be seen as directly relevant. The programme has as its objectives the development of local industry; promotion of industries; establishment of linkages in industry; incentives to industry; support to industries; development of management and technical manpower; and monitoring and evaluation. The intention to stimulate the food processing sector could be perceived through the priorities established for the agricultural and industrial sectors. Under the subsectoral development objectives, the priority areas of industrial and agricultural activities include: (a) production, protection, processing and preservation of crops and livestock (b) manufacturing based on use of local raw material and (c) manufacturing of mechanization equipment, spare parts and land machine tools.

In 1987, the food processing sector had the third largest number of enterprises as well as employment in manufacturing, after textiles and wood. It had the largest value added of the manufacturing sector. A high proportion of the employment was accounted for by large enterprises, with 73% of total food processing employment by medium and large scale firms. The sector since 1985 has experienced steady growth, although its index of production of 59.3 in 1991 is still below the 1977 level of 100 and also below the manufacturing average of 71.3.[4] Table 4.3 shows the production of some selected important manufactured foods. Most of these are produced by large scale firms using imported foreign technologies.

The sector relies heavily on local raw materials. Thus availability of raw materials is linked with the production levels of agricultural production. With the sector's reliance on local raw materials its orientation to local taste, competition is less severe, although there are certain processed foods and drinks which face strict competition from imports. The sector produced under high protection barriers in the pre-ERP period, but during the seventies and early eighties, import constraint hurt the industry. The liberalization has helped producers to get access to spare parts, and import dependent raw materials.

Existing Technologies in the Farming and Food Processing Sectors

Agricultural Implements and Equipment

The four different ecological zones entail the use of different methods of land preparation and machinery, equipment and implements. In the pure forest zone, it is difficult to mechanize; mechanization brings out all forms of environmental problems; thus the use of methods of land preparation which do disturb the soil, necessitating the use of manual method which involve the use of hoes, cutlasses, axes, and the mattock. In the coastal savanna, the grass specie lends itself to tractorization and not the slash-and-burn method.

The transitional zone does not require the use of too much mechanization. The zone makes itself permissible for animal traction and it is also tsetse free. The guinea savanna lends itself to tractorization and animal traction. Farm sizes beyond five acres use tractor, while the smaller ones depend upon the hoe.

Prior to the period of independence, technology in the agricultural sector was mainly traditional. The back-breaking hoes and cutlasses dominated the sector. However, some animal drawn ploughs were used minimally. The technology for the production of these hoes and such harvesting implements like sickles and knives were mainly traditional. Blacksmiths used their hand tools and scrap metals to turnout these goods.

Table 4.3: Production of Some Selected Important Manufactured Foods

Industry	Unit	1985	1986	1987	1988	1989	1990	1991
1. Milk (Reconstituted)*	Million Litres	14.6	7.7	23.4	27.5	22.1	20.8	24.5
2. Ice Cream	Thousand Litres	1,152.0	686.0	792.0	628.0	303.0	993.0	1,041.0
3. Edible Fats & Oil	Tonnes	941.0	999.0	2,396.0	3,205.0	3,747.0	3,560.0	16,293.0
4. Wheat Flour	Tonnes	45,306.0	62,818.0	71,444.0	95,215.0	88,112.0	108,422.0	96,236.0
5. Cocoa Butter	Tonnes	7,674.0	6,399.0	8,114.0	5,626.0	5,887.0	7,743.0	7,967.0
6. Cocoa Liquor	Tonnes	3,000.0	3,676.0	4,931.0	6,988.0	6,129.0	6,328.0	7,544.0
7. Cocoa Cake	Tonnes	9,178.0	7,490.0	10,313.0	6,713.0	6,367.0	9,137.0	10,046.0
8. Cocoa Powder	Tonnes	475.0	578.0	665.0	618.0	557.0	830.0	1,078.0

Source: Statistical Service, *Quarterly Digest of Statistics*, March 1992.

At independence, the industrialization and modernization drive led to the introduction of power driven agricultural equipments. These include ploughs, disc harrows, row planters and combine harvesters. With time varieties of these machines were either locally developed or adapted to local conditions from imported equipments.[5] However, the introduction of the power driven equipments to Northern Ghana with the hope of increased output and employment met with problems.

The problems include lack of spare parts, bureaucratic delays in ordering and paying for spare parts, land clearing practices resulting in damage to equipments, poor service facilities and shortage of skilled operators. The impact of the high powered equipments on the fragile tropical soil added its own dimension to the problem. These combined engendered the search for an appropriate technology and renewed interest in animal drawn equipments after two decades.

The handtools of cutlasses, knives, pick axes, hoes, pluckers, and other agricultural implements are made of scrap iron as no other source of raw materials is available for local blacksmith and are thus of low quality. There is a need for improvement of the quality of locally manufactured tools to provide farmers with better equipment.

Food Processing Technology

Existing technology in food processing in Ghana comprise a wide range of processes and products;

(i) There are the traditional (indigenous) technologies for simple processing and preservation of farm produce and beverages. In the traditional sector a wide variety of locally designed and manufactured equipments are seen in the grain milling comprising small units of maize milling machines, rice milled in traditional mills of small capacity, smoking of fish using local technologies and tuber processing sector. As noted by the UNDP/TTC report (1990) on the food processing sector, the proliferation of indigenous technology on these subsectors indicates the importance accorded the traditional Ghanaian diets like palm oil, gari and milled corn.

(ii) Simple technologies using a mixture of second hand, and unsophisticated imported equipment and locally made equipment by urban based firms for urban market; the technologies are improvement on the traditional ones; the locally-made equipment has been developed in response to the technological needs of both the rural and urban sectors, a local machinery manufacturing capacity emerged to produce the basic equipments (very often with limited skills) but very practical methods.

(iii) Modern factory-based technologies using basically imported technology to produce dairy products, meat processing, fruit and vegetable canning and refined oil producing industries.

Technologies (i) and (ii) are designed to meet local demands and packaging is not important here. It will be difficult for firms using these technologies to change their production processes without dramatically changing their technologies and making large investments.

Future Demand for Food Processing Equipment and Farm Implements

The needs and future equipment requirements of the food processing and agricultural sectors will depend on several factors, which include the growth of the economy, the success of agricultural programmes, growth in incomes and population.

Mechanization, the Search for Appropriate Technology and Metal Manufacturing

Assuming that the 1993 growth rate of agricultural output of 2.5% continues, the need for agricultural implements would need to be satisfied. Current traditional tools still have a role to play in small-scale agriculture, but considerable improvements should be made to ensure their efficiency. A more appropriate technology for the rural areas must be chosen to reduce reliance on urban areas which in turn depend on imported technology.

By FAO (1992) definition "agricultural mechanization" embraces the manufacture, distribution and operation of all types of tools, implements, machines and equipments for agricultural land development, farm production and crop harvesting and primary processing. These processes require human, animal or mechanical power. As such mechanization operations are conveniently classified by these power sources into mechanization technologies. These include hand tools technology, draught animal technology and mechanical power technology (FAO, 1990). For a sustainable cultivation of the land, the mix of technology applied to the land and climate factors are very important. This leads us to the issue of appropriate technology.

The current policy of the Ministry of Agriculture is to emphasize the development and use of appropriate technology; encourage the manufacture of hand tools, animal and tractor drawn implements, processing machines and simple windmills for the installation at appropriate places for pumping water from streams and wells for irrigation purposes and also power generation (MOA, 1987).

The concept of appropriate technology itself is difficult to define. The FAO, 1992 Document No. 99/1, 1991 defines it as mechanization which is best suited for introduction and use in specific development situation. Appropriate technology for farmers in developing countries is defined to be characterized by the following set of conditions:

(i)   low in capital cost;

(ii)   labour intensive rather than capital intensive;

(iii)   use locally available material as much as possible;

(iv)   should use local labour and skills and create jobs;

(v)   should be affordable by the beneficiaries, i.e. small farmers;

(vi)   need a low level of skill to operate, be able to be operated controlled and maintained by local population;

(vii)   can be produced by a small metal-working shop or in village itself;

(viii)   must be compatible with local values, attitudes and preferences

(ix)   be subject to high degree of control and initiative by users;

(x)   be flexible to suit changing circumstances;

(xi)   facilitate the involvement of the beneficiaries;

(xii)   be amenable to dispersal and have a demonstration effect.

These complex requirements of what constitutes appropriate technology underscore the Ministry of Agriculture's effort to collaborate with donor agencies on such programmes as the Ghana-German Agricultural Development Project (GGADP). The collaboration is to lead to:

(a)   manufacture animal drawn equipment. This has become necessary because of the near destruction of the fragile top soils which accompanied the introduction of tractors, combine harvesters and harrows and ploughs in the decades of the 1960s and 1970s. During this period, mechanical power was introduced with the aim of modernizing agriculture. The German project was established to work on ploughs, carts and hoes. The local blacksmiths still have a role to play. When the tractors started dying out in the northern parts of the country, the farmers went back to traditional local blacksmiths to produce the carts and hoes, to the extent that the implements produced by the GGADP are modified by local blacksmiths. The local blacksmiths are a very vital link to make appropriate tools moulding the factory-made tools to suit local conditions.

(b) Apart from the manufacture of animal drawn equipments the GGADP also offers training in the use of animal traction which has been found to be economical and efficient in the Northern and Upper regions.

The Ministry's programme of transferring appropriate technology also entails disseminating information, knowledge and skills on farm implements and tools to the farmer. The Agricultural Engineering Services Department (AESD) of the Ministry of Agriculture is very instrumental in this area. The AESD is in collaboration with local universities, research institutions and FAO/UNDP to reach out to farmers with suitable and standardized equipments that match the various soil and vegetational zones.

To ensure that farmers receive the right message and improve upon their productivity the Ministry also introduces:

(a) A Unified Agriculture Extension System as part of the policy reform. The Unified Agriculture Extension System of Ghana (UAESG) is defined as a system which;

(i) Only one extension agriculture called the Frontline Staff (FLS) of the Department of Agricultural Extension Services DAES) would deliver technological messages on crops, animal husbandry, fisheries, agricultural mechanization, irrigation extension, nutrition and home economics to farmers.

(ii) At the institutional level only DAES will be responsible for planning and security agricultural extension services in collaboration and consultation with other institutions.

(iii) All agricultural extension related activities under donor or NGO-supported projects will be coordinated by DAES.

(iv) DAES would be made professional and confined to technology transfer and be relieved of all non-extension functions such as credit disbursement and recovery and input distribution; extension staff would however, facilitate the work of others undertaking the non-extension functions.

The design, research and collaborative activities between the AESD and industry and the innovation in extension could enhance knowledge and dissemination of information on existing technology. This is a possible starting point of a revolution in the use of labour saving devices and increased market for the farm implements and tools industry.

The FAO observes that farmers in developing countries do not have enough tools and simple equipments, machines and implements to meet their needs. This suggests that there is considerable scope for an increase in local manufacturing (FAO, 1992). Thus, as long as the industry reflects technology response to indigenous farm and food habits, the demand for its products will continue to grow.

Future Demand and Need for Food Processing Equipment

The demand for food processing equipment is difficult to estimate. If we project that the modest growth rate of 2.5% of agricultural production of raw materials of 1993 will continue, then the equipment need of the food processing sector will grow and a large market for local machinery producers will be created. The sector will also require improvements in the quality of equipment used. The Technology Transfer Centre (CSIR) (1990) has made demand projections for processing needs in the country till 1995, which indicate a positive trend. The increased processing needs will require increased processing technology. If the sector is to go into exports, an improved form of technology whether indigenously produced or imported will be required to achieve competitiveness.

Capacity utilization has generally been low in food processing activities. It gradually increased from a low of 25% in 1983 to 55% in 1990. The problem has been attributed among other things to foreign exchange problems, obsolete machinery and spare parts, especially for firms dependent on imported technology and raw materials. Those dependent on local raw materials have sometimes faced supply problems of agricultural products. While capacity still exists in the food processing sector, the equipment is so obsolete that most of the firms when faced with expanded demand would require replacement with new and improved equipment. Thus, the future demand for food processing equipment is promising.

While the increased agricultural production will require increased use of agricultural implements and equipment, the rate of increase in agricultural implements requirements will be far exceeded by the increased need for agricultural processing equipment. The Rural Electrification Programme going on will increase the need for electrically powered food processing equipment. Thus there is more scope for the production of food processing equipment than farm implements and tools.

IMPACT OF RECENT POLICY AND INSTITUTIONAL ENVIRONMENT

The launching of the Economic Recovery Programme (ERP) has changed the direction of government policy from controls to liberalization and has added impetus to the promotion and development of the SME sector. This has taken the form of certain legal, physical, institutional and economic measures, all aimed at strengthening the SME sector.

The industrial policy under the ERP was aimed at increasing capacity utilization of existing factories from 20% to at least 50%. This target was to be achieved by enhancing the availability of foreign exchange for the importation of raw materials spare parts and plant and equipment.

The history of the development of Ghana's capital goods sector (of which agricultural and food-processing equipment manufacture firms form a part) indicates an apparent neglect of the sector, especially during the pre-ERP era. This may be explained by the fact that Ghana's post-independence economic policy was biased towards the promotion of large State-Owned Enterprises (SOE's). This philosophy implied that the Small and Medium Scale Enterprises (SME) sector was discriminated against. The significance of this development lies in the fact that in Ghana, most (if not all) of the firms engaged in the manufacture of agricultural and food-processing equipment are in the SME sector. Thus, relatively little attention was paid to this important sub-sector of the economy.

The agricultural and food processing equipment sub-sectors however attracted some attention in the late 1970s. This was in the wake of the realization of the importance of SMEs as the engine of growth in the economy, a development which was in turn, triggered off by the decline in the economy and the dismal performance of many large State-Owned Enterprises.

Before looking at the impact of recent economic policy measures on the agricultural and food processing equipment manufacturing sectors, it should be noted that these sectors have hardly enjoyed any considerable independent policy support. This is because to a large extent, apart from policies aimed at improving the SME sectors in general, no separate policies have been formulated for the agricultural and food processing equipment sectors.

One of the earliest attempts by Government to support the growth of the SME sector was the establishment, in 1970 of the Ghanaian Enterprises Development Commission (GEDC). This commission was to promote and develop small-scale firms by providing technical and financial support. At the same time the government established a credit guarantee scheme to assist institutions lending to small-scale enterprises. Even though this scheme was to some extent successful, it was abandoned because the central bank was reluctant to shoulder the liabilities of defaulters.

The agricultural and food processing equipment production sub-sectors have also received a boost with the rehabilitation of economic infrastructure, especially the electrification projects under the ERP. This is because some of the machines produced are capable of being powered by electric current, and as a result, the demand for such machines are enhanced by the electrification projects.

In pursuance of the Government's policy to promote the growth of SMEs, the National Board for Small Scale Industries (NBSSI) was established in 1985 specifically to offer support to the small and medium scale enterprises. A major objective of the NBSSI was to encourage and assist local small-scale machinery and tools for the agricultural selector. The Board has also helped indigenous food processing industries to improve upon their technology for processing, storing and handling agricultural produce.

The NBSSI's Modernization of Iron Smelting Project was also expected to contribute significantly to the growth of the agricultural and food processing equipment sub-sectors. This project was aimed at improving indigenous technology in the iron smelting industry in the Northern and Upper regions. As part of the project, training programmes were to be organized to improve upon existing skills, as well as introduce new ones. The training programmes would also introduce standardization systems and upgrade technology through the transfer of appropriate technology.

Furthermore, in 1987, the Government approved the Ghana Regional Appropriate Technology Industrial Services (GRATIS) project. This project was aimed at establishing Intermediate Technology Transfer Units (ITTUs) in every region in the country. Those ITTUs were to assist in transferring technology to small-scale industries. In this connection, the ITTUs were to establish and operate engineering workshops to demonstrate the use of new appropriate technologies in small-scale production to enhance quality and productivity. The expected income from the sale of the products so produced were to be used by the ITTUs to pay off part or all of their operating costs. Another aspect of the ITTU programme is that small-scale industrialists wishing to adopt the ITTU technology are given on-the-job training. In addition, they are permitted to hire workshop space and machine tool services of the ITTUs for their own manufacturing activities.[6] In establishing ITTUs, the GRATIS project links up with various interest groups in the regions, such as local technical institutions and small-scale industrialists.

Another institution that has been set up as part of efforts to enhance the technology of small-scale industrialists is the Development and Application of Intermediate Technology (DAPIT) project. DAPIT which was set up in 1984 is jointly sponsored by the Government of Ghana and the United States of America. As part of the project, the results of research and development were to be made available to small-scale entrepreneurs. This would hopefully enhance the operation of agricultural and food processing equipment manufacturers.

The issue of equipping entrepreneurs in the SME sector with working knowledge of modern management practices has also been addressed. This important role is played by the Management Development and Productivity Institute (MDPI) through periodic seminars and courses that it organizes for SME entrepreneurs.

The impact of the ERP on the manufacturing sector of Ghana has been described as mixed,[7] and this observation applies equally well to the agricultural and food processing equipment manufacturing sectors.

Trends in Imports of Agro-Machinery and Equipment

On the positive side, the ERP helped in eliminating wide-ranging economic controls, as well as enhancing the access to inputs especially imported spare parts. For example, for the first half of 1991, 2,254 kgs of parts of agricultural machinery (excluding tractors) were imported into the country, whilst for the first six months of 1993, as much as 43,469 kgs of such imports was recorded. There was a general increase in the availability of inputs like spare parts, non-ferrous metals land iron and steel for the sub-sectors under review. Furthermore, the ERP (through the financial sector reforms) has the potential of improving in the long-run, the accessibility of local producers of agricultural and food processing equipment to long-term capital.

On the negative side, firms in the agro-metals sector should have suffered severely as a result of these economic reforms. The trade liberalization policy has generally encouraged competition from imports, some of which are of questionable quality. A look at the Table 4.4 indicates a general increase in the importation of agricultural and food processing machinery in recent times. For example, for the first six months of 1991, 56,769kg of agricultural machinery (excluding tractors) were imported into the country. In 1992, imports jumped to over 10 million kg. It should be noted that such a trend should have had the potential of stifling the local production of these machinery. Imports of food processing machinery has also shown increasing trends in the nineties, increasing from only 81,354kg in the first half of 1991 to over 3 million kilogrammes in the first half of 1993.

But large sections of the agro-metals sector are not exposed to direct import competition because they serve local markets for goods of a kind not readily provided by foreign producers. For example, many of farm implements imported to be used on small farms sometimes have to be remoulded by local blacksmiths to suit the local environment. Thus, the increased imports of the machinery did not serve to drive out local producers, but came in to supplement domestic production. Although, the quality of locally produced equipment is crude, and there are imported equipment from India which are better designed and finished, local firms are to able to compete on prices.[8] It also indicates existence of a large local market for food processing and agricultural equipment which cannot be adequately satisfied by domestic producers alone. Local producers could be encouraged to produce to fill the gap presently satisfied by imports. The bank-credits regulation has also resulted in severe liquidity constraints on the producers of agricultural and food processing equipment.

Table 4.4: Imports of Agricultural and Food Processing Machinery

Imports (kg) of	1991 (January–June)	1992 (January–December)	1993 (January–July)
1. Agricultural Machinery (excluding tractors) and parts thereof	56,769	10,741,296	386,318
2. Food Processing Machinery	81,354	1,685,538	3,277,594
3. Iron and Steel	4,702,277	42,063,161	22,229,743
6. Non-ferrous Metal	390,687	4,391,326	2,329,043

Source: Ghana Statistical Service.

The liberalization of the exchange rate has also dealt a big blow to the producers in question. This is because it has led to a consistent depreciation of the cedi, with its associated import cost implications. Thus, for a local producer of the machinery in question who imports inputs on credit, the product has to be priced highly to guarantee that he would be able to fulfil his debt obligations. This is because, the cedi might have depreciated considerably by the time payment is due.

LOCAL PRODUCTION CAPACITY OF AGRO-METALS SECTOR

The success of agricultural mechanization and improvement in the technology and equipment for the food processing sector is contingent upon the performance of the metal sector of which agro-metals is part. This metal sector is estimated to have produced 3.5% of manufacturing valued added in 1989 (Berger, 1989). The agro-metal subsector consists of various industries producing agricultural implements and food processing equipment.

Table 4.5: Value of Imports of Metal Products (in Cedis)

Items	1983	1984	1985
67 Iron and Steel	173,602,685	465,348,989	888,076,646
68 Non-ferrous Metal	70,974,028	121,120,187	220,579,175
69 Manufactures of Metal, NES.	274,697,100	417,104,360	898,217,205

Source: Statistical Service.
* Data for 1986–1990 were not available.

The metal sector is very diverse, consisting of rural artisans and blacksmiths making simple metal products with a minimal of tools, using traditional techniques with little precision"[9] and highly sophisticated plants. Every country has some form of metal industry, which has significance for industrial development, in terms of providing the base for engineering skills needed by other industries, providing parts and components for repairs, providing the information needed for adaptation and improvement of equipment and providing inter-firm linkages through sub-contracting[10] The structure of technologies used and products vary across countries. Because of the wide diversity of firms and techniques used which is a function of size of firm we analyze in this section, the present local capacity to produce farm implements and food processing equipments by distinguishing between micro, small and medium scale producers.

Structure of the Agro-Metals Sector

To study the present structure of the metals sector, especially the agricultural implements and food processing equipment sectors we shall make use of the Ghana Industrial Census (1987) conducted by the Ghana Statistical Service, and Key Enterprise Survey of a sample of 25 firms conducted in 1994. What are the characteristics of the firms in the sector? Table 4.6 gives some relevant data on the structure

Table 4.6: Characteristics of the Agro-Machinery Sector (1987)

(a) Number of Establishments by Size Class (Employment)

		Total	Micro 1-4	Small 5-9	Medium 10-29	Large 30-99	100+
371	Iron and steel basic	6	–	1	–	3	2
372	Non ferrous metal basic	4	–	–	–	2	2
381	Fabricated metals	668	205	325	101	25	12
3811	Cutlery, hand tools etc.	166	74	57	29	1	5
3819	Fabricated except M&	302	69	174	41	13	5
382	Non electrical machinery	135	33	60	34	6	2
3822	Agricultural machinery	21	3	7	7	2	2
3824	Special industrial machinery	54	15	17	20	2	–
3829	M&E except elect. nec.	50	12	30	6	2	–
371/372/381/382/383/384		1166	290	569	214	67	26
Total agro-metals sector		593	173	285	103	20	12
Percent		100	29.2	48.0	17.4	3.4	2.0

(b) Number of Establishments for Selected Towns

		Total	Sekondi Takoradi	Accra	Tema	Kumasi	Other
371	Iron and steel basic	6	1	3	2	–	–
372	Non ferrous metal basic	4	–	2	1	–	1
381	Fabricated metals	668					
3811	Cutlery, hand tools etc	166	–	8	7	43	108
3819	Fabricated except M&E	302	5	49	26	145	77
382	Non electrical machinery	135					
3822	Agricultural machinery	21	–	5	–	4	12
3824	Special industrial mach.	54	–	11	4	2	16
3829	M&E except elect. nec.	50	–	4	1	6	39
371/372/381/382/383/384		1166					
Total agro-metals		593	5	77	38	220	252
			1.0	13.0	6.4	37.1	42.5

Table **4.6** *(cont'd.)*

(c) Nationality of Ownership

		Total	Ghanaian	Non-Ghanaian	Mixed
371	Iron and steel basic	6	4	–	2
372	Non ferrous metal basic	4	3	–	1
381	Fabricated metals	668			
3811	Cutlery, hand tools etc	166	158	5	3
3819	Fabricated except M&E	302	284	9	9
382	Non electrical machinery	135			
3822	Agricultural machinery	21	20	1	–
3824	Special industrial machinery	54	49	3	2
3829	M&E except elect. nec.	50	47	1	2
371/372/381/382/383/384		1166			
Total agro-metals sector (%)			94.1	3.2	2.7

(d)   Persons Engaged by Size Class (Employment)

		Total	1–4	5–9	10–29	30–99	100+
371	Iron and steel basic	808	–	5	–	166	637
372	Non ferrous metal basic	2043	–	–	–	89	1954
381	Fabricated metals						
3811	Cutlery, hand tools etc.	2314	191	341	396	30	1356
3819	Fabricated except M&E	3807	208	1099	607	592	1301
382	Non electrical machinery						
3822	Agricultural machinery	463	10	40	107	93	213
3824	Special industrial machinery	598	41	111	334	112	–
3829	M&E except elect. nec.	363	32	171	79	81	–
Total agro-metals sector		7545	482	1762	1523	908	2870
	(%)	100	6.4	23.4	20.2	12.0	38.0
Average size (employment)		12.7	2.8	6.2	14.8	45.4	239.2

Source: Statistical Service, Ghana Industrial Census, Phase I, 1987.

of agro-industrial machinery sector derived from the 1987 Industrial Census undertaken by the Statistical Service of Ghana.

(i)   From the table it can be observed that the bulk of establishment in the tools and agricultural machinery manufacturing sector are micro firms employing less than 10 workers. The remainder are small and medium enterprises. Large firms in the sector are rather few. This is consistent with UNDP/TTC (1990) description local producers as consisting of two relatively disconnected groups of relatively small group of medium scale enterprises in the formal sector and a large group of small enterprises in the informal sector. The dominance of small and micro firms in the sector is an indication of thwarted growth. This is the result of type of ownership, which is mainly sole proprietorship.

(ii) The largest concentration of firms (37.1%) is found in Kumasi (Suame Magazine).

(iii) About 94% of the agro-metal firms are indigenously owned with 3.2% owned wholly by foreigners and 2.7% being joint ventures.

The Key Enterprises Survey

The purpose of this survey was to explore technologies in use in agro-metal firms in Ghana and the potential for local development of technological capability. The survey was undertaken in January and March 1994. The key enterprise survey covered 25 agro-metals firms in three major clusters — Accra-Tema, Kumasi, Cape Coast/Sekondi-Takoradi. The key informants survey covered 7 institutions and firms. Several firms refused to cooperate, arguing that they had been over-interviewed and have not gained anything from previous interviews. The questionnaire provided information on the characteristics of the firms and the entrepreneur, products, production and sales, inputs, constraints, regulations and the impact of structural adjustment.

Owing to the non-existence of a complete list of all agro-metal firms in the country, we had to resort to the 1987 Industrial Census list of firms provided by the Statistical Service. The selection of firms was not random but was based on previous knowledge of the firms acquired through earlier surveys and was not meant to achieve statistically representative results.

The type of technologies in use and the type and quality of the machines produced are all related to firm size. Thus we attempted to survey a mix of firms of different sizes. We considered three size categories, micro (subdivided into blacksmiths and non-blacksmiths), small and medium. The term "micro-enterprise" is sometimes used to describe firms with fewer than 5 workers. For the purposes of this study we adopted the following classification of size:

1-4   workers termed "micro-enterprises" (blacksmiths) or micro 1;

5-9   workers, termed "micro-enterprises" (non-blacksmiths) or micro 2;

10-29   workers, termed "small";

30-99   workers, termed "medium".

The distribution of the 25 firms by size and location is given in Table 4.2. Fifty-six percent of the firms were located in Accra/Tema, 20% in Kumasi and 24% in Cape Coast/Takoradi area. Of the 25 sample firms, 4 (16%) are blacksmiths, 6 (24%) are micro 2, 11 (44%) are small, and 4 (16%) are medium firms.

Table 4.8 describes the characteristics of the entrepreneurs. There is a wide variation in the age of sample firms, ranging from 1 year to 33 years. Both the oldest and youngest are all micro firms. Almost all the micro enterprises are sole proprietorship, while the small firms are split between sole proprietorship and limited liability. All the medium scale firms are limited liability companies.

The agro-metals industry is dominated by males; not a single female was found in any of the 25 firms interviewed, working there as an entrepreneur, a paid worker, or an apprentice. The average age of the entrepreneurs or managers was found to be lower in the micro enterprises than in the small and medium scale enterprises. Entrepreneurs in the small and medium scale enterprises were more educated than those in the micro enterprises. Apprenticeship as an additional form of training was more common for entrepreneurs in the micro enterprises.

Types of Workshops, Existing Technology, Equipment and Other Capital Inputs

As observed in many developing countries the machinery for production of agro-metals is mainly imported. Domestic suppliers of machinery start with repair and maintenance of imported machinery followed by manufacture of machines and equipment in response to needs of customers. This is evidenced by the list of machine tools and hand tools used in the industry.

Table 4.7: Distribution of Sample Enterprise by Size, Location and Legal Status

	Bblacksmiths	Micro	Small	Medium	Total
Location					
Accra/Tem a	–	4	6	4	14
Kumasi	2	1	2	–	5
Cape Coast/Takoradi	2	1	3	–	6
Total	4	6	11	4	25
Legal status					
Single ownership	4	5	5		
Family business	1	1			
Limited liability	5	4			

Table 4.8: Entrepreneur Characteristics

	Blacksmiths	Micro	Small	Medium
Age (years)	40	42	50	50
Range	32–63	24–70	36–74	32–68
Highest Education (years)	6.5	8	12.2	12.5
No. with Additional Training				
Apprenticeship	4	4	2	2
Technical School	–	2	2	–
Gender	male	male	male	male

The local manufacture of mechanization equipments involves some foundry, forging, sheet, tube and profile working, fabricating, casting heat treatment, machining, surface finishing and design facilities.[11]

(i)   It has been observed that *rural blacksmith/metal workers* outside the cities/towns work sheet-metal and tubes, in addition to forging and several bench fitting activities in the form of filling. This involves the use of hand tools and earth hearth with bellows or hand blowers. Their production is manual. They make use of hand tools such as hammer, spanner, file etc. (Table 4.9)

(ii) The mode of production and nature of equipment of *Urban-based blacksmith/metal workers* are identical to that of their rural counterparts. They however, have access to electricity. In our key enterprise survey, for example, one blacksmith was found to be making use of a lathe machine.

(iii) We can also identify *micro 2 enterprises*. They engage in metal forming and machine shop jobbing. Their processes involve sheet metal and tube forming, metal cutting, machinery, welding and assembling using mainly general hand tools including electric drills and grinders and acetylene gas or electric welding. They also use hand tools similar to what the blacksmiths use.

(iv) *Small* industrial enterprises are engaged in forging, metal working, welding, machinery, heat treatment and product assembling. This group normally uses electricity powered machine tools. Within this group are what one might term "dynamic entrepreneurs" with better capabilities to be able to produce machinery for local markets. They use intermediate technologies.

(v)   a few *medium scale metal working firms* are also engaged in forging, metal working, welding, machinery, heat treatment and product assembling. They also normally use electricity powered machine tools. They have larger workshops. The equipment is imported tools.

Table 4.9: Tools Used in the Agro-Metals Industry by Size of Firm

Micro 1 (Blacksmith)	Micro 2	Small	Medium
*Lathe machine**	Electric/ Gas Welding	Lathe Machine	Lathe machine
Bellows/hand blowers	Spraying machine	Sanding Machine	Electric welding
Hearth	Gas cutting machine	Press machine	Gas welding
	Guillotine machine	Spraying machine	
	Electric Welding	Grinding machine	
	Spraying Machine	Rolling machine	
	Gas Welding	Cutting machine	
	Temperature Furnace	Drilling machine	
	Drilling Machine	Generating plant	
	Grinding Machine	Shaping machine	
	Shaping Machine	Milling machine	
	Milling Machine	Bending machine	
	Bending Machine	Hacksaw	
	Power Hacksaw		
	Rolling Machine		
	Punching Machine		
	Electric Saw		

List of Hand Tools

Hammer	hammer	File	Hammer
Chisel	spanner	Vice	Chisel
File	chisel	Clamps	Clamps
Anvril	cutlass	Anvil	Punch
Punch	scissors	Hammer	Drilling machine
Drilling machine	plier	Chisel	Grinding machine
Grinding machine	grinding machine	Punch	
Spanner	drilling machine	Drilling Machine	
File	punch	Spanner	
Clamp	Grinding Machine		
Punch	Plier		

Source: 1994 key Enterprise Survey Data.
          *There was one blacksmith who was also using a lathe machine.

Labour Inputs

The labour supply to the sector and the level of skills, like technology appears to be influenced by locational factors. The implement producers located in the rural areas have very little or no education. They have acquired their skills mostly through apprenticeship.[12] Similarly the city based implement producers have very little education (mainly primary and middle school leavers). They also acquire their skills through apprenticeship.

The artisanal shops, small and medium scale industrial establishments, mainly found in the urban areas, have two levels of skilled manpower. These are the Artisans/Engineering Technicians from the Technical Schools and Polytechnics and the Professional Engineers with degrees and diploma in special discipline of Science and Technology from the Universities. These categories hold the prospect for growth in the sector. When sufficiently motivated they could be innovative. The supply of professional engineers and engineering technicians appear to combine favourably with the apprenticeship system to provide in pool of qualified manpower for the Agro-Industrial machinery and implements manufacturing sector. Table 4.11 shows the percentage of persons engaged in the sector by level of skills.

From Table 4.10, even though apprentices constitute about 21% of persons engaged in the sector, unskilled workers are about 6%. It is sector dominated by skilled workers. This is a very positive development. Although, a large percentage of these agro-metal workers are relatively lacking in professionals with engineering training, their creativity and flexibility, ingenuity in adaptation and copying is a great asset for the sector.

Raw Materials Inputs

Table 4.11 lists by size the type of raw materials used by our sample of agro-metal firms. The evidence is that iron and steel and steel products constitute the main inputs of the metal/equipment manufacturers. The steel and steel products are obtained from two sources viz. importation and scrap obtained from the local market. Imported raw materials are limited to well established firms with huge capital outlay and producing on very large scale with modern methods and machinery.

Table 4.10: Persons Engaged by Level of Skill

	Total	Professional/ Managerial	Technical/ Clerical	Skilled	Apprentices	Unskilled
371 Iron and steel basic	808	135	125	460	23	65
372 Non ferrous metal basic	2043	138	608	1171	–	126
381 Fabricated metals						
3811 Cutlery, hand tools etc	2314	246	295	1104	504	165
3819 Fabricated except M&E	3807	465	400	1618	1122	202
382 Non electrical machinery						
3822 Agricultural machinery	463	65	69	194	113	22
3824 Special industrial mach.	598	77	39	240	206	36
3829 M&E except elect. nec.	363	56	17	105	181	4
TOTAL	10396	1182	1553	4892	2149	620
Percentage	100	11.4	14.9	47.1	20.7	6.0

Source: Statistical Service, Industrial Census, 1987. Part I.

Table 4.11: List of Raw Material Requirements by Size of Firm

Micro 1 (Blacksmith)	*Micro 2*	*Small*	*Medium*
Scrap metals	Scrap metals	Scrap metals	Mild steel plates
Galvanised pipes	Steel plates	Steel plates	Galvanised sheets
Steel plates	Galvanised plate	Iron rods	Aluminium sheets
Brass.	Aluminium sheets	Square pipes	Shafts
Iron plates	Iron rods	Iron sheets	Iron rods
Iron rods	Electrodes	Mild steel rods	Pipes
Electricity	Angle iron	Galvanised sheets	Flat bars
	Flat bars	U channels	Angle iron
	Galvanised pipes	Shaft	Electrodes
	Gas	Bore bearing	Steel pipes
	Electricity	Electrodes	Galvanised pipes
	Compressor Tanks	Stainless steel	Gas
		Gas	Electricity
		Electricity	Compressor Tanks
		Compressor Tanks	

Source: 1994 Key Enterprise Survey Data.

Medium size firms use some imported raw materials and scrap, whilst the small and micro producers who are in the majority rely on scrap metal. The adaptation to the use of scrap makes entrepreneurs flexible with the input situation but it limits their range of products.

Output of the Sector

Firms in the agro-metals sector are multi-product establishments with each firm producing more than one product. A recent study by the Industrial Research Institute (IRI) of the Council for Scientific and Industrial Research (C.S.I.R) (Damptey *et al.* 1989) listed 50 products that are being locally produced to aid mechanization. These equipment are produced for the following sectors:

    (i)   Farming Sector
        (a) Farm implements
        (b) Farm machinery
    (ii) Food processing sector
        (a) Edible oil sector
        (b) Fruits and vegetable sector

(c) Roots and tubers
(d) Sugar cane
(e) Other equipment

As noted earlier, these machines are either locally developed or adapted to local conditions from imported equipments. The adaptations have been undertaken by entrepreneurs who have had little or no formal training in equipment development, using scrap metal (Aboagye, 1991). The products of the agro-metals sector by size of firm are given in Table 4.12.

The range of products for the blacksmiths are limited. They include hoes, chisels, hand forks, cutlasses and cocoa harvesting

Table 4.12: List of Products of the Agro-Metals Sector by Size of Firm

Micro 1 *(Blacksmith)*	*Micro 2*	*Small*	*Medium*
Hand Fork	Flour mixing machine	Gari mill	Flour mixer
Hoes	Flour rolling machine	Sugar cane crusher	Flour roller
Cutlasses	Kokonte crusher	Pepper mill	Kokonte cracker
Cocoa plucker	Cassava grater	Cassava mill	Gari mill
Cocoa harvesting	Corn mill	Corn mill	Corn mill
sickels	Pepper grinder	Tomato mill	Cassava grater
	Fish mill	Coconut mill	Coconut grater
	Nut cracker	Hammer mill	Hammer mill
	Oil extractor	Poultry feed mill	Sugar cane crusher
	Oil palm digester	Shea butter processing	Rice sheller
	Palm kernel cracker	Palm kernel cracker	Animal feed mill
	Baking cans	Dough presser	Palm kernel cracker
	Poultry cans	Juice extraction	Tomato mill
	Buckets	Bean driers	Pepper mill
	Hoes	Rice mill	Palm oil mill —
	Groundnut thresher	digester	
	Palm oil mill —	presser	
	digester	boiler	
	presser	stripper	
	boiler	bullock ploughs	
	stripper	Tractor trailers	
	Cutlass		
	Hoe		

Source: 1994 Key Enterprise Survey Data.

sickels; the blacksmiths produce mainly agricultural implements. The micro non-blacksmith firms produce a few agricultural implements, but concentrate on food processing machines. The difference between the small and medium sized firms is in the diversity of the products of individual firms. While the small firms concentrate on a few food processing equipment, the medium firms are more diversified, producing in addition to food processing machines, agricultural equipment such as tractor trailers and ploughs.

Production and Capacity Utilization

Value added is the most important indicator of the relative economic importance of an industry. Table 4.13 shows the share of metal working subsector in Manufacturing value added together with the value of output, wages and salaries and level of employment.

From Table 4.13 it is clear that manufacturing value added accounted for about 67% of industry value added. Also over 66% of people engaged in industry are in manufacturing. The corresponding shares of fabricated metal products, machines and equipments in manufacturing value added is rather low.

The analysis reveals that non-electrical machinery (including for instance agricultural machinery) appear to have always been completely marginal in terms of providing value added to the domestic economy. Despite its current performance, it should be clear that as long as the growth of the industry is dependent on structural shifts in production technology in agriculture, there is a way ahead.

Employment has been used as an indicator of size in this analysis in place of production or value of machinery and equipment because of the problems of measurement of the value of capital. The problem is less serious with output measurement; but in our sample the micro firms never kept any books, and one had to make guesstimates of output levels. It is interesting to note that in our sample the three indicators will give a similar classification of firm with a few exceptions. For example, two of the medium-sized firms have production which would have placed in the small scale group, while two of the small firms produced output of more than $100 million in 1993. Capacity utilization in the metal sector as a whole in 1990 was 49%. The average rate for the sample of key enterprises in the agro-metals was not very different; it ranged from as low as 5% to 100%, averaging about 50% (Table 4.14).

Table 4.13: **Principal Indicators of Industrial Activity in the Metal Working Subsectors Relative to Total Manufacturing and Total Industry**

	No. of Persons Engaged	No. of Employees	Wages or Salaries ¢million	Value of Output ¢million	Census Value-Added ¢million
Total Industry (1)	126,985	177,535	18,807	218,662	112,180
Total MFG (2)	87,577	78,188	11,697	167,074	75,732
MFG of Metal Products Machine Equipments (3)*	7,423	6,343	874	8,559	4,284
(2) ÷ (1)x100	69.0	66.5	62.2	76.4	67.5
(3) ÷ (2)x100	8.5	8.1	7.4	5.1	5.7

Source: Ghana Industrial Census, Phase II, 1987.
   * The group covers all of ISIC 38.
Note.   The Phase II results cover only firms employing 10 or more persons.

In almost all the firms surveyed entrepreneurs combine production with repairs. When asked about the desirability or profitability of production vis-a-vis repairs, most of the respondents indicated that despite the constraints facing them, production was more desirable and profitable. Only one medium sized firm had moved entirely from production, and was concentrating only on repairs.

CONSTRAINTS ON PRODUCTION AND PRODUCTIVITY GROWTH

It has been found that the response of the manufacturing sector to the economic reforms have been impeded by a number of institutional, structural, technological and financial constraints inherent in the present stage of Ghana's economic development.[13] One would therefore expect the agro-metals sector to face similar problems. The removal of these constraints could increase the agro-metals sector's capacity for expansion. Thus there is the need to identify the type and severity of restrictions, in order to be able to devise appropriate policies for the sector.

Table 4.14: Production, Utilization and Capital in Sample Firms by Size of Firm

Employee		Production 1993 ¢Million	Capacity Utilization %	Replacement Value of Machinery and Equipment ¢Million
Medium scale firms				
01	32	12.0	70	60.0
02	73	675.0	80	175.0
03	94	427.0	75/60/55	60.4
04	38	18.2	50	10.5
Small scale firms				
05	11	17.1	n.a	83.8
06	20	8.3	60	14.4
07	15	2.0	50	9.8
08	24	348.6	50	817.3
09	22	n.a	50	25.0
10	13	1.4	100	12.0
11	22	n.a	50	n.a
12	14	21.0	33	12.0
13	22	106.0	50	55.0
14	10	n.a	n.a	n.a
15	25	n.a	50	n.a
Micro firms (Blacksmiths)				
16	5	n.a	-	12.5
17	3	1.82	50	0.9
18	7	n.a	50	0.05
19	6	n.a	100	0.1
Micro firms (Non-blacksmiths)				
20	3	2.52	50	0.5
21	9	1.05	-	2.0
22	5	0.75	50	0.4
23	4	2.4	5	0.06
24	6	7.2	50	0.04
25	2	2.5	40	0.77

Source: Key Enterprise Survey, 1994.

Several surveys have been conducted to find out what firms perceive as the major constraints to their operation and expansion. Industrial surveys in Ghana have found a high proportions of firms citing lack of access to credit as a major constraint. Studies by Thomi and Yankson (1985), Anheir and Seibel (1987) Webster and Steel (1991), Sowa and others (1991), Osei and others (1993), Baah-Nuakoh and Steel (1993), Baah-Nuakoh (1993) emphasize the importance of finance especially working capital as the major constraint; Another important constraint which most of these studies do not bring out is the capability needed to set up and efficiently manage an enterprise — management, skills and technology. Although, management is considered a serious constraint especially within small and medium scale firms, as evidenced by the establishment of training institutions such as the National Board for Small Scale Industries' (NBSSI) Entrepreneurship Development Programme and EMPRETEC, entrepreneurs themselves do not perceive management as a problem. Baah-Nuakoh and Steel (1993) found out that only 0.8% of the 133 firms interviewed in 1991 indicated that management was a problem.

We examine how Ghanaian firms in the agro-metals perceive the impact of the problems of raw materials, technology and equipment, finance, labour and management, infrastructure, demand, business environment, and marketing and distribution and other problems which have constrained the performance of firms in the agro-metals sector. This section makes use of the 25 key enterprise survey conducted in January–March 1994.

Entrepreneurs' Perception of Constraints

The 25 enterprise survey approached the question of constraints by asking the entrepreneurs to identify the main constraints to the expansion of their firms development. Firstly, the entrepreneurs were to rank the severity of each constraint listed on a scale of 1 (not important) to 5 (very important). Secondly, the entrepreneurs to rank the three most serious problems which affect expansion of their firms. These problems relate to growth potential of firms. Table 4.15 summarizes the major groups of constraints. Table 4.16 lists the detailed responses. Irrespective of size, finance is considered the single most serious constraint facing firms (45%) in the agro-metals sector. The problem was cited more frequently by micro 2 firms (60%) than large firms (50%), small (44%) and blacksmiths (25%).

Table 4.15: Major Constraints on Expansion by Firm Size

	Total	Micro 1	Micro 2	Small	Medium
First Ranking					
Raw materials	2(9.1)	1(25.0)	1(20.0)	–	–
Technology, Equipment	7(31.8)	1(25.0)	1(20.0)	–	1(25.0)
Finance	10(45.5)	1(25.0)	3(60)	4(44.4)	2(50.0)
Demand	1(4.5)	1(25.0)	–	–	–
Marketing and Distribution	1(4.5)	–	–	–	1(25.0)
Others	1(4.5)	–	–	1(11.1)	–
No. of responding firms	22	4	5	9	4
Aggregate of Top Three Responses					
Raw materials	4(18.2)	1(25.0)	3(50.0)	–	–
Technology, Equipment	13(59.1)	3(75.0)	4(66.7)	5(55.6)	1(25.0)
Finance .	22(100)	4(100)	6(100)	8(88.9)	4(100)
Infrastructure	2(9.1)	–	–	–	2(50.0)
Demand	8(36.4)	1(25.0)	–	6(66.7)	1(25.0)
Business Support Services	4(18.2)	–	–	3(33.3)	1(25.0)
Marketing and Distribution	1(4.5)	–	–	–	1(25.0)
Others	1(4.5)	–	–	1(11.1)	–

Source: Key Enterprise Survey data.
 Percentage of respondents in each category in parentheses.

When the problems mentioned by the firms are aggregated, finance still remains the commonly cited problem. All the responding firms irrespective of size considered this a serious problem.

. The second most important constraint to the expansion of agro-metals firms is technology. About 32% of sample firms considered this as the principal constraint, while 59% of firms mentioned it as a problem. The machines used by most of the firms in the sector are outdated and there was a strong desire for the firms to upgrade their machinery.

In the agro-metals sector although demand is a problem (36.4%), it is not the most serious. Only one firm in the sample (a blacksmith) considered demand as the principal constraint. Although, the problem of demand may exist in the sector, the problem is glossed over by the firms; for example, imports which is a demand related problem

Table 4.16: Detailed Constraints on Expansion by Firm Size

	Micro 1		Micro 2		Small		Medium	
	P	A	P	A	P	A	P	A
No. of responding firms	4		5		9		4	
Raw materials								
Inadequate or unreliable supply of local materials	1	1	–	1	–	–	–	–
High price of local raw materials	–	–	1	1	–	–	–	–
Price of imported raw materials too high	–	–	–	1	–	–	–	–
Technology, Equipment								
Equipment is old and replacement costs of equipment is too high	1	2	1	2	1	2	1	1
Replacement costs are too high	–	–	–	1	–	–	–	–
Workshop space is inadequate	–	1	–	1	3	3	–	–
Finance								
Cannot get credit for raw materials or working capital	1	3	3	4	1	3	1	1
Cannot get credit for equipment	–	1	–	2	1	2	–	–
Interest rates are too high	2	3	1	3				
Infrastructure								
Interruption of electricity supply	–	–	–	–	–	–	–	2
Demand								
Inadequate domestic demand	1	1	–	–	–	3	–	1
Too many imports	–	–	–	–	–	3	–	–
Business Environment								
Taxes	–	–	–	–	–	3	–	1
Marketing and Distribution								
Too few distributors	–	–	–	–	–	–	1	1
Others								
Stealing	–	–	–	–	1	1	–	–

Source: Key Enterprise Survey, 1994. P - principal constraint A — aggregated constraint

was not cited by even a single firm as constituting a problem. The entrepreneurs believe that their sector, unlike the textiles industry where demand is a problem because of import competition, their products are such that they consider them as differentiated products which are better (durable) and cheaper.

Many of the firms complained that the workshop space was too small, but the banks were not prepared to provide investment capital.[14]

The Severity of the Constraints

We then tried to find out the severity of the constraints on expansion by asking the entrepreneurs on a scale of 1 to 5 (not important to important) to measure the extent of the severity. For each constraint the score was averaged to derive a rough index of severity. Table 4.18 provide information on the firms' perception of the severity of the individual constraints.

Survey scores range from 1 to 5. Figures are averages for firms surveyed in each category than imported equipment. They argue that the problem is inadequate domestic demand.

The constraints of finance, technology and demand revealed in Table 4.15 and 4.16 seem to be confirmed by Table 4.17. The constraints seem to be more severe for the blacksmiths and the medium firms than for the micro 2 and small enterprises. The problem of finance is basically getting credit to finance raw materials and equipment. The medium sized firms also complained about high interest rates. Inadequate domestic demand faced all categories of firms, but the medium firms complained about too many imports being allowed into the country by the liberalization policy.

Other Problems Facing the Sector

From the interviews with firms and key informants, other problems facing the sector emerged. It was strongly pointed out that:

(i) Although, there is demand for the products of the agro-metals sector, there is lack of coordination between producers;

(ii) There is no clear government policy on technology for the sector;

(iii) Entrepreneurs with knowledge in processing are not available;

Table 4.17: Severity of Constraints

	Micro 1	Micro 2	Small	Medium
No. of responding firms	1	5	5	4
Raw materials				
Inadequate or unreliable supply of local materials	3.0	1.8	1.4	1.8
High price of local raw materials	1.0	3.6	1.6	2.0
Price of imported raw materials is too high	1.0	2.6	2.8	2.8
Inadequate or unreliable supply of imported materials and spares	1.0	1.2	1.6	2.0
Technology, Equipment				
Equipment is old and replacement costs of equipment is too high	5.0	3.2	2.2	3.5
Lack of technological information	1.0	2.0	1.4	2.3
Cannot get spare parts	1.0	1.0	1.6	2.0
Replacement costs are too high	1.0	2.8	2.8	4.0
Workshop space is inadequate	5.0	3.0	2.8	1.5
Poor machine tools	4.0	3.2	2.2	2.5
Finance				
Cannot get credit for raw materials or working capital	5.0	3.2	2.4	2.8
Cannot get credit for equipment	5.0	3.8	1.8	3.0
Interest rates are too high	1.0	1.6	3.6	4.8
Banks are difficult to deal with	1.0	3.4	2.2	3.0
Profits are too low to finance new equipment	4.0	3.0	2.8	3.8
Profits are too low to finance raw materials	3.0	3.0	2.2	3.3
Have to give too much credit to customers	1.0	2.6	1.2	1.0
Labour, Management				
Lack of skilled workers	1.0	2.0	1.2	1.0
High labour costs	1.0	1.2	1.6	2.0
Unable to attract management with necessary skills	1.0	1.6	1.0	1.5
Lack of unskilled workers	1.0	1.0	1.2	1.3
Not allowed to lay off workers	1.0	1.0	1.2	1.3

Table 4.17 (*cont'd.*)

	Micro 1	Micro 2	Small	Medium
Infrastructure				
Interruption of electricity supply	1.0	1.2	2.2	2.8
Inadequate water supply	1.0	1.0	1.0	1.8
Transportation costs are too high	1.0	1.6	2.2	1.5
Demand				
Inadequate domestic demand	5.0	3.2	2.8	3.3
Too many firms in the same business	1.0	2.4	2.2	1.8
Too many imports	1.0	2.0	2.2	3.5
Business Environment				
Taxes	1.0	1.4	4.0	3.8
Regulations, licensing, permits	1.0	1.0	1.6	2.5
Obtaining foreign exchange	1.0	1.0	1.6	2.3
Rules and policies change too often	1.0	1.0	2.0	1.8
Standard and quality requirements	1.0	1.0	1.2	1.0
Marketing and Distribution				
Too few distributors	1.0	1.0	1.0	1.8
Distributors wont handle firms products	1.0	1.0	1.0	1.8
Distributors will pay too little for the products	1.0	1.0	1.0	1.3

Source: Key Enterprise Survey data.

   (iv)   Production is not attractive.

   (v)   Specifications of the products are rough and lack standardization.

   (vi)   There is lack of inter-firm linkages. The SMEs sector of the industry has few linkages with the large scale sector. Thus, sub-contracting which could improve the technology and skill levels in the smaller firms is minimal or almost non-existent. Presently, the level of technologies used in the smaller firms is far below that required by the larger firms.

   (vii)   The SMEs do not have technological links with foreign companies and do not produce under licence from foreign companies. It seems they are satisfied with their present technological capability geared towards the local market.

(viii) There is lack of expertise in plant design and lack of a developed steel industry there is thus dependence on imported
materials and scraps and engineering support facilities such
as foundries, forge shops etc. Skill acquisition is through
apprenticeship

RECOMMENDATIONS AND AREAS OF INTERVENTION

This section discusses the strategies to be adopted in devising
programmes and polices to improve the environment for the
development of a dynamic agro-metal industry in Ghana. The
economy has the capacity, potential skills and dynamism to develop
a viable agro-metals industry. But this will require policy support
and interventions. While the blacksmiths have a role to play in the
sector producing agricultural implements, they can also continue to
serve as a link between the locally mass-produced and imported
implements, serving to remould these implements to suit local
environments. The medium scale sector has problems competing with
imports. It seems the sectors which have the capacity to grow are the
micro non blacksmiths and the small scale firms producing food
processing equipment.

The previous section has summarized the constraints facing the
agro-metal sector. Lack of capital, technology as well as lack of
demand, have been found to be among the serious constraints facing
the sector, and were cited more often by the entrepreneurs. To
remove or reduce these constraints would require some assistance
from the government, donor agencies and NGOs.

Review of Policy Towards the Sector

The agro-metal sector in Ghana has potential for development.
Changes in the official policy of the government directly or indirectly
which would help to remove the numerous constraints facing the
sector could enhance its capacity to expand the production of
equipment and implements to feed the food processing and
agricultural sectors. In Ghana, like in many countries on the African
continent, government policy and attitudes towards the sector is
ambiguous. While there is official acknowledgement of the potential
of the sector to generate the intermediate technologies, there is
complete absence of overall policy priorities in the area of capital
goods production.

Integrated Programme of Agro-Metal Industry Development

There is a need for an integrated programme of agro-metal development. This requires:

  (i) identifying one sector at a time and identifying which machinery to be developed;
 (ii) defining which parts to be built locally — for it will be difficult to try to produce everything at the same time;
(iii) then isolating organizations to produce a set of machines; GRATIS and CSIR could be made to support the project with given deadlines;
 (iv) organizing the food processing firms and farmers who are the consumers of the final products, to be able to identify the demand for the agro-metal equipment;
  (v) helping the food processing firms and farmers with a funding programme to purchase the machinery and implements produced by the agro-metals sector.

Increased Access to Finance

The survey asked the entrepreneurs to provide information on the type of intervention they require. The information coming from the entrepreneurs themselves could be useful in helping to evolve the design suitable programs and policies for the agro-metal sector. Since the most serious problem facing the sector is the lack of capital, with the sector relying on internal financing from the entrepreneurs' own savings or borrowing from friends, relatives and money lenders, one would expect the entrepreneurs to ask for increased access to finance.

The problem of capital whether, fixed or working reduces the capacity of the sector to expand. The entrepreneurs rely on their own savings and resort to borrowing from their friends and relatives to relieve them of the financial requirements. They see the banks and other financial institutions and structures which are impersonal and hostile and which exist for foreign businesses. These banks ask for collateral which they know the entrepreneurs do not possess.

According to the survey, only a few of the entrepreneurs will solve the problem of business expansion through the use of bank loans. They will rely on suppliers' credits and customers' advances.

Support from the financial institutions could come from the development of an intermediate mechanism which is aimed at facilitating the access of entrepreneurs to credit for the establishment and operation as well as improvement of their enterprises. Thus, interventions which involve sudden injection of capital into especially an economic system where only a small number of artisans make attempts to obtain bank loans should be avoided; this could lead to accelerated development of a few privileged entrepreneurs and penalize small enterprises. It should be noted here that while external funds are necessary to help the expansion of the sector, this should not serve to stifle the internal financing arrangements which already exist. For producers in the agro-metals sector external funding should be in the form of suppliers credits for equipment and raw materials, provided to identifiable groups of producers.

Increased Access to Raw Materials

The raw materials required to make these technologies functional do not exist locally. It is evident that steel and steel products are the main inputs in the metal working sector. Steel sheets and bars are imported and because of foreign exchange constraint, the supply is inadequate, consequently a large group of metal working firms obtain their iron and steel requirements from local scrap (UNDP/TTC Doc 16, 1991). This observation is borne out by the fact that at the time of the 1987 Ghana Industrial Census there were only six (6) iron and steel basic industries. They were made up of one(1) micro firm with less than 10 employees, two (2) medium scale firms engaging between 30-49 employees and three (3) large scale firms, employing 50 and above. Apparently all these firms were recycling scrap. For the firms that depend on imported raw materials, customs procedures and duties increase the cost of materials. Although, the drawback mechanism has been put in place, lack of coordinationbetween various government institutions make the processes for refund unbearable.

Role of Markets

Some key informants think there is competition from imports of food processing and agricultural implements, the survey results show that demand is a constraint to the expansion of business in Ghana especially for blacksmiths and the larger firms.

There is a need to introduce measures that will enlarge demand. One problem that the small scale sector faces is the lack of publicity, and there might be the need for aggressive salesmanship by the sector enterprises to popularize their products.

The government could devise a strategy to stimulate its demand for SME sector products. The government should revise its procurement policies to include the informal sector enterprises, breaking its bids into smaller units to attract small enterprises.

Another method of increasing demand would be through the promotion of sub-contracting with modern sector firms; this will also introduce new technology and skills to the sector as well as improve the quality of the products of the sector.

The metal working companies produce and/or have the capabilities to produce the farm implements and the food processing equipments. But the end users most of the time do not have knowledge of the existence of these products. It is our hope that the collaboration between farmers, Agricultural Engineering frontline staff and manufacturers as a result of the unified extension system will help abate this problem.

Institutional Assistance

Smaller firms are held back by the lack of institutional assistance for testing, design and training. Any institutional assistance to improve production capacity and productivity in the agro-metals sector would involve looking at all the stages from the acquisition and storage of raw material to the intermediate stage of production of the equipment to the final stage of marketing the product.

Technology

(i) Technology is very relevant for the agro-metals sector and the development of the sector would require high level engineering knowledge and skills

(ii) There is a need for a well developed iron and steel industry to supply raw materials; lack of this has meant reliance on imported materials and scraps, which takes time.

(iii) Engineering support facilities such as foundries, forge shops, heat treatment shops are absent. Foundries are capital intensive units which cannot be provided by small and medium scale firms. While most of the work in Ghana is fabrication, the imported units use the casting method. GRATIS has set up small foundries, and this should be encouraged; but these cannot accommodate big units. Encouragement should be given to the foundry in Takoradi — Western Casting — to be able to start casting big units. The emphasis should be on ferrous metal foundries. Suame Foundry should be reactivated and replaced with a ferrous metal foundry.

(iv) While the finishing of most locally produced equipment is unattractive due to the lack of appropriate machines for polishing, in the short-run, one can do with this type of packaging for the local market.

(v) It is not feasible to establish a large implements factory in the country in the short run. Since the needs of implements differ from region to region, small factories could be built in the regions to suit local conditions, for whatever mass-produced implement that is produced in the country or imported from abroad will be remoulded by the local blacksmiths.

(vi) Government should intervene in Research and Development (since the SMEs cannot fund R&D) by seriously funding already established institutions, such as Industrial Research Institute, Food Research Institute, University of Science and Technology, and others.

(vii) The Capital Good Sector study (TTC 1990) also cited lack of coordination in the indigenous research and development efforts and duplication of research projects. We might attribute the problem to the absence of an Applied Agricultural Engineering Research Institute. There might be the need for an institution which will bridge the gap between the academic pursuits of the engineering faculties and industry.

Provision of Infrastructural Facilities

Industrial estates should be established with adequate infrastructural facilities to the metal firms at low cost. The concentration of these enterprises will facilitate exchange of experiences within the sector.

The legally approved sites and premises could serve as collateral in the acquisition of loans from banks. In the 1994 Budget Statement the government mentioned its intention to go in this direction.

Training Needs

Low level skill acquisition in the country is through the apprenticeship system in the informal sector and technical and vocational schools in the formal sector. Apprentices who acquire their skills in the informal sector end up in the same sector. Most entrepreneurs acquire their training from the informal sector itself and only a few are trained in the formal sector. At the same time only a handful of trainees from vocational schools enter the informal sector. The informal sector would need the infusion of new skills and methods of operation through the training of the graduates of vocational schools to enter the informal sector as entrepreneurs or apprentices or even as paid employees, and the upgrading of skills of entrepreneurs and apprentices from the informal sector through training programmes.

Skill training in micro and small-scale sector could also get support from the formal vocational schools, upgrading the master craftsmen and apprentices through organizing training programmes.

In addition to the technical skills provided, enterprise management skills should be emphasized in the technical and vocational schools, while at the same time the master craftsmen in micro and small enterprises could improve their management skills through short term courses.

Several serious problems identified in the method of skill acquisition include the short duration of the training programme, the fact that the training of the apprentices is carried out through imitation by apprentices, the failure of the system to check or even test the apprentices' understanding of the techniques embodied in the operation of a machine, and the problem of enterprise management. There is a need for manpower training measures in the informal sector which involve not only technical training but also the training in organization and running of business. The technical training should include the introduction of new products.

A majority of entrepreneurs in the sector do not keep account of their business, depending upon mental retention of data on the business, thus for example confusing revenues with profit. There is thus the need for programmes for the artisans on the need for good management. Simple management techniques should be introduced to the master craftsmen to that these will be incorporated in the training process.

Coordination of Efforts or Assistance to the Sector

It may be argued that there is a need for government recognition of the agro-metals. Government assistance may be required to remove the constraints identified. It has been suggested that a structure be set up to meet the needs of the sector and mediate between the artisans of the sector and other institutions, especially financial institutions, and also coordinate with other relevant ministries. The problem with such state run bodies that are usually recommended is that they are ill-adapted to the dynamics of the sector. Such state institutions may meet with indifference on the part of the entrepreneurs and apprentices. The type of assistance they require from the government is usually loans.

Any sort of institutions or intervention for the sector should utilize resources (human, material, and technical) available within the sector, all these coordinated not by a government body but by a body established within the sector. Thus there is a need to encourage the formation of associations such Association of Metal Firms to promote the objectives of entrepreneurs of the sector.

Trade and Industrial Policies

The ERP and SAP has provided a uniform set of incentives for all firms in the manufacturing sector. But the liberalization has been costly to many firms. Some form of revision in the policy is required if industry is to survive and viable agro-metals industry is to develop.

Other Recommendations

The institution of annual fairs (dubbed Grand Sales) to boost the patronage of locally manufactured goods is also a step in the right direction. This could be extended to the regions and even the districts. It is expected that local producers of agricultural and food processing equipment would take full advantage of the opportunities these fairs provide. Furthermore, these fairs expose the producers to new and more efficient technology. Thus an ideal intervention required in both the production of food processing equipment and agricultural tools will involve increasing the productivity of local producers through the identification of these producers including the local artisans and blacksmiths, and providing them with support in the form of training and equipment to let them improve on their work.

NOTES

1. Technology Transfer Centre (CSIR) (1991c) p.15.
2. *Ibid.*
3. TTC (1990a).
4. See Table 2.2.
5. Aboagye (1991).
6. UNDP/TTC (1991)
7. Sowa *et al.* (1991)
8. Some of the larger machinery manufacturers are now in the export market.
9. Lall *et al.* (1993).
10. Lall *op. cit.* p.177.
11. TTC (1990) and Damptey *et al.* (1989).
12. See Baah-Nuakoh, A. (1992).
13. Baah-Nuakoh, A. (1993c), Steel and Webster (1993), Baah-Nuakoh and Steel (1993), RPED (1992).
14. One of the very successful firms in the agro-metals complained about space, and has been trying to relocate, but banks have refused to help with finance. The question then is whether smaller and unsuccessful firms will ever get finance from local banks.

REFERENCES

Aboagye, A. A. (1982) "Technology and Employment in the Capital Goods Industry in Ghana," ILO *World Employment Programme*, WEP 2–22/wp 91.
—— (1991) *Creation of Appropriate Technology by Domestic Capital Goods. Industry and the Effect on Rural Population in Ghana*, Univ. of Ottawa, October 1991.
Anheir, Helmut and Hans Seibel. (1987) *Small Scale Industries and Economic Development in Ghana: Business Behaviour and Strategies in the Informal Sector Economies.* Verlag Breintenbach Publishers. Scarbruken.
Baah-Nuakoh, A. (1993a) *Development Policies and Institutional Environment for Employment Promotion in the Informal Sector in Ghana.* JASPA, Addis Ababa.
—— (1993b) "Industrial Sector ," a paper in ISSER's *The State of the Ghanaian Economy, 1992.*
—— (1993c) "Constraints on the Growth and Expansion of the Manufacturing Sector in Ghana," in Baah-Nuakoh, A. and Francis Teal (ed.) *Economic Reform and the Manufacturing Sector in Ghana. RPED Report*
—— and Steel, W. F. (1993) *Background Paper on SME Demand for Finance.* Report prepared for NBSSI, Accra.

Baah-Nuakoh, A. and Teal Francis (ed), (1993) *Economic Reform and the Manufacturing Sector in Ghana*. Report prepared for World Bank. RPED.

Baark, E. (1991) "The Capital Goods Sector in Ghana: Options for Economic and Technological Development," *Industry and Development*, 29, pp. 37–61.

Berger, Louis (1989) "Draft Report on the Metal-Working Subsector." Prepared for the Republic of Ghana and UNIDO as part of the Industrial Sector Adjustment Programme in Ghana, Project GAA/86/001, Paris, 1989.

Damptey, M. F. *et al.* (1989) *Study to Identify the Production and Technology Constraints in the Local Manufacturing of Agro-Industrial Machinery and Implements*. IRI, CSIR, August.

Dawson, Jonathan (1990) "The Wider Context: The Importance of the Macroenvironment for Small Scale Enterprise Development," *Small Enterprise Development, An International Journal*, Vol. 1 No. 3 pp. 39–46.

ECA/FAO (1989) *Role of Technology in Small Farmers' Productivity in Africa*, Addis Ababa, July.

FAO (1992) *Agricultural Engineering in Development: Mechanization Strategy Formulation Vol. 1 Concepts and Principles*, Technical Bulletin No. 99/1, Rome.

—— (1990) *Agricultural Engineering in Development: Selection of Mechanization Input*, Technical Bulletin No. 84, Rome, 1990.

Ghana (1992) *Industrial Policy Statement of January*.

Ghana Statistical Service, *Ghana National Industrial Census, 1987 Phase I & Phase II Reports*, Accra.

Government of Ghana, *Investment Code 1985*, Accra.

Grayson, Leslie (1971) "The Promotion of Indigenous Private Enterprise in Ghana," *Journal of Asian and African Studies*, Vol. 1 No. 9 May.

Hakam, A. N. (1976) *Technology Diffusion from Modern to the Informal Sector: Automobile Repair Trades in Ghana*. ILO. Geneva.

Hart, Keith. (1970) "Small Scale Entrepreneurs in Ghana and Development Planning," *Journal of Development Studies*, pp. 104–120.

Hart, Keith. (1973) "Informal Income Opportunities and Urban Employment in Ghana," *Journal of Modern African Studies*, pp. 61–89.

Hemsling A. H. J. and T. Kolstee, *Small Enterprises and Changing Policies* – Structural Adjustment and Financial Policy and Assistance Programmes in Africa.

Killick, Tony (1978) *Development Economics in Action: A Study of Economic Policies in Ghana*, Heineman, London, 1978.

Klu, F. E. (1985) "Technology Diffusion and Linkage Mechanisms in the Small Scale Auto Repair Industry: A case Study of Accra."*Legon Geographer*, Vol. 1 No. 1 August, pp. 54–67.

Lall, Sanjay (1993) *Technological Capabilities and Industrial Development in Ghana*. Regional Programme for Enterprise Development, Technology Module, Report for the World Bank, Africa Technical Department.

Levy, Brian. (1993) "Obstacles to Developing Indigenous Small and Medium Enterprises: An Empirical Assessment," *The World Bank Economic Review*, Vol. 7 No. 1 January, pp. 65–83.

Ministry of Agriculture. *Performance of the Agricultural Sector, 1987*, compiled by PPME, Accra.

Ndlela, Daniel (1987) *Technology Imports and Indigenous Technological Capacity Building: The Zimbabwean Case.,* ILO, Geneva (WEP 2–22).

Planning Commission. (1963) *Seven Year Plan for National Reconstruction, 1963/4 – 1969/70,* State Publishing Corporation, March.

Qazi Kholiquzzana Ahmad *et al.* (1984) *Technology Adaptation and Employment in the Agricultural Tools Equipment Industry of Bangladesh,* ILO, Geneva (WEP 2–22/wp 134).

Steel W. F and Leila Webster (1993) *Small Enterprises under Adjustment in Ghana.* World Bank Technical Paper No. 138. Industry and Finance Series.

Technology Transfer Centre (1989) *Institutions Supporting Scientific and ndustrial Development,* Accra. Ghana. UNDP/TTC Doc.1.

(1990a) *Report on Food Processing Sector,* CSIR, Accra, UNDP/TTC Doc. 15.

Technology Transfer Centre (1990b) *Report on Capital Goods Sector Study,* CSIR, Accra, UNDP/TTC Doc. 5.

—— (1991a) *Technology Profiles on Capital Goods, Energy and Food Processing,* CSIR, Accra.

—— (1991b) *R & D Projects on Capital Goods, Energy and Food Processing,* CSIR, Accra.

—— (1991c) *Report On Small and Medium Enterprises Study,* CSIR Accra UNDP/TTC Doc.16.

CHAPTER 5

Demand for Carbonated Soft Drinks in Ghana

(with William Baah-Boateng)

Introduction

The carbonated soft drink industry in Ghana is one of the few sectors within the beverages sector that has shown growth in the past few years even though growth in manufacturing, in general, after the initial leaps during the initial years of the ERP, has been slowing down. This chapter will identify the factors that influence the demand for soft drinks, design an appropriate econometric framework to study the impact of the determinants of the demand for soft drinks, and test the conventional wisdom that the demand for soft drinks is price inelastic by quantitatively determining the impact of price adjustment on the consumption of soft drinks.

THE STRUCTURE AND PERFORMANCE OF THE CARBONATED SOFT DRINKS INDUSTRY

Industrial Strategy and Performance

The performance of Ghana's manufacturing sector since independence has not been the best although the sector has some success stories to tell. It is undoubtedly the leading sector in the drive for industrialization and has the potential to contribute efficiently to future economic development and help propel the country to reach the desired middle income status by the year 2020. The improved performance between 1984 and 1988 was due to the access to imported raw materials and inputs. Capacity utilisation in manufacturing increased from a low of 18% in 1984 to 46% in 1993. The liberalization of the foreign exchange market eased the flow of imported raw materials as well as essential spare parts and the replacement of obsolete machinery and plants in some cases. All these developments affect the beverage industry and the carbonated soft drinks.

The Beverage Industry

The Beverage Industry consists of firms producing alcoholic and non-alcoholic beverages. The industry although at the time of independence was not broad as it was dominated by small-scale producers of alcoholic beverages whose targets were the local consumers, it formed quite a significant proportion of the manufacturing sector. Beverage products produced by the indigenous people which did not require any heavy investment like *akpeteshie* (local gin), *pito, burukutu* and palm wine were prominent in the eyes of the local consumers and as such dominated the market.

The beverage industry in Ghana comprises four sub-industries and are classified according to the International Standard Industrial Classification (ISIC) as shown Table 5.1.

Table 5.1: The Beverage Industry

Code	Industry	Products
3131	Distilling, rectifying and	whisky, brandy, schnapps, gin, rum, blending spirits and "akpeteshie".
3132	Wine Industries	wine, cider, palm wine
3133	Malt liquors & malt industries	malt, beer, ale, stout, "burukutu" and "pito"
3134	Soft Drinks and Carbonated Water industries	Soft drinks, fruit flavoured and carbonated fruit drinks, and Carbonated mineral waters

The contribution of the beverage industry to the growth of the manufacturing sector in particular and national development effort in general in the 1960s and 1970s cannot be glossed over. Its share of manufacturing value added stood at 16.0% and 15.9% in 1962 and 1965 respectively, declining to about 10.2% in 1974. The annual growth rate of gross value added of the industry averaged 25% between 1962 and 1965 rising to an average of 50% between 1965 and 1971.

In terms of employment, the beverage, food and tobacco industries jointly employs about 28.3% of total labour force engaged in the manufacturing sector. The beverage and tobacco industries are jointly ranked third in terms of the number of establishments and the persons engaged in the manufacturing sector in 1962. In 1962 and 1965, the total workforce of the beverage industry stood at 1427 and 2028 respectively. This increased to 2171 in 1968 and further up to 3361 in 1978 and as at 1987 the total workforce stood at 15944. With the divestiture of state owned, and establishment of new beverage firms, the total workforce of the industry is expected to have been tripled or quadrupled.

The 1987 industrial census put the number of establishments in the beverage industry at 315 out of which 49.5% operate as one-man business. The state owned 6 firms whilst 35 firms operate as private limited companies. Incidentally, 22.9% is owned by co-operative societies with only one firm operating as a public limited liability company (Table 5.2).

Table 5.2: Beverage Establishments by Type of Ownership and Employment

Type of ownership	Number of firms	Employment size	Employment per firm (average)	Scale of operation
State owned	6	1899	316.5	Large
Joint state/Private	3	1286	428.7	Large
Co-operative	72	8814	122.4	Large
Public Ltd. Co.	1	627	627.0	Large
Private Ltd. Co.	35	664	19.0	Small
Partnership	7	48	6.9	Small
Sole Proprietorship	156	858	5.5	Small
Association	35	1748	49.9	Medium
Total	315	15944		

Source: Compiled from Industrial Census (1987), Statistical Service.

Apparently, a high proportion of employment was accounted for by enterprises owned by co-operative societies but on average, the only public limited enterprise in the industry engaged the highest number of people. It is obvious from Table 5.2 that all the enterprises operating as one-man business, partnership and private limited companies were basically small-scale firms with each firm employing 7.9 persons on average. The only public limited company and co-operative firms as well as joint state/private and state owned enterprises were operating on large scale given the strength of the workforce of these enterprises.

In terms of scale of operations, more than 50% of the beverage firms were operating on small scale. Specifically, 193 establishments constituting 61% were small-scale firms with only 25 firms (7.9%) operating on medium scale. Moreover, 63 firms representing 20% were micro enterprises, while 34 firms representing 10.8% operated on large scale.

The picture is different now owing to the fact that, the liberalization of the economy has led to the establishment of many firms and expansion of many existing ones especially those that have been divested. From this point we are narrowing the discussion towards the soft drinks industry which is an umbrella of the beverage industry.

The Structure and Performance of the Carbonated Soft Drinks (CSD) Industry

The Soft Drinks and Carbonated Water Industry (SDCW), which comprises firms producing non-alcoholic beverages (excluding malt drinks) appears to be one of the Beverage Industries in the manufacturing sub-sector of the economy, which is held in a high esteem among the consuming public owing to the nature of the product. There were few firms producing soft drinks and mineral water in the late 1950s and early 1960s when the country was very young and was striving to industrialize. Notable among them were Nkulenu Industries Limited (1959) and GNTC — Bottling Division, now Coca-Cola Bottling Company of Ghana (1962). Currently, there are a lot of companies registered to manufacture soft drinks including fruit juice and mineral water.

The Soft Drinks and Carbonated Water (SDCW) industry forms a significant proportion of the beverage industry in Ghana. Although, the number of persons engaged by the Soft Drink Industry is not as high as those in malt liquors production and malt industry as well as the sub-industry involved in distilling, rectifying and blending spirits, its contribution to the growth of the beverage industry and national development effort in general cannot be overlooked.

The SDCW industry's share of beverage value added stood at 11% and 6.4% in 1975 and 1976 respectively compared to 10% and 6% recorded by the beverage sub-industry involved in distilling, rectifying and blending spirits. However, It has subsequently declined continuously from 5.4% in 1977 to 5% in 1979 and further down to 1.6 percent in 1980 before rising to 3.7% 1981. The annual growth rate of the Gross Value added of the industry was 23% and 1.9% in 1976 and 1977 respectively, declining drastically by 44.9% in 1980, but successfully recovered a year later to record a growth rate of 208% in 1981. The decline in the performance of the industry was not an isolated one since the economy in general and manufacturing sub-sector in particular were all affected by the external shock and drought which exerted much constraints on import dependent industries like SDCW.

Over the years, soft drink products have enjoyed a high degree of patronage from the consuming public. This is because, unlike alcoholic beverages, which are not patronized by Christians especially the "born-again Christians" and Muslims alike, Christians as well as non-Christians patronize the soft drink products very much. This high demand for soft drinks might also be due to rapid population growth and the greater awareness, which has in recent times been created by firms especially Coca-Cola Company of Ghana through advertisements of different kinds. In most cases people consume soft drinks to quench their thirst and above all consume it along with food. Based on the basic economic principle that "goods are produced in anticipation of demand", producers have responded positively to the rise in demand for soft drinks over the last ten years.

The growth in the production of soft drinks between 1975 and 1983 was not consistent, showing a declining trend on average. This was at the time when the economy as a whole and industrial sector in particular, especially manufacturing, was in crisis, performing dismally in terms of growth. Between 1975 and 1979, the total production of soft drinks averaged annually at about 2.17 million crates, declining to an annual average of about 0.97 million crates over a 5-year period between 1980 and 1984. However, after the launching of the ERP in 1983, which brought some light and life into the economy with manufacturing growing at a two-digit rate, the soft drinks industry began to show positive signs of growth. Over a 10-year period between 1985 and 1994, the annual production of soft drinks averaged 2.05 million crates rising sharply to an annual average of 4.83 million crates between 1995 and 1998. The improvement in output growth after 1984 is due among others to the emergence of new firms involved in the manufacturing of fruit flavoured, and mineral water in response to the ERP, and more importantly the reduction in excise tax rate on soft drinks by two percentage points in 1987 and 1988. The sharp improvement in production, which occurred in 1995, was due to the privatization of some state-owned soft drinks firms. For instance, after privatisation of the company in 1995, Coca-Cola Bottling Company of Ghana has experienced an increase production in four-fold from 2.8 million crates in 1995 to 8.4 million crates in 1999.

Interestingly, some of the brewery companies also engage in the production of soft drinks, notable among them are Accra Brewery Limited (ABL), and Ghana brewery Limited (GBL). Apparently, in recent times the production of flavoured fruit drinks like orange and pineapple juice is also gaining popularity among the consuming public. All these changes in preferences no doubt, might have induced the increase in production of soft drinks since 1987.

The major companies engaged in the production of soft drinks include:

- Coca-Cola Bottling Company of Ghana Ltd., which until 1995 (when it was privatised) used to be a division of GNTC Bottling. Soft drink products manufactured and/or bottled by Coca-Cola Company include Coke, Fanta Lemon, Fanta Orange, Sprite, and Krest products (ginger ale, soda, tonic, and bitter lemon). The firm controls about 80% of the market.
- Beverage Investment Company Ltd., which was formerly known as Ghana Bottling Company Ltd. produces 7UP, Pepsi cola and Mirinda, and currently boasts of a total market share of about 9%.
- D and C, producers of Crush and Schweppes. Its market share at present stands at about 2%.
- Accra Brewery Ltd., which manufactures Club Orange, Club Cola, Cclub Soda among others commands a market share of about 2% in the soft drink industry.
- Ghana Brewery Ltd., a merger of Achimota Brewery Company and Kumasi Brewery Limited, produces Bluna Tropic, Bluna Lime, Bluna Orange, Africola among others. They have about 2% of the total share in the soft drink industry.

Some other non-beverage firms engaged specifically in the production of fruit juice include:

- Astek Fruit Processing Limited, producers of pineapple and orange juice and bottled water;

- Kedak Processing Ltd., which produces pineapple juice (Nourisher) among others;
Agromax Limited, manufacturers of exotic fruit drinks;
Athena Foods Limited, manufacturers of fruit juice.

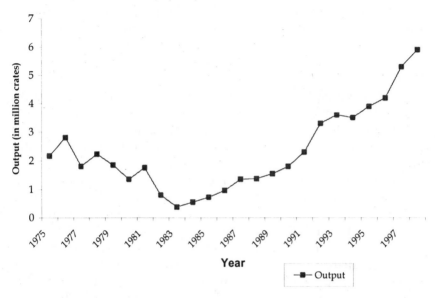

Fig. 5.1: Annual Soft Drinks Production, 1975– 1998 (in million crates)

The Structure and Growth of Employment in the Soft Drinks Industry

Current data on the industry is difficult to come by, and we were forced to rely on the 1987 Industrial Census conducted by the Statistical Service to study the structure of the industry. According to the 1987 Industrial Census, the Soft Drinks and Carbonated water sub-industry forms about 6.4% in terms of number of establishments and employs 912 people representing 5.7% of total employment in the Beverage Industry. It comprises 20 firms, majority of which engage up to 19 employees. Nine of the firms in the industry operate with a workforce of between 10 and 49. Eight firms engage not more than 9 persons each whilst 3 firms each employs workforce of between 100 and 500.

The picture at present looks different from what prevailed before 1987. The liberalization of the economy, which led to the privatization of some state-owned soft drinks firms, has no doubt contributed to the establishment of new firms and the expansion of old ones. Although, there is no formidable data to lean on, it is obvious that the number of firms in the soft drinks industry stands at far more than the level as at 1987. This is due to, of late, the establishment of new firms specializing in the production of fruit juice and mineral water and the involvement of brewery companies in the production of soft drinks.

The changing trend in the share of employment of soft drinks industry in total beverage employment has not been smooth. Available data indicates that the soft drinks and carbonated water industries accounted for 21.8% of total employment of the Beverage industry in 1975 rising to 26.9% and 28.9% in the subsequent years 1976 and 1977 respectively. The employment share however assumed a downward trend, declining continuously to 23.5% and 22.3% in 1979 and 1980 respectively in favour of the other Beverage sub-industries (ISIC Code 3131 and 3133) and further down to 22.1% in 1981. The employment share assumed a positive trend again thereafter recording a share of 21.3% and 21.6% in 1981 and 1982 respectively. The industrial statistics of 1987 puts the employment share of the soft drink industry at 5.7% of total employment of the beverage industry. Given that some of the brewery companies engaged in the production of soft drinks and malt drinks in addition to their main product of alcoholic beverage, it becomes difficult to disentangle the growth of employment in the soft drinks industry vis-à-vis the other sister industries in the beverage industry.

The strength of labour force in the soft drink and carbonated water industry grew by 38.2% and 3.3% in 1976 and 1977 respectively. The 1980 production year saw a drastic decline in employment of 30.7%. It however recovered slightly in 1981, recording a modest growth of 0.2% and 5.7% in 1982 but this declined again recording a growth rate of –2.2% in 1983. The number of people engaged in the industry by 20 firms as at 1987 stood at 912 compared to 2073 in malt liquors and malt industries. The growth of employment in the industry since 1987 can be said to be positive on account of the privatization and the resulting expansion of some key firms as well as the establishment of new ones in the industry. For instance, Coca-Cola Bottling Company of Ghana, which was formed from the

Table 5.3: Ghanaian Soft Drinks and Mineral Water Establishments

Name of Establishment	Location	Year Established	Size of Establishment	Product
Coca-Cola Bottling Co. of Ghana	Accra	1962/1995	G	Soft drinks
Beverage Investment Co. Limited	Accra	1962/1998	E	Soft drinks
D & C Industries	Accra		E	Soft drinks
Accra Brewery Limited	Accra	1975	G	Beer, Malt, & Soft drinks
Ghana Breweries Limited	Accra	1997	G	Beer, Malt & Soft drinks
Astek Fruit Processing Limited	Nsawam	1983		Mineral water and fruit juices
Kadek Limited	Accra			Fruit juice
Rush Farms & Processing Ltd.	Accra	1990		Soft drinks
Aquafresh Limited	Accra			Soft drinks
Soltcoast Industrial Enterprise				Mineral water
GIHOC Cannery Company Ltd.	Nsawam	1960	F	Fruit juice
High Barnet '85 Limited	Accra	1985		Fruit juice
Pro-Bio Laboratory Limited	Accra	1981		Fruit juice
Nkulenu Industries Limited	Accra	1959		Fruit juice
National Industrial Co. Limited	Accra			
Akoto Nzema Industries	Cape Coast			Soft drinks

Table 5.3 (*Cont'd.*)

			A	
Morleme Minerals Enterprise	Ho			Soft drinks
New Kool Bottling Factory	Kumasi	1991	B	Soft drinks
Pedu Soft Drinks Industry	Cape Coast			Soft drinks
Piccadilly Minerals Limited	Nsawam			Minerals
Prospect Mineral Factory	Accra			Minerals
Tetteh Mineral water works	Nsawam			Mineral water
Uni-corp Ltd.	Tema			Soft drinks
Fan Milk Limited	Accra			Fruit drinks etc.
Agromax Limited	Accra			Exotic fruit drinks
Athena Foods Limited	Tema			Fruit juice
COB-A Industries	Accra			Drinking water
Erofrash Fruits Processing Industries	Accra			Fruit drinks
Primo Industries Limited	Accra	1999		Fruit juice
First Watch Limited	Kumasi			Mineral water
Dynasty Beverage Limited	Tema			Mineral water
Jubilee Industries				Fruit and malt drinks

Source: Association of Ghana Industries, Ghana Chamber of Commerce, and Ghana Statistical Service

divestiture of the Bottling section of GNTC in March 1995, has seen its employment level increased from 372 in 1995 to 636 in 1999. This represents an increase in employment of about 71% over 1995 level. Similar stories can be said about other firms in the industry that have been divested in recent years. Beverage Investment Limited (Pepsi) which was formed from the divestiture of Ghana Bottling Company in 1998, New Kool Bottling Ltd. (formerly N.I.C. Bottling) and GIHOC Cannery Limited have all witnessed their employment increased tremendously. The unhygienic manner by which many local ice water sellers operate has given room for the emergence of firms (with less than 10 employees) like Yes Mineral Water Ltd, First Watch Ltd, Dynasty Beverage Ltd among others to produce bottled mineral waters.

The level of labour productivity of the industry measured by Net Value added per person appears to have positive correlation with the level of employment. The industry recorded net value added per person of 5,400 cedis, 20,700 cedis and 23,400 cedis in 1975, 1976 and 1977 respectively when the employment size of the industry stood at 1039, 1436 and 1483 in the same respective years. The labour productivity however declined in 1979 to 8970 cedis of net value added per person and 4393 cedis in 1980 when employment level also dropped to 1028 and 994 in 1979 and 1980 respectively. The net value added shot up again in 1981 to 15108 cedis with an increase in employment level of 2 people to 996.

Apparently, in terms of scale of operations, out of the 20 establishments in the soft drink industry in 1987, 75% (i.e. 15 firms) operated on small scale while 3 firms, representing 15%, were large-scale enterprises. There was only one micro and one medium scale firm in the industry in 1987. The 15 small-scale firms employ a total workforce of 167 persons. A total of 39 persons are engaged by 7 of the small-scale firms, (an average of 5.6 employees by each firm), with 75 engaged by 6 small-scale firms (12.5 persons on average), while 2 of the small scale firms employ a total of 53 persons giving an average of 26.5 persons by each firm. The three large-scale firms employ a total workforce of 710 with an average of 236.7 persons by each firm. Specifically, one large-scale firm engages a total of 159 persons whilst the other 2 employ a total of 551 persons or 275.5 on average by each firm. Incidentally, there hasn't been any significant structural change in the industry as far as scale of operation is concerned since 1987. Almost all the newly established firms are operating on small scale while the medium and large-scale firms are the ones that have been privatized and have registered improvement in employment as well as undergoing expansion. Coca-Cola, the dominant firm in the industry has undertaken a $11 million expansion programme to expand its bottling and warehouse capacity with an installation of a second bottling line in Accra to double its production capacity.

With regard to the skill level of the workforce, 10% have managerial or professional skills, 32% technical skills and clerical skills while unskilled labour and apprentices accounted for 14% and 8% respectively. Incidentally, apart from the brewery firms notably Accra Brewery Limited (ABL) and Ghana Breweries Limited (GBL) and one soft drink firm, Fan Milk Ltd, none of the soft drinks firms is listed on the Ghana Stock Exchange. This poses a great concern about the extent to which firms are involving the general public in the capitalization process. It is gratifying to note that the dominant firm in the industry is not listed on the stock exchange.

Market Competition

Any kind of liquid that passes through human throat is a potential competitor of soft drinks. In Ghana, the soft drinks industry is faced with competition from the domestic producers of alcoholic beverages like beer, spirits and non-alcoholic beverages like malt with foreign competition being reasonably and relatively minimal. Incidentally, all the brewery companies are engaged in the manufacturing of malt drinks. They are:

- Guinness Ghana Limited, established in 1971 and located in Kumasi manufactures Malta Guinness in addition to their main product — Guinness Stout;
- Accra Brewery Limited also produces Vitamalt along side the main product which is beer (Club Beer, Club Shandy, Castle Milk Stout) as well as soft drinks;
- Ghana Brewery Limited, apart from beer (main product) and soft drinks, they also produce malt drink called Amstel Malta. The Kumasi Brewery limited which entered into a merger with Achimota Brewery Company to form Ghana Brewery Company were producing malt drink called Maltina some few years back.
- Jubilee Industries produces fruit and malt drinks.

Location of Soft Drinks Firms

In terms of industrial localization, exactly half of the firms are located in the big cities of Accra, Tema and Kumasi. Out of 20 firms in the industry, 7 are located in Accra, 2 in Kumasi and only one in Tema with the rest located in other towns. The 1987 industrial census indicates that 8 of the soft drink firms are based in Greater Accra region, 7 in Central region and 2 each in the Eastern and Ashanti regions. None of the soft drink establishments is based in the Western, Upper East, Upper West, Northern and Brong Ahafo regions. This gives a wrong and negative impression about the extent to which industries are regionally distributed. Thus, a high proportion of soft drink establishments is concentrated in the big cities of Accra and Kumasi in particular and the southern sector of the country in general. Thus, the regional distribution of the soft drink industry is extremely uneven. The skewness of firms' location in favour of Accra has remained unchanged since 1987. Almost all the newly established soft drinks and mineral water firms are located in the capital city of Accra with few operating in the Harbour City of Tema and Kumasi. This is due to the fact that the market in Accra is larger compared to other places in the country, and given the fragile nature of the products (in bottles) it becomes less surprising that a greater number of soft drinks firms are located in Accra.

Raw Material Inputs

As far as inputs of raw materials are concerned, the soft drink industry is heavily dependent on imported inputs. Between 1975 and 1977, the percentage of foreign material to total materials consumed in the industry averaged 74.0% compared with an average of 75.7% used between 1979 and 1983. Between 1975 and 1983, the year which saw the industry use a higher percentage of foreign materials in production was in 1980 with a percentage of 92.9% and the least of 39.4% in 1983. Thus, over the years the foreign input component of the industry has varied between a low of 39% and a high of 93%. This ratio varies from firm to firm, for example Coca-Cola in 1998 imported 95% of its raw materials.

Tax Contribution to National Economy

The modest contribution of the industry to national development effort in terms of tax revenue to the state is worth noting. Since 1985, the ratio of total tax revenue (excise duty and sales tax) from the production and sale of soft drinks to real GDP has experienced an upward trend as observed from Fig. 2. It rose from a modest of 0.008% in 1985 to 0.571% in 1997 yielding an average of about 0.192 percent annually over the 13 year period. The ratio began to rise steadily after 1990 when excise tax rate was increased from 42% to 50.4% in 1991. This contributed to an increase in total revenue to the government at the expense of the industry. The sharp increase in the ratio in 1996 could be attributed to the increased tax revenue paid to the government by Coca-Cola Bottling Company, the dominant firm in the soft drinks industry just one year after privatization. In 1996, total tax revenue paid to the government by Coca-Cola Bottling Company rose by 67.7% over the 1995 figure, the highest ever recorded after privatization. This in no doubt contributed to a drastic increase in total tax revenue from the soft drinks industry.

Concluding, although the soft drinks sector accounts for a relatively smaller proportion of enterprises in the beverage industry and constitutes 5.7% of total workforce in the beverage industry in 1987, its contribution, in terms of total output, has been on the ascendancy since 1987. Whilst most of the soft drink enterprises are found to operate on small scale, the few large scale ones are located in the big cities of Accra, Kumasi and Tema. The regional distribution of firms in the industry is skewed in favour of the south.

AN ANALYSIS OF DEMAND FOR SOFT DRINKS

On the basis of traditional economic theory of demand, one expects the level of consumption of soft drinks to change negatively in response to price changes. However, the price elasticity of demand for soft drinks, which underlies the degree of responsiveness of consumption to changes in price is an empirical issue and thus calls for a thorough empirical investigation. The conventional wisdom is that the demand for soft drinks is price inelastic.

Based on traditional economic theory, a model to estimate and examine the causes of changes in soft drinks consumption in Ghana is constructed. The demand for soft drinks can be explained, among others, by the following factors:

- *The price of soft drinks, inclusive of any taxes:* It is expected that higher prices will discourage consumption whilst lower prices

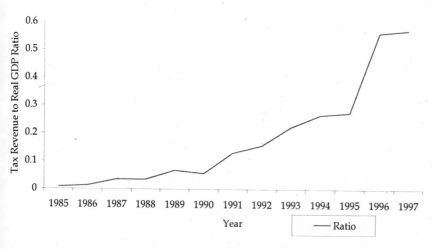

Fig. 5.2: **The Ratio of Tax Revenue from Soft Drinks to Real GDP (1985–1997)**

will boost consumption. Thus, the price — consumption relationship of soft drinks is expected to be negative. The crucial, issue here is the level of sensitivity of consumption of soft drinks to price changes.

- *Price of related goods:* The level of consumption of soft drinks could be affected by changes in the prices of related goods, which serve as substitutes or complements to soft drinks. The prices of goods that serve as substitutes will have positive relationship with the level of consumption of soft drinks whilst that of the prices of complements will have negative relationship with the consumption of soft drinks.

- *Tastes of consumers:* Consumers' tastes for soft drinks are strongly influenced by weather and thus consumption. In Ghana, during the chilly and/or rainy season, consumers' taste for soft drinks declines while in the hot and dry season as well as Christmas and Easter periods the level of consumption rises. Therefore, to obtain a true measure of response of soft drinks consumption to changes in price, we should have control factors such as weather, which have the tendency to affect demand for soft drinks.

- *Population:* The consumption of soft drinks is expected to rise in response to an increase in national population.

- *The Level of Income:* Given that soft drinks are considered as a "normal" consumer good, it is expected that the consumption level of soft drinks would increase over time with the growth in the economy measured by rate of increase in GDP.

- *Weather:* the consumption of soft drinks is also affected by the weather, for example one would expect greater consumption of soft drinks during periods of high temperatures.

In the process of constructing and estimating demand function, it is necessary to carefully analyze the status of the price as explanatory variable in the function. Theoretically, it is a fact that price shown as explanatory variable in the demand function is not exogenous. From the methodological standpoint both prices and quantity are endogenously determined in the market, although individual consumers may regard product prices as exogenous.

In order to obtain consistent estimates of demand elasticities, the interaction of demand and supply forces in the determination of market prices and quantities must be taken into account. In the consumer theory, demand for a product is based primarily on own price, the price of related commodities (substitutes or complements), consumer's income, and taste or fashion. A structural equation is therefore specified as:

$$\text{Log}Q_t/POP_t = \beta_0 + \beta_1 \log PSD_t + \beta_2 \log PF_t + \beta_3 \log PB_t$$
$$+ \beta_4 \log GDP_t/POP_t + \beta_5 \log W_t + e_t$$

where:

Q_t = quantity of soft drinks purchased, measured in bottles,
POP_t = the population of Ghana,
PSD_t = the average retail price of soft drinks,
PF_t = the consumer price index of food products,
PB_t = average retail price of beer, measured in bottles,
GDP = Real Gross Domestic Product,
W_t = weather, and e_t = the error term, which is normally distributed with zero mean.
The t subscript represents the observation year (or time period).

Thus, we specify per capita consumption of soft drinks as a nonlinear function of the price of soft drinks, price of related goods — food and beer, per capita GDP (as a proxy for income) and weather. The specification of demand model in log form, which is common in demand analysis, implies that constant price elasticity of demand is β_1 — the coefficient of log (psd). Since the price variable is endogenously determined in the model, and therefore correlated with the error term, application of Ordinary Least Square (OLS) method of estimation will yield inconsistent estimates. Therefore, we used Two-Stage Least Square (2SLS) method to estimate the model.

Two-Stage Least Square method of estimation is a single equation method applied to one equation of a system at a time. Theoretically, 2SLS may be considered as an extension of Indirect Least Square (ILS) and of the Instrumental Variables (IV) methods. It aims at eliminating as far as possible the simultaneous-equation bias. The demand equation is over-identified after satisfying the order and rank conditions.

Although the specification of a structural supply equation is not necessary in our analysis, it was used to specify an equation for price, which is reported below:

$$\text{Log (psdt)} = \alpha_0 + \alpha_1 \text{logEXC}_t + \alpha_2 \text{logSLT}_t + \alpha_3 \text{logbevind}$$
$$+ \alpha_4 \text{logPF}_t + \alpha5 \text{logQ}_{t-1} + \alpha_6 \text{logGDP}_t + \mu_t$$

Where psd, GDP, fd, and POP are as defined earlier.

EXC = excise tax rate;
SLT = sales tax rate or
VAT, Bev ind = consumer price index of beverage and tobacco
    (used as a proxy for cost of production,
Qt-1 = lag value of per capita consumption and
μ_t = the error term assumed to have constant variance and
    zero mean.

The lag consumption is used in the estimation rather than current consumption because, it is assumed/believed that, last year's consumption affects current prices more than current consumption since price takes time to adjust to changes in consumption.

Prior to the estimation of the system of equations a Granger-

Causality test at the non-stationary as well as stationary levels of the price and quantity variables was carried out to prove the simultaneity of the model. It was observed that, while a One-way causality was observed between price and quantity of soft drinks at their stationary levels (first difference) there was no causality between the two variables at their non-stationary levels at 5% or 1% significant level. However, a two-way causality could be established at about 10% significant level. The results of the causality test is reported in Table 5.4.

Table 5.4: Granger-Causality Test Between the Two Explanatory Variables in the Model (Price and Quantity of Soft Drinks)

(1) Granger-Causality test for adding $\Delta logQt$ to Dlogpsdt
     $F (2, 18) = 8.3213 [0.0028]^{**}$

     Granger-Causality test for adding $\Delta logPsdt$ to DlogQt
     $F (2, 17) = 2.2688 [0.1322]$

(2) Granger-Causality test for adding logQt to logPsdt
     $F (2, 19) = 2.4967 [0.1090]$

     Granger-Causality test for adding logPsdt to logQt
     $F (2, 19) = 2.5894 [0.1013]$

The test was based on null hypothesis that there is no causality between price and quantity of soft drinks, whilst the alternative states that there is a causality between the two variables. The test was performed with lag 1 for Autoregressive part and 0–1 for distributed lag part under Autoregressive-distributed lag model. The first test was carried out at the stationary levels (first difference) of the variables while the second test was performed at their non-stationary log levels. The results of the test indicate that, consumption causes variation in prices at their stationary levels at 1% significant level, but not the other way. At their non-stationary levels, there is no causality between the two variables at either 5% or 1% level of significant.

Apparently, the failure of the causality test to prove significant and attest to the fact that there is a two-way causality between the two explanatory variables means that, the two equations could have been estimated separately by Ordinary Least Square (OLS) method. However, based on the theory that price and quantity are determined endogenously in the market and also on the fact that there was a two-way causality between the two endogenous variables at 10% level of significant at their non-stationary level, we went ahead to estimate the model by 2SLS method. The exclusion of weather as one of the pre-determined variables in the estimation was due to unavailability of data on weather (average temperature or rainfall figures of the entire country).

The negativity of the parameter of the food index implies that food and soft drinks are complements and are consumed together. This means that an increase in the price of food will negatively affect the consumption of soft drinks. Therefore, based on the results, it seems clear that the precise estimate of the cross price elasticity of demand for soft drinks with respect to beer is 3.04 (elastic) and –1.45 with respect to food. Of course, people consume soft drinks together with food especially during festive occasions.

The estimation results for demand and price equations using data from 1975 to 1997 are provided in Table 5.5. The estimated price elasticity for soft drink is –1.5095 at 1% significant level. This means that a 10% decline in the price of soft drink would lead to a 15.1% rise in the number of bottles consumed, holding all other factors constant. This means that the demand for soft drinks is price elastic. That the price elasticity of demand is greater than one indicates the demand for soft drinks is more elastic than the assumed price inelasticity that has been used by policy makers. A similar study on Ireland obtained a price elasticity of 1.10. (Bahl and Walker 1998).

The sign of the coefficient of beer (3.0416) is positive and statistically significant at 1% implying that it is a substitute to soft drinks. The results thus show that the price was significantly different from zero. The effect of changes in price of beer on consumption of soft drinks is strong, a 10% increase in the price of beer leads to a 30.4% increase in the demand for soft drinks. Apparently, it becomes difficult as to how one defines a substitute for soft drinks in spite of the economic importance attached to price of substitute products.

The estimated income elasticity of demand for soft drinks is 0.77 and is statistically significant. A ten- percent growth in per capita real GDP would lead to a 7.4% increase in the consumption of soft drinks holding all other factors constant. The results so far suggest that the demand for soft drinks is price elastic. It was observed that one percent decline in the price of soft drinks would cause a 1.5095% increase in the purchase of soft drinks by consumers.

Table 5.5: Estimating the Model by 2SLS: (The Present Sample is 1976 to 1997)

Equation 1 for LogQt

Variables	Coefficient	Standard error	t – value
Average Retail Price of Soft Drinks #	-1.5095	0.53056	-2.845 **
Food Index	-1.4547	0.36256	-4.013 **
Average Retail Price of Beer	3.0416	0.75840	4.011 **
Per Capita Real GDP	0.77046	0.24444	3.152 **

Equation 2 for LPsd

Variables	Coefficient	Standard error	t – value
LfoodIndex	- 1.2042	0.27954	- 4.308 **
LBevIndex	2.2310	0.27008	8.261 **
LEXCRate	0.48338	0.56295	0.859 ♣
LSalesTax	0.11810	0.21277	0.555
LRPCGDP	-0.85704	0.13797	- 6.212 **
LQt_{-1}	-0.13769	0.10811	- 1.274

** ⇒ 1% significant level   # Endogenous variable in the demand equation
* ⇒ 5% significant level
♣ ⇒ 40% significant level

Conclusion

The study has examined the impact of excise taxes on the soft drinks industry in Ghana. The results of the study might be summarized as follows:

- The important question relates to the price elasticity of demand. Beverages, tobacco and petroleum have been grouped together for discriminatory excise tax. Is the demand for soft drinks price inelastic like these other products? The econometric analysis of the demand for soft drinks in Ghana revealed that changes in soft drinks consumption in Ghana can be explained by changes in prices of soft drinks, the prices of related goods such as food and beer, and income.

The demand for soft drinks is highly price elastic, with a coefficient of 1.5095; that is a 10% reduction in the price of soft drinks will lead to a 15% increase in the consumption of soft drinks.

The income elasticity of demand for soft drinks is 0.77, that is, a 10 percent increase in GDP will lead to 77% increase in the consumption of soft drinks.

REFERENCES

Baah-Nuakoh, A. and Francis Teal. (1993) *Economic Reforms and Manufacturing Sector in Ghana*, World Bank RPED Study.

Baah-Nuakoh, A. (1997) *Studies on the Ghanaian Economy-The Pre-Revolutionary Years*, Ghana Universities Press, Legon.

Bahl, R. and Walker, M. B. (1998) "Discriminatory Taxation of Carbonated Beverages: The Case of Ireland," Georgia State University, School of Policy Studies.

Bolnick Bruce and Jonathan Haughton. (1998) Tax Policy in Sub-Saharan Africa: Examining the Role of Excise Taxation. African Economic Policy Discussion Paper No. 2. Harvard Institute of International Development.

Chipeta, C. (1998) *Tax Reform and Tax Yield in Malawi*. AERC Research Paper 81, March.

Duffy, M. (1983) "The Demand for Alcoholic Drinks in the U.K.: 1963–78," *Applied Economics*, Vol. 15, pp. 125–40.

Godfrey, C. (1988) "Licensing and the Demand for Alcohol," *Applied Economics*, Vol. 20 pp. 1541–58.

Government of Ghana. *Budget Statements*, various issues from 1970 to 1998.

Kapur, I. *et al.* (1990) *Ghana: Adjustment and Growth 1983–91*. IMF Occasional Paper. No. 86. Washington D.C.

Kusi, N. (1998) *Tax Reform and Revenue Productivity in Ghana*. AERC Research Paper 74. March.

MacGuiness, T. (1980) "An Econometric Analysis of Total Demand for Alcoholic Beverages in the U.K: 1956–75," *Journal of Industrial Economics*. Vol. 29, 1980, pp. 85–109.

CHAPTER 6

Factor Intensities in Manufacturing Establishments

Introduction

Technology in industry can be studied by means of fitting production functions to cross-section or time series data. There are several conceptual and statistical problems involved in the fitting of production functions. In this chapter we adopt a method of measuring technology which examines observed factor intensities in Ghanaian manufacturing industries. The paper has two main objectives: firstly, the examination of observed factor intensities as a guide to studying inter-industry differences in technology, and secondly, we examine the relationship between factor intensities and nationality of ownership and scale (Forsyth and Solomon 1977b).

Various statistical measures have been suggested for the measurement of factor intensity in production, but none is generally acceptable as an ideal measure; for example, capital-output ratio, labour-output ratio, value added per worker. The problem of finding an appropriate measure of capital has led to the use of surrogate measures such as installed horse-power capacity, electricity consumption, fire insurance value of fixed assets. These measures are used interchangeably, but it is possible for the measures to give different rankings of industries. We shall discuss some of the alternative measures of factor intensity, before they are applied to Ghanaian manufacturing.

We also adopt more than one measure, in the empirical section, to get a good indicator of the nature of factor intensity and reduce the problem of the sensitivity of the results to the particular shortcomings of each measure. A new variable — *energy per employee* — which permits a fuller treatment of the flow of capital services is derived and used in conjunction with fixed assets per employee as a guide to factor intensities. The relationships between technology and nationality of ownership and scale are examined.

ON THE MEASUREMENT OF FACTOR INTENSITY

We consider here some of the measures of factor intensity in the literature. Five measures are treated:

(i) book value of fixed assets (plant machinery and equipment) per employee,
(ii) installed horse-power capacity per employee,
(iii) value added per employee,
(iv) two fuel measures of capital per employee — electricity consumption per employee and energy consumed per employee, and
(v) human capital per employee.

Fixed Assets per Employee

A measure of factor intensity that is generally used is observed capital per worker. But the problem that arises is the valuation of capital in use. Our survey data gives the book value of fixed assets and its components. The book value which is the written down value of fixed assets does not reflect the productive capacity of the assets because of the following factors:

(i) the prices of capital goods have increased over time, while the reported figures are not adjusted for the increase in the price of capital stock. Thus, identical plants may differ in book value merely because of different price levels at the time of purchase;
(ii) the reported figures on fixed assets are arrived at by applying the depreciation rates allowed by the government, often tempered with differential incentives considerations, rather than the actual patterns of depreciation which differ from the accelerated depreciation rates;
(iii) machines of different vintages are not of the same quality; machines of recent vintages embody more advanced technology and may thus have higher productive efficiency. Thus, if older machines are compared with the more recent ones, on the same footing, there will be an element of over-estimation.

Thus, it is argued that replacement costs of capital should be used instead of book values. The replacement cost of capital is the cost of replacing an existing unit by a new functional equipment. But a problem arises here too. It is not meaningful to speak of replacement costs, for it may not be possible to obtain any functional equivalent for an obsolete unit. Secondly, when the equipment is fairly old its modern functional equivalent may well be technologically superior to the original unit. All capital are not equally scarce. Observed capital-labour ratios may conceal widely-divergent uses of machinery, buildings and other equipment in different industries. Thus, if two industries using different amounts of machinery and buildings show identical capital per worker ratios, this by itself does not mean that the two industries have the same capital-intensity.

Installed Horse-power Capacity per Worker

A proxy for physical capital-intensity is the number of horse-power of installed power equipment per worker. Horse-power capacity is an indicator of the quantity of machinery used which is one aspect of fixed capital. Though machinery is in most cases the largest component of fixed assets, we cannot ignore buildings, vehicles and other such fixed assets.

Even as an indicator of machinery used, horse-power data has some limitations:

(i)   it does not say anything about the age and actual performance of the machinery;

(ii) horse-power is a very comprehensive physical characteristic of machinery, but it does not necessarily indicate the labour using character of the equipment;

(iii) with technical progress, the performance of machinery appears to be increasing without a corresponding increase in the number of horse-power; and

(iv) the degree of utilization varies after machinery has been installed. Thus, the use of horse-power per worker alone, by itself as an index of capital-intensity, may not be reliable.

Lary's Generalized index of capital-intensity: Value added per Employee

Value added per employee is an index which permits an integrated treatment of the flows of services rendered by both capital and labour.

Capital is not measured as a stock, but the services performed by the factor, while skill differences implicit in labour is taken account of. An industry with a higher value added per employee uses either a large capital equipment per employee or a higher proportion of skilled employees or both. This index was first used by Lary (1968) and is adopted for two main reasons. Firstly, value added data are easier to obtain and more reliable than data on fixed assets; and secondly, the use of value added per employee as a measure of capital-intensity allows for both physical and human capital.

Lary's basis for using value added per employee as an index was the strong correlation found between wage value added and the proportion of skilled workers in total employment. The implication of this finding is that industries paying higher wage rates employ a higher proportion of the skilled workers available. A strong correlation was also found between the non-wage component of the value added per employee and the amount of physical capital used per employee. Thus, an industry is defined to be labour (capital) intensive if value added per employee is less (more) than the average value added per employee for the manufacturing sector as a whole.

But this measure of capital-intensity is not faultless. The measure implies that both the product and factor markets are fully competitive and the productivity of factors are matched by returns to the factors. But these assumptions may not hold especially in developing economies.

Imperfections in the product market affect the non-wage component of value added. This influence being independent of inter-industry differential in the non-wage component may be due to differential tax and credit policies affecting industry, especially in developing countries where selective credit control and varying tax ratios are used as instruments for encouraging some industries and discouraging others.

Labour market imperfections which arise from such factors as differences in the strength of unionized labour as well as government interference with the fixation of wages, do affect inter-industry differences in the wage component of value added independently of the skill component of the industry's labour force.

The correspondence between the inter-industry differences in the value added per employee and factor intensity is also based on the assumption that value added per employee is not related to economies of scale. An industry enjoying economies of scale would yield a higher value added than another even though the latter uses more skilled labour and capital equipment per employee.

A final weakness of the Lary index is that it does not provide an absolute measure of factor intensity, but only a relative measure — that is ranking of the one industry compared with the average for the entire manufacturing. Thus, this index does not help one to evaluate whether factor proportions chosen are optimum in the context of prevailing factor endowments in a given country, and it does not give any clue as to whether a given industry in, say, country A needs more or less capital per unit of labour as compared to the same industry in country B.

Capital Services — Fuel Link

The use of unadjusted capital stock as a measure of capital services is based on an assumption that capital is utilized at the same rate across establishments and industries. But evidence from several less developed countries (LDCs) suggest that the level of capital utilization varies considerably. To account for differences in capital utilization, a link has been found and established between fuel consumption and capital services; electricity consumption is this fuel measure (Foss, 1963; Heathfield 1972; Moody, Jr. 1974; Kim and Kwon, 1977). Thus, electricity consumption per employee gives a measure of capital intensity.

Electrical energy is complementary to utilized equipment and a high correlation is expected between utilized capital stock and electricity consumed. The premise of this measure is that since electric motors account for most of the mechanical work done in factories, the intensity of usage of machines can be estimated by finding the intensity of usage of electric motors which drive the machine. Moreover, the intensity of usage of machinery will reflect the intensity of some other forms of capital, for example, plants which "house" the machine. Thus, electricity consumption is related to the flow of capital services.

The characteristics of electricity have been put forward as a case for its usefulness as a measure of capital services. Firstly, electricity consumption is more easily measured than data necessary to calculate capital. Secondly, electricity is a perfectly homogeneous input of unvaried quality and thus, does not present aggregation problem. Thirdly, electricity cannot easily be stored and so the flow corresponds exactly with what is currently used up by the process, thus, there is no problem of "hoarding", as there is, with say, labour.

There are, of course, problems associated with the use of electricity as capital input. Electricity has additional use as a raw material in certain processes, for example, in steel, copper and aluminium industries, where electrolysis or electric furnaces are used. There is also the problem that relationships between capital services and electricity consumption may change with time, so that one capital hour in time period t, but two capital hours in time period t_2. It is therefore insufficient simply to use electricity consumption as a measure of capital services. The problem of usage of electricity consumption as a measure of capital is compounded in developing economies. Plants are operated by electric power as well as non-electric power, such as steam engines or gasoline engines. Thus, the use of electricity consumption alone as a measure of capital services may be a source of under-estimation of capital. In a sample of 59 establishments in saw-milling and wood industry taken from Central Bureau of Statistics (CBS), 1974 annual returns in Ghana, 45 establishments were found to use more non-electrical fuels than electrical fuel, measured in cost terms.

Another argument usual made against the use of electricity consumption as a measure of capital services is the lack of data on the composition of electricity consumption — lighting, driving electric motors, heating and air-conditioning, the actual consumption varying with the industry group.

However, in developing economies in tropical areas, the greater intensity of sunlight and the greater inability of trade unions to demand better working conditions (e.g., for air-conditioning) means that the percentage of electricity consumed for use other than driving motors is small.

A more adequate fuel measure of capital services is needed. The use of non-electric power may not be important in the advanced economies, but it may be widespread in less developed economies where electric power may not be available. We thus derive a new measure by defining a new capital service variable ENERGY which is a composite of all fuels used by an establishment to account for the use of non-electric motors. Capital-intensity is thus, measured by energy per employee. This measure exhibits all the limitations of the electricity measure, but has the added advantage that is takes account of the use of non-electric motors.

Human Capital-intensity

The factor intensity measures that we have considered with the exception of the Lary's generalized index, neglect human capital. Most of the empirical studies on factor use in developing economies have not used a framework which explicitly incorporates measures of human capital, physical capital, and unimproved labour. The Lary index aggregates human capital into a labour input, considering the wage component of value added as due to human capital. This aggregation eliminates the possibility that entrepreneurs in developing economies may use less human capital, in production but more physical capital per labour [Hirschman's "machine paced" hypothesis]. For it seems unlikely that the two types of capital are close substitutes [Griliches (1969)]. If we assume complementary, then the ranking of industry by their skill intensities may approximate that by physical capital intensities. Thus, in a study of factor input use, there is a need to consider the independent influences of physical capital, human capital and unimproved labour. This necessitates the use of a three-input production function.

$$Q_i = I_i\, L_i,\, H_i,\, K_i$$

where

Q_i is output of establishment i;
L_i is unimproved labour;
H_i is human capital and
K_i is physical capital.

In the following sections, we present estimates of factor intensities for Ghanaian manufacturing based on some of the measures discussed, despite their limitations. For as Joan Robinson has put it, the difficulty of measuring capital "is not a reason to fall into a state of intellectual nihilism and refuse to say anything. The crudest measures' — say, cost written down at the rate permitted by the tax authorities, the businessman's own valuation as shown by the books of the firms, or estimated replacement costs with a rough allowance for age — are better than none . . . Questions of this kind (capital-intensity and capital per unit of output) are of the greatest interest, and it is worthwhile to try to answer them, no matter that the measurements are crude, imprecise or even ambiguous when it comes to fine details.[1]

DATABASE AND CHARACTERISTICS OF THE SAMPLE

Successful testing of hypotheses depends upon the amount and quality of available data. This and the following chapters are based on unpublished surveys of Ghanaian manufacturing establishments which the Central Bureau of Statistics (CBS) annually conducted to collect input and output data. The information was gathered in the form of a questionnaire sent to the establishments, and where required assistance for filling the questionnaire was provided by the staff of the CBS. The CBS questionnaires were designed to obtain information on the general characteristics of the establishments, type of ownership and nationality, employment, intermediate inputs and other costs of production, production, sales, inventories, exports, fixed assets and other several characteristics. Access was granted to files of 420 establishments for 1974, for different size groups, nationalities, and 53 4-digit International Standard Industrial Classification (ISIC) groups. Forty-five establishments were excluded from the analysis, since these did not satisfy our selection criteria.

The following criteria for selection were used to discard some of the establishments;

  (i)   establishments with incomplete data;
  (ii) number of persons less than or equal to 4;
  (iii) book value of plant, machinery and equipment was nega-
        tive or zero;
  (iv) payments to capital obtained as the difference between
        value added and total labour cost was negative or zero;
  (v)   value added was negative;

Thus, our analysis has been based on data for 375 manufacturing establishments. Our information concerning certain characteristics of the establishments and industries is limited. Unfortunately, there is no way around this shortage of information, but the problem lies within reasonable tolerable limits, and we have had to rely on surrogate measures. No attempt was made to gather information from the establishments themselves, because it was thought unlikely that more detailed or more reliable information would be obtained, and any improvements would not have made up for the cost of gathering the information.

The quality of the data used was high; but since the data were

taken as supplied by the respondents, some respondent biases may
be involved. Firstly, the respondents might mis-report, purposely
thinking they might gain or lose from the survey. But if the assumption
is made that the errors made are normally distributed over the
sample, the data can be used for examining our hypotheses. We may
also take refuge in the fact that the annual publication, *Industrial
Statistics* published by the CBS is based on this questionnaire. Secondly,
the data on fixed assets may be subject to some errors because
depreciation may not reflect the wear and tear of equipment. But as
long as all establishments overstate depreciation and therefore
understate the value of their assets by more or less the same
percentage, this does not distort the analysis. Thirdly, the reliability
of the information provided by each establishment may be
significantly and positively correlated with the size of the
establishment.

It should be noted here that the files of the various establishments were supplied on a strictly confidential basis. It was agreed
that the establishments would not be identified and that none of the
materials supplied in confidence would be released in a form which
might reveal the identity of individual establishments. Thus, we
adopted an identification showing the industry group and region of
establishments but not their names.

On the basis of the questionnaire information a number of
variables to be used in the study were derived. Several practical
problems evolved and in some cases several experimentations had
to be made, for example the capital intensity variable. These variables
and their construction are discussed in the text of the various chapters.
As well as continuous variables, zero/one dummy variables were
developed, dichotomizing the sample establishments into groups.

Some Characteristics of the Sample

Though the sample is limited in terms of the biases towards large
and medium scale and more successful establishments, the range of
the observations is still quite large. Establishments in our sample
range in persons engaged from as low as 4 to as many as 3668. Table
6.1 shows the distribution of the 375 establishments among three
size groups, three ownership categories and 25 3-digit industry groups.

    (i) To compare the size of the establishments serious —
        measurements arise, and various measures have been

Table 6.1: Cross Classification of Establishments by 3-digit Industry, Nationality and Size

Name of Industry Group	n	nationality of Ownership			size (measured) by number of persons		
		DOE	FOE	JOE	<30	30-99	>100
Food processing	39	26	7	6	17	8	14
Beverages	14	6	3	5	2	4	8
Tobacco	1		1				1
Textiles	25	8	10	7	4	8	13
Wearing apparel	32	14	12	6	11	18	3
Leather and products	14	7	7		5	9	
Footwear	10	7	3		2	4	4
Wood, cork and products	55	25	21	9	8	24	23
Furniture and fixtures	24	18	3	3	8	11	5
Paper and products	8	4	2	2	3	4	1
Printing/Publishing	23	22		1	9	7	7
Industrial chemicals	8	2	5	1.00	2	5	1
Other chemicals	24	5	9	10	4	15	5
Rubber products	6	1	3	2	2	1	3
Plastics	10	1	4	5	2	6	2
Pottery, china,	1		1				1
Glass and products	3	1	2			1	2
Other non metallic	15	10	3	2	2	9	4
Iron and steel	2	1		1			2
Fabricated metals	27	11	12	4	6	13	8
Nonelectrical machinery	1		1				
Electrical	11	2	6	3	4	5	2
Transport	14	3	7	4		6	8
Professional, scientific	1		1		1		
Other manufacturing	7	4	3		4	3	
Total Manufacturing	375	178	126	71	96	162	117

Notes: n   — number of establishments
    DOE — domestic owned establishments
    FOE — foreign owned establishments
    JOE — jointly owned establishments

suggested in the literature — sales, gross value of production, value added, fixed assets and employment. These measures are usually used interchangeably because of the often made assumption that the different measures are correlated. As a measure of size We have used the number of persons engaged in the establishments because of the following considerations; employment is an important indicator of an establishment's capacity; it is straightforward to measure. To avoid objections to the use of persons engaged as a measure of size, the coefficients of correlation between the number of persons engaged and other possible indicators of size: total fixed assets, plant, machinery and equipment, total energy consumption and value added — were estimated. The simple correlation coefficient values obtained were all significant at the 0.01 probability level.

We divided the sample establishments into 3 size-groups (<30, 30-99, and >100). The sample is biased towards large establishments. These constitute about 70% of the sample, since proportionately, more of the larger-sized establishments receive the questionnaires and also tend to have the staff capable of filling the questionnaires.

(ii) industrial composition — wood, cork and products account for the bulk of the sample establishments. This is also true of the population of establishments, this being a natural consequence of the availability of the raw material in the form of the natural resource (timber). This is followed by food processing, wearing apparel, chemicals, fabricated metal products and textiles.

(iii) nationality of ownership — out of the total of 375 establishments, 47% are wholly Ghanaian owned, 34% wholly foreign owned and 19% jointly owned. If we make the assumption that foreign control exceeds domestic control in the joint ventures, this brings the total foreign controlled establishments to 197 (53%). It is being assumed that even where foreign equity holding is minimal, foreign control is still exercised. A point that we should take note of here is that some of the establishments considered foreign are really resident expatriates. We included these in the category of foreign owned for three reasons: (a) they considered themselves to be foreign owned; (b) the questionnaire on which the analysis is based does not identify this group of resident expatriates; (c) and more significantly, the decisions taken by these resident expatriates are usually based on interests foreign to the domestic economy.

Our sample reflects the importance of foreign dominated establishments in Ghanaian manufacturing. The wholly foreign owned establishments are concentrated in textiles and wearing apparel, tobacco, wood and products, rubber, fabricated metals and transport equipment. We tested for the association between ownership category and the type of industry using the X^2-test. The null hypothesis of no association is rejected at the 0.005 probability level.

(iv) When we compare the size distribution of sample establishments for the three ownership groups, we observe from Table 6.2 identical size distribution patterns for the ownership categories, with most of the establishments in the 50–99 size group, and tapering off in the smaller and larger-sized groups.

Table 6.2: Distribution of Sample by Ownership and Size

Size	Ownership			Average Number of Years
In operation	DOE	FOE	JOE	(AGE)
1 – 9	11	4	0	12.8
10 – 29	38	26	7	9.6
30 – 49	23	25	14	10.2
50 – 99	38	36	20	10.4
100 – 249	20	27	15	10.9
250 – 499	10	7	4	11.7
500 +	11	11	3	12.2
Age (as of 1974)	10.8	10.8	9.4	

On the average, there is no difference between the age of domestically owned establishments and foreign establishments. Joint enterprises are of more recent origin. With respect to age and-size, with the exception of the 1–9 category, there is a tendency for age to correlate with size.

ESTIMATES OF FACTOR INTENSITIES IN GHANAIAN MANUFACTURING

The data used in the analysis of this chapter have been drawn from unpublished surveys of manufacturing establishments kept by the Central Bureau of Statistics of Ghana discussed in the previous section. The analysis is based on data for 375 establishments of different size groups. The number of large scale establishments in our sample constitutes about 75% of the large scale manufacturing establishments on which the CBS publication *Industrial Statistics* is based. The data pertains to the year 1974.

This section reports the results of our attempts at estimating factor intensities in Ghanaian manufacturing industry based on the sample of cross-section data for 1974. We had to aggregate the establishment data for each 3- and 4-digit industry group for the analysis in this section. We use three factors, labour, capital and skill. Skill is measured by the number of man-years of non-production labour, Four definitions of capital is used — book value of plant, machinery and equipment (KPME), book value of total fixed assets, electricity consumption and energy consumption. Thus, in all, we have six measures of factor intensity:

(i) physical capital-intensity — plant machinery and equipment per employee, total fixed assets per employee, electricity consumption per employee and energy consumption per employee;
(ii) skill intensity;
(iii) Lary's generalized factor intensity measure.

Comparison of the Measures

The results of the estimates for all the six factor intensity measures are summarized in Appendix Table 6.A1 for twenty-five 3-digit and fifty-four 4-digit industry groups. From the Table, we found substantial inter-industry differences in factor intensity with either measure. For example, if we consider the total fixed asset measure (KINT2) we observe capital intensity ranging from ¢990 for the manufacture of rubber products to ¢12,374 for tobacco industry. Table 6.3 presents the ranking order of the results in Appendix 6.A1 for the 3-digit industries. The ranking number 1 is attached to the highest values and the highest spanking number is given to the lowest values.

The difference between factor proportions under the different measures has been calculated by testing to find out whether the measures give uniform ranking of industries by using two non-parametric tests: Spearman rank correlation test r for the pairwise comparison, and Kendall's coefficient of concordance (W) for overall uniformity.[2] The coefficient of concordance is 0.4738 which is significant at 0.001 probability level, and implies that there is similarity in the ranks given by the various measures.[3] Given the significant concordance among the ranking, the ranking of the sums of the ranks can be used as a composite ranking.

Spearman's rank correlation coefficient (s) for pairs of factor intensity measures for twenty-five 3-digit industry are presented in Table 6.4 with critical levels at 1 percent, 5% and 10% probability at 0.466, 0.337 and 0.265 respectively. The average rank order correlation coefficient[4] among all possible pairings of the factor intensity measure is 0.5686.

On the basis of the average ranking, it can be seen that a number of industries such as tobacco, beverages, iron and steel, electrical machinery, food manufacturing, pottery and china, other chemical are clearly capital-intensive, while a number of others such as furniture, leather, footwear, rubber, miscellaneous manufacturing, non-electrical machinery and paper products are labour-intensive.[5] It can also be seen that many of the component industries do not possess the same degree of capital intensiveness as the major industry group to which they belong (Appendix Table 6.A1).

While there is strong concordance in the rankings there are few notable reversals in the rankings. For example, while KINT2 ranks tobacco as the most physical capital-intensive industry, according to the energy-labour ratio, tobacco ranks the fifteenth. Another example is the wood industry. According to electricity measure, this industry ranks the fourth, while the plant machinery and equipment measure ranks it the twentieth. A closer look at rank comparisons by Spearman's rank correlation reveals that while the physical intensity measures are closely correlated, a meaningful association is not found

Table 6.3: Ranking of Manufacturing Industries According to Factor Intensity

Average Rank Ordering	ISIC Code	Industry Group	KINT1	KINT2	KINT3	KINT4	KINT5	SKINT
(4)	311/12	Food Manufacturing	5	6	4	4	12	13
(2)	313.	Beverages	3	4	5	8	5	9
(1)	314	Tobacco	1	1		7	8	22
(17)	322	Clothing	13	12	10	19	21	23
(24)	323	Leather	23	20	17	23	20	21
(23)	324	Footwear	22	15	21	25	24	12
(11)	331	Wood	14	14	20	6	4	14
(25)	332	Furniture and fixtures	20	22	22	24	22	20
(11)	341	Paper	7	13	13	21	17	1
(19)	342	Printing & Publishing	17	19	16	16.5	15	17
(18)	351	Industrial Chemicals	15	18	23	16.5	19	7
(8)	352	Other Chemicals	9	16	15	5	9	2
(22)	355	Rubber Products	21	25	24	10	11	25
(6)	356	Plastics Products	4	3	3	11	6	18
(7)	361	Pottery, China, etc.	19	2	2	1	3	24
(9)	362	Glass and Products	24	5	7	2	1	8
(10)	369	Other Non-Metallic	12	9	12	91	19	
(3)	371	Iron and Steel	18	7	8	3	2	3
(16)	381	Fabricated Metal Product	11	17	14	13	16	16
(20)	382	Non-Electrical Machinery	10	24	25	12	25	11
(4)	383	Electrical machinery	2	8	6	14	10	4
(15)	384	Transport equipment	6	11	18	18	18	15
(13)	385	Professional etc.	8	21	11	20	14	5
(21)	390	Other Manufacturing	16	23	19	22	22	10

between the skill intensity measure and the physical capital-intensity measures, suggesting a sort of non-complementarity between physical capital and human capital, and supporting Hirschman's (1958, p.145) categorization of technology into "machine-paced" and "operator-paced". Industries that are physical capital-intensive tend to use lower skill intensity. This finding, to some extent, is in the same vein as Mason's (1973) finding for Philippines and Mexico. He found that although United States firms in these countries used more physically capital-intensive production methods than the domestically-owned firms, they employed lower levels of skills than their domestically-owned counterparts.

Table 6.4: Spearman Correlation Coefficients for Pairs
of Factor Intensity Measures

	KINT1	SKINT	KINT2	KINT3	KINT4	KINT5
KINT1	1.000					
SKINT	0.449	1.000				
KINT2	0.348	0.114	1.000			
KINT3	0.335	0.122	0.877	1.000		
KINT4	0.010	0.009	0.532	0.501	1.000	
KINT5	0.196	0.032	0.660	0.625	0.751	1.000

KINT1   Value added per employee;

KINT2   Total fixed assets per employee;

KINT3   Plant, machinery and equipment per employee;

KINT4   Energy consumed per employee;

KINT5   Electricity consumed per employee;

SKINT   Skill intensity.

W   = 0.4738

X^2 (calc) = 68.233 > $X^2_{0.001,25}$ = 52.620

TECHNOLOGY, SCALE AND NATIONALITY OF
OWNERSHIP RELATIONSHIP RECONSIDERED

We examine here the effect of scale and nationality of ownership on technology since most of the studies on technology (except those which involved estimating elasticities of substitution) have touched on the two questions of technology and nationality of ownership and scale and technology, but the conventional wisdom is that foreign firms use more capital-intensive technology than domestically-owned firms because of the limited search behaviour of the foreign firms and their desire to use technology closer to their domain of competence.

Hakam (1972) in a study based on limited survey evidence and mainly concerned with the access to finance, maintains that nationality of ownership and scale operation are joint determinants of factor proportions with private large- and medium-scale factories tending to be more capital-intensive than in the small scale sector. In a series of articles, Forsyth and Solomon (1977a, 1977b, 1978) find that foreign firms are more capital-intensive than local firms within given sectors, but they are markedly less, skill intensive. Steel (1977), hypothesized that small scale firms use less capital per worker than large firms, and found this hypothesis supported by 1973 Ghanaian manufacturing evidence.

Nationality of Ownership

We re-examine here the influence of nationality on the choice of technology in manufacturing using 1974 survey data. We compare the capital intensity of foreign and local establishments differentiating between twenty-four 4-digit industries. Table 6.5 presents evidence on capital-intensity for local and foreign-owned establishments for 24 industry groups which had observations on foreign and local establishments (all jointly-owned establishments were excluded), technology measured by fixed capital per person engaged. From the Table we found that, for 13 industries, domestically-owned establishments (DOEs) used more capital-intensive technology, foreign-owned establishments (FOEs) with the ratio of average fixed capital per person, engaged in DOEs to that in FOEs varying between 109 percent to 1,914%.

A non-parametric test, Wilcoxon matched pairs signed rank test, was applied to test the hypothesis that DOEs used more capital-intensive techniques than FOEs.

Table 6.5: Capital Intensities of Foreign-Owned and Domestic-Owned Establishments in Manufacturing Industries in Ghana 1974

Code	Name of Industry	Average Capital Intensity		Domestic as % of Foreign
		Domestic	Foreign	
3113	Canning and Preserving of Fruits and Vegetables	733	1,821	40.3
3115	Vegetables and Animal Oilds and Fats	7,798	1,792	435.2
3116	Grain Mill Products	1,646	86	1,914.0
3119	Cocoa, Chocolate, and Sugar Confectionery	6,946	915	759.1
3131	Distilling, Rectifying and Blending Spirits	1,550	2,970	52.2
3212	Made up Textile Goods	412	3,423	12.0
3213	Knitting Mills	1,195	4,804	24.9
3220	Wearing Apparel	4,603	2,808	163.9
3233	Products of Leather	1,230	845	145.6
3240	Footwear	1,320	528	250.0
3412	Containers and Boxes of Paper	2,599	2,382	108.1
3512	Fertilizer and Pesticides	1,494	1,677	89.1
3521	Paints, Varnishes and Lacquers	1,194	1,274	93.7
3522	Drugs and Medicines	3,841	2,437	157.6
3559	Rubber Products (nec)	200	674	29.7
3560	Plastic Products	4,267	8,548	49.9
3620	Glass Products	5,146	1,499	343.3
3691	Structural Clay products	1,504	1,124	133.8
3699	Non-Metallic Mineral Products (nec)	2,688	455	590.8
3811	Cutlery, Hand Tools, etc.	8,334	2,299	362.5
3812	Furniture and Fixtures Primarily of Metal	1,573	2,876	54.6
3819	Fabricataed Metal (nec)	1,232	2,532	48.7
3822	Radio, Television	2,342	4,002	58.5
3901	Jewellery, etc.	1,219	1,007	575.0

Note. (nec): Not elsewhere classified.

This test has been applied for similar purposes by Mason (1973) and Agarwal (1976). The test has a power efficiency equal to 95% of the normal t-test. It takes into account the direction and relative magnitudes of capital-intensity differences between DOEs and FOEs.

The null hypothesis (H_o) states that there is no difference in capital-intensity between DOEs and FOEs, while the alternative hypothesis (H_A) states that DOEs are more capital-intensive than FOEs. Though, we have a sample of 24 matched pairs which is smaller than 25 (the lower bound for use of normal approximation with Wilcoxon test) we use here the normal approximation. We shall reject the null hypothesis if the calculated probability is less than or equal to 0.05 in a one tailed test. The calculated probability is 0.0764; thus, we cannot reject the null hypothesis.

The evidence tends to suggest that in Ghanaian manufacturing there is no difference in technology used by foreign and indigenous establishments. Physical capital intensity seems not to differ between the two nationality categories, and contradicts Solomon and Forsyth, and Hakam's finding for earlier periods that foreign firms are more capital intensive than indigenously owned firms.

The effects of nationality of ownership on technology were also studied at the individual establishment level, irrespective of the industry group. The 375 establishments were classified into three ownership groups — foreign-owned, jointly-owned by foreigners and domestic businessmen, and wholly-domestically-owned.

We estimated a model,

$$KINT_{ij} = a + b_1 DNAT_1 + b_2 DNAT_2$$

where

> $KINT_i$ is capital intensity measure
> j for establishment
> i (j = fixed assets per employee, energy consumed per employee);
> $DNAT_1$ is a dummy = 1 if the establishment is wholly-foreign-owned, and = 0 otherwise; $DNAT_2$ is a dummy = 1 if the establishment is jointly-owned, and = 0 otherwise.

The results of the estimation are as follows (with t-statistics in brackets below the regression coefficients);

$$log\ KINT1 = 0.1788 + 0.1790\ DNAT_1 + 0.5433\ DNAT_2$$
$$(1.2757) \qquad\quad (3.1933)$$
$$r = 0.1636$$

$$log \ KINT2= -2.6428 + 0.6260 \ DNAT_1 + 0.5220 \ DNAT_2$$
$$(3.7840) \qquad\qquad (4.289)$$
$$r = 0.2170$$

The results from the fixed assets measure of capital-intensity do not support the contention that foreign-owned firms choose less appropriate technology than domestically-owned firms by selecting capital-intensive techniques. The jointly-owned firms tend to use more capital-intensive technology than domestically-owned ones. The energy regression ($KNIT_2$) seems to suggest that foreign-owned firms use more capital-intensive production methods than wholly-domestically-owned firms, but the domestically owned firms use more energy intensive techniques, than the jointly owned firms. The different results revealed by the fixed assets measure of factor intensity and the energy measure may reflect the different utilization rates of capital by the different ownership groups, implying that foreign-owned establishments keep less idle capacity than their indigenous counterparts.

Scale and Technology

The hypothesis that capital-intensity increases with size is examined briefly here. The average size of establishments is measured by the arithmetic average of employees in all establishments in a given industry. Appendix Table 6.A2 presents data on establishment size and capital-intensity. To test for relationship between size and capital-intensity, we used the non-parametric Spearman correlation tests. The rank correlation coefficient is 0.53 which is statistically significant at 1% level. Thus, there appears to be a relationship between the two variables which suggests that capital-intensive industries tend to be industries with large establishments. The 25-industry groups have been further sub-divided into 7-size groups. The evidence suggests that there is variation in capital-intensity by size class for a number of industries.

Conclusion

This chapter has sought to analyze technology in the manufacturing industry of Ghana. The chapter had two objectives: (a) examining inter-industry and intra-industry factor intensities; and (b) the relationship between factor intensities and nationality of ownership and scale.

Various measures of factor intensities were suggested and adopted. A new factor intensity measure — energy consumed per employee — which permits a fuller treatment of the flow of capital services was used in conjunction with other measures. Strong concordance in the rankings suggested by the measures were obtained although there were notable reversals. An examination of the rank comparisons by Spearman's rank correlation reveals that while the physical intensity measures are closely correlated, such correlation does not exist between skill intensity measure and the physical intensity measure, suggesting that industries that are physical capital intensive tend to use lower skill intensity in their operations. On the basis of average rankings such industries as tobacco, beverages, iron and steel, electrical machinery and food manufacturing stood out as the most capital-intensive, while furniture, footwear, rubber and paper products were the most labour-intensive. Thus, the emphasis of industries in the labour-intensive group would help reduce the unemployment problem.

Our results on factor intensities and nationality of ownership revealed that one cannot reject the null hypothesis that factor intensities are identical in foreign-owned and domestically-owned establishments. What seems clear is that capital intensive industries tend to be the industries with large establishments. There is a need to re-examine the question of factor intensities when better data become available.

APPENDICES

Table 6.A1: Ranking of Manufacturing Industries According to Factor Intensity

ISIC Code or Sub-group	KINT1 Value Added/ Employee (1)	KINT2 Fixed Assets/ Employee (2)	KINT3 Plant, Machinery & Equipment/ Employee (3)	KINT4 Energy/ Employee (4)	KINT5 Electricity/ Employee (5)	SKINT Skill Intensity (6)
311/12 FOOD MANUFACTURING	8.582	4.224	2.524	0.484	0.055	0.222
Dairy Products (3112)	12.355	9.362	6.001	0.514	0.114	0.415
Canning and Preserving of Fruits and Vegetables (3113)	1.575	1.718	1.407	1.390	0.149	0.254
Canning, Preserving & Processing of Fish, etc. (3114)	2.122	10.463	4.591	0.165	0.161	0.277
Vegetable and Animals Oils and Fats (3115)	3.971	6.726	3.010	0.250	0.060	0.371
Grain Mill Products (3116)	7.293	3.669	1.825	0.143	0.056	0.150
Cocoa, Chocolate, and Sugar Confectionery (3119)	12.821	4.613	2.987	0.300	0.046	0.185
Other Food Products (3121)	4.487	0.627	0.165	1.148	0.016	0.186
13 BEVERAGE INDUSTRIES	11.816	5.187	2.277	0.273	0.112	0.264
Distilling, Rectifying and Blending Spirits (3131)	.372	2.048	0.811	0.170	0.021	0.319
Malt, Liquors and Malt	18.224	8.243	3.366	0.384	0.190	0.255
Soft Drinks and Carbonated Waters (3134)	3.974	0.473	0.357	0.072	0.031	0.168

Table 6.A1 (*cont'd.*)

314	TOBACCO MANUFACTURES	57.622	12.374	7.798	0.139	0.090	0.295
321	MANUFACTURE OF TEXTILES	1.518	3.282	1.690	0.308	0.087	0.132
322	Spinning, Carving and Finishing Textiles (3211)	1.460	3.377	1.745	0.364	0.097	0.129
	Made up Textile Goods Except Wearing Apparel (3212)	4.167	2.947	1.222	0.055	0.036	0.096
	Knitting Mills (3213)	1.310	3.474	2.661	0.105	0.044	0.126
	Carpets and Rugs (3214)	0.532	1.312	0.835	0.038	0.023	0.118
	Cordage, Rope and Twine (3215)	1.461	2.465	0.624	0.065	0.052	0.173
	MANUFACTURE OF WEARING APPAREL	2.741	2.972	1.631	0.080	0.027	0.126
	MANUFACTURE OF LEATHER AND PRODUCTS	1.948	1.568	0.850	0.056	0.028	0.141
	Tanneries and Leather finishing (3231)	5.130	5.623	3.158	0.208	0.091	0.145
	Products of Leather and leather substitutes (3233)	1.488	0.983	0.516	0.034	0.091	0.140
3240	FOOTWEAR	1.967	2.578	0.728	0.054	0.022	0.234
331	WOOD AND CORK AND PRODUCTS	2.632	2.688	0.751	0.364	0.141	0.221
3320	FURNITURE AND FIXTURES	2.040	1.447	0.692	0.055	0.025	0.162

Table 6.A1 *(cont'd.)*

Code	Industry						
341	PAPER AND PRODUCTS	5.328	2.869	1.160	0.061	0.035	0.397
	Containers and Boxes of Paper Board (3412)	5.64	2.720	1.050	0.064	0.037	0.427
	Pulp, Paper Board articles (nec) (3419)	3.969	3.507	1.634	0.049	0.026	0.267
3420	PRINTING, PUBLI	2.235	1.619	0.953	0.092	0.040	0.206
351	INDUSTRIAL CHEM	2.589	2.296	0.586	0.092	0.029	0.278
	Basic Industrial Chemicals except Fertilizers (3511)	2.280	2.673	1.247	0.033	0.009	0.026
	Fertilizer and Pesticides (3512)	2.610	2.264	0.529	0.097	0.031	0.300
352	MANUF OF OTHER CHEMICALS	4.469	2.566	0.974	0.404	0.063	0.371
	Paints, Varnishes and Lacquers (3521)	4.265	1.073	0.211	0.081	0.035	0.479
	Drugs and Medicines (3522)	2.723	2.682	0.928	0.082	2.723	0.309
	Soap and Cleaning Preparations, Perfumes, Cosmetics (3523)	5.604	2.988	1.232	0.693	0.083	0.391
	Chemical Products (nec) (3529)	3.382	1.532	0.545	0.095	0.064	0.298
355	MANUFACTURE OF RUBBER PRODUCTS	1.969	0.090	0.494	0.215	0.056	0.067
	Tyre and Tube (3559)	9.320	1.430	0.403	0.130	0.055	0.182
	Rubber Products (nec) (3559)	1.912	0.988	0.495	0.216	0.056	0.066
3560	PLASTIC PRODUCTS	9.496	6.184	5.057	0.185	0.110	0.193

Table 6.A1 *(cont'd.)*

Code							
	POTTERY, CHINA AND EARTHWARE	2.114	11.176	6.020	2.011	0.184	0.124
362	Glass and Products	1.609	5.163	2.134	0.829	0.050	0.269
369		3.177	3.450	1.182	0.272	0.205	0.188
	Structural Clay Products	0.887	1.298	0.568	0.177	0.030	0.238
	Cement, etc. (3692)	4.907	7.725	2.478	0.755	0.701	0.276
	Non-Metallic Mineral Products (nec) (3699)	3.144	2.015	0.733	0.053	0.100	0.122
3710	IRON AND STEEL	2.200	3.736	1.786	0.680	0.190	0.335
381	FABRICATED METAL PRODUCTS	3.526	2.314	1.114	0.164	0.039	0.211
	Cutlery, Hand Tools, etc. (3811)	1.933	4.922	2.017	0.193	0.053	0.235
	Furniture and Fixtures Primarily of Steel (38121)	4.943	2.608	0.779	0.119	0.024	0.148
	Structural Metal Products (3813)	3.709	1.629	1.107	0.066	0.240	0.106
	Fabricated Metal (nec) (3819)	3.376	2.107	0.985	0.222	0.048	0.230
382	NON-ELECTRICAL MACHINERY	3.782	1.051	0.343	0.177	0.016	0.258
	ELECTRICAL MACHINERY, etc.	26.119	3.598	2.143	0.140	0.061	0.321
	Radio, T.V, etc.	4.290	2.708	1.119	0.115	0.050	0.311
	Electrical Appliances and Housewares (3833)	93.457	1.978	1.765	0.106	0.062	0.341
	Electrical Appliances (nec) (3839)	8.729	5.364	3.477	0.176	0.067	0.279

Table 6.A1 *(cont'd.)*

382	TRANSPORT EQUIPMENT	6.908	3.070	0.786	0.085	0.032	0.220
	Ship building and Repairing (3841)	1.201	0.541	0.262	0.023	0.010	0.168
	Motor Bicycles (3843)	7.983	3.547	0.885	0.097	0.036	0.230
385	PROFESSIONAL AND SCIENTIFIC, etc.	4.922	1.548	1.52	0.075	0.045	0.304
390	OTHER MANUFACTURING	2.552	1.296	0.752	0.060	0.025	0.261
	Jewellery, etc. (3901)	2.161	0.976	0.638	0.038	0.13	0.213
	Manufacturing (nec) (3909)	2.766	1.471	0.815	0.072	0.032	0.288

Table 6.A2: Establishment Size and Capital Intensity, 1974

Industry	1-9 (1)	10-29 (2)	30-49 (3)	50-99 (4)	100-249 (5)	250-499 (6)	500+ (7)	Average Est. size (Employees) (8)	Average Capacity Intensity (¢) (9)
Food	411	1,713	6,537	4,705	5,212	3,353	4,283	149 (11)	3,988 (6)
Beverages	–	85	982	3,867	2,970	4,328	7,924	253 (5)	5,814 (4)
Tobacco	–	–	–	–	–	–	12,374	732 (1)	12,374 (1)
Textiles	500	2,249	7,434	1,885	2,627	6,527	3,468	570 (2)	3,512 (9)
Wearing Apparel	–	2,148	1,218	2,751	353	–	7,710	68 (21)	3,536 (8)
Leather and Products	–	845	1,098	2,185	–	–	–	42 (23)	1,698 (18)
Footwear	561	–	884	893	1,036	–	–	69 (19)	944 (25)
Cocoa, Cork and Products	2,561	3,502	1,374	2,263	1,913	1,426	4,257	156 (8)	2,796 (12)
Furniture and Fixtures	767	2,386	846	2,447	688	–	–	71 (18)	1,460 (21)
Paper and Products	–	2,050	3,323	–	1,228	–	2,761	112 (13)	2,534 (14)
Printing & Publishing	694	1,837	1,232	881	2,420	–	1,468	156 (8)	1,534 (20)
Industrial Chemicals	–	2,259	4,314	2,610	373	–	–	69 (19)	2,102 (17)
Other Chemical Products	–	1,539	1,680	2,740	1,203	–	3,203	124 (12)	2,512 (15)
Rubber Products	200	1,430	–	4,316	579	1,933	390	309 (6)	1,151 (23)
Plastics	–	–	1,653	7,079	7,188	–	–	81 (17)	6,046 (3)
Pottery, China, etc.	–	–	–	–	11,176	–	–	186 (7)	11,176 (2)
Glass and Products	–	–	1,449	–	1,512	5,612	5,857	302 (4)	5,141 (5)
Other Non-metallic	–	1,642	1,090	2,015	325	2,342	–	100 (15)	3,408 (10)
Electrical	220	916	2,693	3,741	–	4,957	0	63 (22)	2,662 (13)
Transport	–	–	3,720	8,145	1,828	–	–	152 (10)	3,102 (11)
Iron and Steel	–	–	–	4,393	–	–	3,666	466 (3)	3,730 (17)
Fabricated metals	–	1,090	7,233	3,369	2,716	1,557	509	106 (14)	2,363 (16)
Non-Electrical Machinery	–	–	–	1,051	–	–	–	89 (16)	1,051 (24)
Professional & Scientific Instruments	–	1,548	–	–	–	–	–	23 (25)	1,548 (19)
Other Manufacturin	216	1,400	1,835	1,137	–	–	–	32 (24)	1,279 (22)
ALL MANUFACTURING	779	1,754	2,454	2,154	2,425	3,405	3,695	157	3,310

Sources: Computed from Central Bureau of Statistics files of manufacturing establishments.

NOTES

1. Joan Robinson pp. 203–204
2. For a discussion of the sample, see Baah-Nuakoh [1980].
3. The coefficient of concordance (W) is defined as

$$W = \frac{125}{k^2 N (N^2 - 1)}$$

where k is number of measures, N is number of industries, and S is sum of squares of the deviation of the k sums of ranks around their mean. The test of significance is given by the X^2 statistic:

$$X^2 = \frac{125}{kN (N + 1)}$$

For a discussion of the coefficient of concordance and Spearman rank correlation, see for example S. Seigel (1956).

4. Pairwise comparisons of the measures were also made by simple correlation analysis for all the 375 establishments in our sample. These coefficients of correlation are all statistically significant at 0.01 probability.
5. The average rank order correlation coefficient R is related to W by the formula:

$$R = \frac{(kW - 1)}{R - 1}$$

6. Industries are classified as capital/labour intensive according to the value of their average rank relative to the median rank for all industries in the sample.

REFERENCES

Agarwal, J. P. (1976) "Factor Proportions in Foreign and Domestic Firms in Indian Manufacturing," *The Economic Journal*, Vol. 86, pp. 589–594.

Central Bureau of Statistics, *Industrial Statistics*, Accra periodical series.

Forsyth, J. C. and Solomon, R. F. (1977a) "Substitution of Labour for Capital in Foreign Sector: Some Further Evidence," *Economic Journal*, Vol. 87, June, pp. 283–289.

—— (1977b), "Choice of Technology and Nationality of Ownership in Manufacturing in a Developing Economy," *Oxford Economic Papers*, Vol. 29, July, No. 2, pp. 258–82.

—— (1978) "Restrictions on Foreign Ownership of Manufacturing industry in a

Less Developed Country: The Case of Ghana," *The Journal of Developing Areas*, Vol. 12, April pp. 281–296.

Foss, M. F. (1963), "The Utilisation of capital Equipment: Post-war Compared with Pre-war," *Survey of Current Business*, pp. 8–16.

Griliches, Z. (1969) "Capital-Skill Complementarity," *Review of Economics and Statistics*, Vol. 51, No. 4, November, pp. 465-468.

Hakam, A. N. "Impediments to the Growth of Indigenous Entrepreneurship in Ghana 1946-68", *Economic Bulletin of Ghana*, Second Series, Vol. 2, No. 2.

Heathfield, D. F. (1972) "The measurement of Capital Usage Using Electricity Consumption Data for U.K," *Journal of Royal Statistical Society*, No. 2, pp. 208-220.

Hirschman, A. O. (1958) *The Strategy of Economic Development*, Yale University Press, New Haven and London.

Kim, Y. C. and Jene Kwon (1977) "The Utilization of Capital and the Growth of Output in a Developing Economy: The Case of Korean Manufacturing," *Journal of Development Economics*.

Krueger, Anne O. (1978), "Alternative Trade Strategies and Employment in LDCs", *American Economic Review Papers and Proceedings*, Vol. 68, No. 2, May pp. 270-274.

Lary, H. B. (1968) *Imports of Manufactures from Less Developed Countries*, National Bureau of Economic Research, New York.

Mason, R. H. (1973) "Some observations on the Choice of Technology by Multi-national Firms in Developing Countries," *Review of Economics and Statistics*, Vol. 3, August, pp. 349-55.

Moody, Jr., C. E. (1974) "The Measurement of Capital Services by Electrical Energy," *Oxford University Institute Bulletin of Economics and Statistics*, Vol. 36, No 1, February, pp. 45-52.

Robinson, Joan (1958) *The Accumulation of Capital*, Macmillan Company Limited, London.

Steel, William F. (1977) *Employment Small-Scale and Production in Developing Countries: Evidence from Ghana* (Praeger Publishers, New York, London).

CHAPTER 7

Factor Substitution in Multi-Input and Non-Competitive Environment

Introduction

This chapter examines the pattern of technology in use in Ghanaian manufacturing using industrial establishment data belonging to 53 4-digit industries obtained through a survey conducted by the Central Bureau of Statistics (CBS) of Ghana. The data pertains to the year 1974. We examine whether alternative techniques are available, especially labour intensive type. We use the capital-labour ratio estimates in various establishments within given industries to study the range of technologies available to produce given goods. The finding of significant differences in techniques across establishments in a given industry are used to establish the fact that the range of techniques is wider than probably each establishment thinks it is.

An attempt is then made to understand and quantify at the establishment level the relationship between factor costs and choice of techniques by rank correlation and estimation of elasticities of substitution. The framework that we adopt to estimate elasticities of substitution tends to reduce some of the biases implicit in the assumptions made by Roemer (1974) and Steel (1977) for Ghana by the incorporation of imperfection in both the product and factor markets and the possibilities of non-constant returns. A three input production function which disaggregates the labour input into production and non-production labour is utilized in the estimation of elasticities of substitution.

In the following sections we examine the shelf of techniques for eight 4-digit industries the relationship between factor costs and choice of techniques. An attempt is made at quantitatively estimating elasticities of substitution.

The data employed in this chapter has been discussed in the previous chapter.

THE SHELF OF TECHNIQUES

From our sample of 375 manufacturing establishments, eight 4-digit industries involving 105 establishments were selected to make systematic comparisons of techniques used by various establishments within the industries. We calculated the value of plant, machinery and equipment per production worker for each establishment in each industry. The capital-labour ratios were used to represent the type of techniques for producing a given good. The purpose is to see whether the techniques for producing a given good vary substantially or whether the shelf of available techniques is in fact limited.

Before we present the empirical results, we briefly comment on their limitations as a guide to technological alternatives available in an industry, and warn that the evidences produced against the hypothesis of rigid technological coefficients are only crude and tentative.

    (i)   We must distinguish between technological possibilities available, which gives the knowledge about methods of production, and the technology in use or the methods being used. The latter is only a subset of the former and the technology in use may not fully reflect the technological possibilities if some of the known methods still remain unused. The data we have at the moment represent the technology in use because they come from already existing establishments. Hence, the range of alternatives indicated by our data may be narrower than the range that could be available.[3]

    (ii)   The data does not claim to represent the full range of techniques in use in Ghana, since our sample does not give an exhaustive list of technologies actually in use, and this may further limit the range of alternatives shown by our data.

    (iii)   Several factors may account for differences in capital-labour ratios such as scale, age and management.

    (iv)   Some of the establishments reported are very old, and it is not certain whether the type of equipment used by them is still produced in the contemporary world.

We now look at the data. Table 7.1 (i) to (viii) show the range of technologies for the eight selected 4-digit industries: bakery products (3117), knitting (3213), products of leather (3233), foot wear (3240), furniture and fixtures (3320), drugs and medicines (3522), plastics (3560), and transport and equipment (3843). The industries show large variations in technologies among establishments. In the bakery industry, for example, the variation is from 0.071 thousands to 5.69 thousands, with a coefficient of variation of 106.8%. In the knitting industry, the coefficient of variation is 82%. In plastics, we observe a capital-intensity as low as 381 cedis and as high as 21,667 cedis, while similar significant variation in capital-intensity is found in other industries. But one must be careful in drawing policy implications from the data assembled. But identifying the various technologies within an industry as alternatives is not easy, since different alternatives may not be providing the same amount of output, for lower capital-labour alternative may not be efficient. Whatever the limitations of the data, it seems the available evidence can be depended upon to cast doubts on the limited substitution possibilities hypothesis.

The evidence assembled has revealed a wide range of variation in capital-intensity employed by different establishments. The question that we ask is, "do these alternatives provide labour-intensive technologies?" To answer this question for our sample of 375 establishments, we classified the technologies into "capital-intensive", "intermediate" and "labour-intensive" categories. The technological strata is defined, according to whether capital-intensity, used as a proxy for technological level, is higher than total manufacturing average, lower than 65 percent of it or whether it is located between these two, as capital-intensive, labour-intensive and intermediate respectively.[4] Table 7.2 gives the number of establishments in each technology stratum by industry. It must be noted that footwear is made entirely by utilizing labour-intensive techniques. The remaining industries show establishments in more than one stratum, suggesting the existence of technological options in the production of almost all the industrial products in Ghana. The results show the presence of heterogeneity conditions.

The labour-intensive industries include almost all the establish-ments in clothing, leather and rubber. The capital-intensive stratum includes a variety of food products, plastics, transport equipment, textiles. It seems the empirical evidence on choice of techniques in Ghanaian manufacturing points towards labour-intensive industries.

There exists technological alternatives in most industries, and the evidence suggests that most of the alternatives are concentrated within the labour-intensive stratum, but choice of technology still has important implications for employment in various industries.

Table 7.1: Capital-Labour Ratios in Selected Establishments in Manufacturing, 1974

	PME (¢'000)	LP (¢'000)	K/L		PME	LP	K/L		PME	LP	K/L
(i)	**Bakery Products Establishment**			**(ii)**	**Furniture Establishment**			**(iii)**	**Leather Products Establishment**		
A	15.8	8	1.975	A	3.2	10	0.229	A	83.5	56	1.491
B	0.5	7	0.071	B	17.0	29	0.586	B	20.0	60	0.333
C	0.6	8	0.075	C	144.5	88	1.642	C	6.7	14	0.479
D	33.2	24	1.383	D	14.0	86	0.163	D	12.3	23	0.535
E	13.2	16	0.825	E	36.4	22	1.655	E	21.6	27	0.800
F	3.8	6	0.633	F	4.0	81	0.049	F	37.9	44	0.861
G	160.8	101	1.592	G	28.6	53	0.540	G	13.6	29	0.469
H	1.6	10	0.160	H	103.2	73	1.414	H	3.5	21	0.167
I	6.0	13	0.462	I	289.1	78	3.706	I	8.6	36	0.239
J	5.2	14	0.371	J	24.0	36	0.667	J	13.0	57	0.228
K	5.6	12	1.467	K	18.4	15	1.227	K	22.6	16	1.413
L	16.0	12	1.333	L	144.7	149	0.971	L	14.9	19	0.784
M	17.7	12	1.475	M	4.8	18	0.267	M	13.5	50	0.270
N	955.9	168	5.690	N	2.9	8	0.363				
O	27.9	18	1.550	O	5.3	40	0.133	Mean			0.628
P	31.0	18	1.722	P	3.6	40	0.090	S.D.			0.415
Q	3.3	6	0.550	Q	27.3	125	0.218	Coeff. of var			66.1%
				R	24.6	32	0.769	Range			0.167–1.491
Mean			1.196	S	49.6	77	0.644				
S.D.			1.277	T	40.0	100	0.400				
Coeff. of var			106.8%	U	39.0	78	0.500				
Range			0.071–5.69	V	39.0	9	4.333				
				W	1.1	11	0.100				
				X	4.6	4	1.150				
				Mean			0.909				
				S.D.			1.056				
				Coeff. of var			116.2%				
				Range			0.049–4.33				

Table 7.1 (*cont'd.*)

	PME	LP	K/L		PME	LP	K/L		PME	LP	K/L
(iv)	*Transport Establishment*			(vi)	*Footwear Establishment*			(viii)	*Drugs and Medicines Establishment*		
A	27.4	134	0.204	A	94.0	104	0.903	A.	33.0	33	1.000
B	35.2	140	0.204	B	69.3	114	0.608	B	4.9	37	0.132
C	37.5	155	0.242	C	585.2	353	1.659	C	26.0	118	0.220
D	47.9	120	0.399	D	103.5	124	0.835	D	144.0	38	3.789
E	81.3	29	2.803	E	29.9	64	0.467	E	22.9	12	0.908
F	40.8	29	1.407	F	10.2	18	0.567	F	28.5	29	0.983
G	53.2	239	0.224	G	25.2	43	0.586	G	13.2	51	0.259
H	639.3	58	11.022	H	6.4	83	0.077	H	59.4	69	0.861
I	110.1	172	0.640	I	3.5	3	1.167	I	244.0	46	5.304
J	20.7	34	0.609	J	4.9	5	0.980	J	5.6	62	0.090
K	337.4	143	2.359					K	147.8	41	3.605
L	86.9	36	2.414								

Mean	1.881			Mean			0.780	Mean			1.100
S.D.		2.907		S.D.			0.410	S.D.			0.410
Coeff. of var	154.5%			Coeff. of vąr	52.2%			Coeff. of var		52.2%	
Range	0.204-11.022			Range	0.077-1.659			Range	0.090-3.789		

	PME	LP	K/L		PME	LP	K/L
(v)	*Knitting Establishment*			(vii)	*Plastics Establishment*		
A	48.1	48	1.002	A	95.1	30	3.170
B	1,779.4	298	5.971	B	36.1	50	7.226
C	209.8	203	1.033	C	12.2	32	0.381
D	179.2	40	4.480	D	1,824.2	181	10.078
E	429.5	97	4.428	E	292.6	100	2.926
F	16.4	159	0.103	F	428.0	49	8.730
G	12.9	35	0.369	G	195.6	46	4.252
H	171.6	61	2.813	H	64.6	30	2.153
				I	65.0	3	21.667

Mean		2.525	Mean		6.186
S.D.		2.075	S.D.		6.000
Coeff. of var	82.2%		Coeff. of var	97.0%	
Range	0.103-5.971		Range	0.381-21.667	

Notes: PME — Plant Machinery and Equipment
Lp — Production Labour
K/L — CapitalIntensity

Table 7.2: Number of Establishments by Technology and Industry

| Industry | Technology Strata | | | |
	Capital-Intensive	Intermediate	Labour-Intensive	Total
Food	14	2	23	39
Beverage	4	2	8	14
Textiles	9	6	10	25
Clothing	5	1	26	32
Leather	1	1	12	14
Footwear			10	10
Wood	12	7	36	55
Furniture and Fixtures	4	2	18	24
Paper and Paper products	2	2	4	8
Printing and Publishing	3	3	17	23
Chemicals	7	7	18	32
Rubber	1		5	6
Plastics	6	1	3	10
Non-metallic minerals	4	4	11	19
Fabricated metal products	8	3	16	27
Electrical machinery	3	2	6	11
Transport and equipment	5	3	6	14
Miscellaneous[a]	3	1	8	12
Total	91	47	237	375

[a] Includes establishments from industries 314, 371, 382.

DIFFERENTIAL FACTOR COSTS AND CHOICE OF TECHNIQUES

The preceding section has revealed the substitution possibilities in manufacturing. It is of interest to investigate further the factor proportions of the establishments and effects of different factor costs. Factor price distortions are evident in Ghana. Thus the range of technologies that we have observed for Ghanaian manufacturing may be attributed to distortions in factor markets that lead establishments to have different factor costs. We find the relationship between factor cost levels and capital-intensiveness of establishments, by testing the hypothesis that, capital-intensive technology is concentrated in establishments, which use an expensive labour input. Data on relative labour costs are needed to conduct this test.

Table 7.3 shows the structure of manufacturing wage costs by six skill categories. Inter-industry differences adjusted for skill levels are significant, ranging from a coefficient of variation of 35.2% for unskilled production labour to 115.4% for the "other" category. Intra-industry differentials are also important and could influence factor combinations. Other hypotheses can be tested by comparing wage cost levels[5] with capital-intensity in establishments. Ranks were

Table 7.3: Wage Rates in Cedis per Man-Made by Industry and Skill Category, 1974

Industry	ISIC CODE	I	II	III	IV	V	VI	VII
Food	311/12	1,094	1,631	6,524	1,662	9,447	1,132	1,616
Beverages	313	566	961	9,973	1,432	6,960	332	1,442
Textiles	321	640	665	7,280	967	4,436	1,236	792
Clothing	322	521	594	7,614	5,947	3,078	351	797
Leather	323	373	400	1,923	782	4,098	–	526
Footwear	324	689	841	7,118	711	5,286	254	949
Wood	331	386	859	4,159	1,727	4,975	334	916
Furniture	332	466	618	4,021	934	6,679	284	760
Paper	341	567	823	3,882	855	6,053	226	980
Printing and Publishing	342	390	1,006	4,222	1,554	6,922	929	1,008
Industrial Chemicals	351	381	896	5,295	1,540	4,161	497	1,156
Other Chemicals	352	738	758	5,081	1,267	6,146	795	297
Rubber	355	226	691	6,179	1,017	4,244	150	735
Plastics	356	510	513	3,181	1,016	2,621	–	766
Non-metalic minerals	36	788	1,049	5,092	1,362	4,915	449	1,144
Fabricated Metals	381	535	957	6,843	1,732	3,494	415	1,220
Electrical Machinery	383	626	828	6,645	1,443	5,997	4,297	1,538
Transport	384	668	738	5,937	771	10,464	970	957
Other	39[a]	850	1,214	9,962	1,676	3,082	1,197	1,967

Source and Notes: Computed from CBS 1974 establishment files.

a. Included in 'other' category are 314, 371, 385, and 390.

  I   *Unskilled production workers.*

 II   *Semi-skilled and skilled production workers.*

III   *Professional, managerial and administrative workers.*

IV   *Technical, clerical and sales.*

 V   *Working proprietors.*

VI   *Other category.*

VII   *All persons engaged.*

assigned to establishments in Table 7.1 in order of magnitude of wage cost levels with 1 assigned to the largest rank and n the lowest. The degree of correlation is confirmed by statistical analysis. Spearman rank correlation coefficient was used to measure the degree of correlation. Table 7.4 gives the Spearman rank correlation coefficients for eight industries. There is statistically significant correlation, though the sensitivity of capital-intensity to factor cost levels varies within the manufacturing sector.

Table 7.4: Correlation of Factor Cost Levels with
Capital-Intensity in Establishments

Industry	Spearman
Bakery	0.436**
Knitting	0.286
Products of leather	0.692***
Footwear	–0.042
Furniture	–0.289*
Drugs and medicines	0.523*
Plastics	0.345
Transport equipment	0.434

*** Significant at 1% level
** Significant at 5% level
* Significant at 10% level

MEASURING ELASTICITIES OF SUBSTITUTION

The previous sections have made observations on the possibilities of factor substitution in Ghanaian manufacturing industries. We make an attempt here to derive quantitative estimates of elasticities of substitution to supplement the information on factor substitution. We do recognize the severe problems involved with empirical elasticities of substitution estimates, and these have been examined in Baah-Nuakoh [2002]. We shall attempt to reduce the biases by relaxing some of the unrealistic assumptions which are usually made in econometric estimation, assume imperfection in both product and factor market and non-constant returns to scale. The biases are further reduced by the use of micro data.

Methods and Problems of Estimation

Assume that the underlying production process can be described by the CES production function with non-constant returns to scale.

$$(1) \quad Q_i = \gamma_i [\, \alpha_i K_i^{-\rho} + \alpha_2 L_i^{-\rho}]^{-v/\rho}$$

where
> Q is value added;
> L is homogeneous labour input;
> K is capital input;
> γ_i is efficiency parameter;
> α_i is distribution parameter;
> v is returns to scale;
> ρ is substitution parameter; and
> σ is $1/(1+\rho)$.

We assume imperfection in both the product and factor markets. The product demand curve is:

$$(2) \quad Q_i = Q_i(P_i)$$

where P_i is the price of the product.

Assuming profit maximization, the factor market equilibrium condition is given by:

$$(3) \quad (\partial Q / \partial L)_i = w/p[(1+E_L)/(1+\eta)]$$

$$(4) \quad (\partial Q / \partial K)_i = r/p[1+EK)/(1+\eta)]$$

where
> η is elasticity of product demand;
> E_L is elasticity of labour supply;
> E_K is elasticity of capital supply;
> w is earnings per employee;
> and r is return on capital.

Partially differentiating equation (1) with respect to L_i and K_i and substituting into equations (3) and (4) respectively we derive equations (5) and (6).

(5) $(\partial Q / \partial L)_i = v\alpha_2 \gamma^{-\rho/v} Qi^{\rho (\rho+v)/v} L_i^{-\rho-1}$

$\qquad = w/p[(1+E_L)/(1+\eta)]$

(6) $(\partial Q / \partial K)_i = v\alpha_1 g^{-\rho/v} Q_i^{\rho (\rho+v)/v} K_i^{-\rho-1}$

$\qquad = r/p[1+E_K)/(1+\eta)]$

Equation (5) can be rewritten as:

(5a) $v\alpha_2 \gamma^{-\rho/v} Q_i Q_i^{\rho/v} L_i^{-\rho-1} = w/p[(1+E_L)/(1+\eta)]$

Multiplying and dividing the LHS by Q^ρ we have

(7) $v\alpha_2 \gamma^{-\rho/v} (Q /L_i)^{1+\rho} Q_i^{\rho[(1-v)/v]} = w/p[(1+E_L)/(1+n)]$

Therefore,

(8) $(Q/L_i)^{1+\rho} = [v\alpha_2 \gamma^{-\rho/v}]^{-1} Q_i^{-\rho [(1-v)/v]} w/p[(1+E_L)/(1+\eta)]$

Likewise equation (6) can be rewritten:

(9) $(Q/K)_i^{1+\rho} = [v\alpha_1 \gamma^{-\rho/v}]^{-1} Q_i^{-\rho[(1-v)/v]} r/p[(1+E_K)/(1+\eta)]$

Taking logs of (8) and (9) and dividing by $(1+\rho)$ we derive equations (10) and (11) respectively.

(10) $\log (Q/L)_i = \sigma \log [v\alpha_2\gamma^{\rho/v}]^{-1} + \sigma \log w + (-\sigma) \log p$

$\qquad + \sigma \log [(1+ E_L)/(1+ \eta)] + [(1-\sigma)(v-1)]/v \log Q$

(11) $\log (Q/K)_i = \sigma \log [v\alpha_1 \gamma^{-\rho/v}]^{-1} + s \log r + (-\sigma) \log p$

$\qquad + \sigma \log [(1+ E_K)/(1+ \eta)] + [(1-\sigma)(v-1)]/v \log Q$

Estimates of elasticity of substitution with standard ACMS model exclude the terms:

(a) product market imperfection term

$\qquad -\sigma \log P_i$ and $\sigma \log (1+\eta)$

(b)   factor market imperfection term

$$\sigma \log (1+E_K) \text{ and } \sigma \log (1+E_L)$$

(c)   non-constant returns to scale term

$$[(1-\sigma)(v-1)]/v \log Q_i$$

and also assumes that $\sigma \log [v\alpha_2 \gamma^{-\rho/v}]^{-1}$ and $\sigma \log [v\alpha_1 \gamma^{-\rho/v}]^{-1}$ are constants or independent of log w_i and log r_i respectively. If these excluded variables are correlated with the included explanatory variables, their omission leads to bias in the estimate of $\hat{s}$. In this case estimate, s will be biased upwards if product and factor market imperfection and non-constant returns to scale prevail, and s is correlated with the wage rate and the price of capital.

Moroney (1970) warns that if one suspects the presence of non-constant returns to scale or imperfect competition in his sample observations, but, their extent is not known, it is desirable to use a method of estimation that is not sensitive to the nature of returns to scale or variation in market imperfection. He suggests a method of estimation that fulfils this requirement — constrained cost minimization. This method is also insensitive to the nature of γ and one does not need to obtain estimates of the γ parameter. The first order conditions for cost minimization is equality between rate of technical substitution and factor price ratio.

(12) $(\partial Q / \partial L)/(\partial Q /\partial K) = w/p[(1+E_L)/1+\eta)]/(1+E_K)/(1+\eta)$

(13) $(K/L) = (\alpha_1/\alpha_2)\sigma (w/r)[(1+E_L)/(1+E_K)]\sigma$

Taking logarithm of equation (13) we obtain the following estimating equation:

(14) $\log (K/L) = \sigma \log (\alpha_1/\alpha_2) + \sigma \log (w/r)$

$$+ \sigma \log [(1+E_L)/(1+E_K)]$$

The salient features of equation (14) are that one does not need data on the nature of returns to scale, and the nature of the product market imperfection.

For empirical analysis, we need estimates of supply elasticities E_L and E_K. We make the assumption that the competition in both the labour and capital markets are equally imperfect, that is, the elasticities of factor supplies are equal. This assumption of equal degree of imperfection is still less restrictive than the perfect competition assumption, and yet effectively simplifies the analysis. Introducing this assumption into (14) we obtain the estimating equation (15).

(15) $\log (K/L)_i = \text{constant} + \sigma \log (w/r)_i$

If we assume a 3-input production function, capital, skilled labour and unskilled labour, the CES production function can be written as

(16) $Q_i = \gamma [\alpha_1 K_i^{-\rho} + \alpha_2 LUS_i^{-\rho} + \alpha_3 LS_i^{-\rho}]^{-v/\rho}$

where, LUS is unskilled labour, LS is skilled labour. For this function, each partial elasticity of substitution is

$$\sigma_{ij} = 1/(1+\rho) = \sigma$$

for all i . . . j

that is, all pairs of the partial elasticity of substitution have the same constant value. From this flows the following equations:

(17) $\log (LS/LUS)_i = \text{constant} + \sigma \log (wus/ws)_i$

(18) $\log (K/LUS)_i = \text{constant} + \sigma \log (wus/r)_i$

(19) $\log (K/LS)_i = \text{constant} + \sigma \log (ws/r)_i$

The theoretical property of the CES function with multi input is $\sigma_{LUS/K} = \sigma_{LUS/LS} = \sigma_{LS/K}$. But we expect the empirical estimates to differ. For, whereas unskilled labour can sometimes be easily replaced by machinery, skilled labour may be difficult to replace. We might therefore hypothesize that the elasticity of substitution between capital and unskilled labour ($\sigma_{LUS/K}$) exceeds that between capital and skilled labour ($\sigma_{LS/K}$).

Alternative Estimates of Elasticities of Substitution

Equations (15), (17), (18) and (19) have been estimated for sample of 375 manufacturing establishments in 1974. The empirical results are presented in Table 7.5. We also report the results obtained for the elasticity of substitution using the ACMS methodology of regressing the log value added per employee on the log of the wage rate. Three different measures of capital were used: total fixed assets, energy, and plant, machinery and equipment. The cost of capital used here is the ratio of value added minus payrolls to capital stock.

There are differences in the results yielded by alternative specifications, and it is clearly evident that the form of the estimating equation exerts a noticeable influence on the range of estimates. The ACMS equations give higher estimates of the elasticity of substitution than the generalized equation (15) which incorporates imperfection in both the product and factor markets, and thus adds weight to Moroney's (1970) argument that the ACMS model has serious mis-specification problems. The lower estimates could also be attributed to measurement errors in the factor prices especially in the cost of capital.

The lower estimates of the log of value-added capital equations than in the log of value added employee equation could be attributed to the measurement errors in capital. Theoretically, the two equations should give identical estimates of elasticity of substitution. The fixed assets measure of capital gives higher estimates than the other measures of capital. Using the results in Table 7.5, a few hypotheses were tested.

Hypothesis I: Capital is not substitutable for labour.

We perform the test which corresponds to the hypothesis of fixed proportions function:

$$Ho : \sigma = 0 \qquad\qquad H_A : \sigma \neq 0$$

Table 7.5 shows the null hypothesis is rejected at the 0.01 probability level for 12 out of the 13 cases examined. These results indicate that Ghanaian manufacturing does not present a rigid technological struc- ture of fixed proportions.

Hypothesis II: Unskilled labour is not substitutable for skilled labour

We test the hypothesis that the elasticity of substitution between skilled labour and unskilled labour is zero:

$$H_0 : \sigma_{LUS/LS} = 0 \qquad\qquad H_A : \sigma_{LUS/LS} \neq 0$$

Table 7.5: Regression Equations for Total Manufacturing

Dependent Variables	Constant Term	w	r	w/r	R^2	F
1. Q/L	1.072	0.717 (9.415)			0.192	88.6
2. Q/KFASSET	0.671		0.552 (17.889)		0.462	320.0
3. Q/KENERGY	3.311		0.322 (8.021)		0.147	64.3
4. Q/KPME	1.516		0.478 (11.883)		0.275	141.2
5. KFASSET/L	0.345			0.280 (8.053)	0.148	64.8
6. KENERGY/L	−2.366			0.099 (2.698)	0.019	7.2
7. KPME/L	−0.523			0.205 (4.995)	0.063	24.9
				wus/r		
8. MFASSET/LUS	0.721			0.273 (7.517)	0.132	56.5
9. KENERGY/LUS	−2.045			0.089 (2.301)	0.014	5.3
10. KPME/LUS	−0.165			0.2118 (5.051)	0.064	25.5
				ws/r		
11. KFASSET/LS	1.860			0.146 (4.926)	0.061	24.3
12. KENERGY/LS	−0.749			0.008* (0.280)	0.0002	0.08
13. KPME/LS	0.986			0.155 (4.606)	0.054	21.2
				wus/ws		
14. LS/LUS	−1.213			0.113 (5.306)	0.070	28.2

Notes. t-statistic in parenthesis below coefficients.

All variables are transformed into natural logarithms.

All coefficients are statistically significant at 0.01 probability level except where starred

The coefficient of log wus/ws in regression 14 measures the elasticity of substitution between skilled and unskilled labour. The null hypothesis can be rejected at the 0.01 probability level.

Regression 8–13 give estimates for $\sigma_{LUS/K}$ and $\sigma_{LS/K}$, the elasticities of substitution between skilled and capital, and unskilled labour and capital respectively. Theoretically, $\sigma_{LUS/K} = \sigma_{LS/K}$, but as we argued, they are not empirically and $\sigma_{LUS/K}$ exceeds $\sigma_{LS/K}$, which suggests that the substitutability between unskilled labour and capital is stronger than between capital and skilled labour.

Hypothesis III: The production function is Cobb Douglas

We test the null hypothesis, $\sigma = 1$ (Cobb-Douglas function) against the alternative hypothesis of $\sigma \neq 1$. We estimate the production functions, Cobb-Douglas and CES:

Cobb-Douglas: $log\ Q/L = log\ \gamma_1 + \alpha_1\ log\ K/L + \alpha_2\ log\ L$

CES : $log\ Q/L = log\ \gamma_2 + \alpha_3\ log\ K/L + \alpha_4 logL + \alpha_5[logK/L]^2$

We form the test statistic

$F = [(RSS_1 - RSS_0)/\ m]\ /[RSS_0\ /(n-k)]$

where RSS_0 is total (unconstrained) residual sum of squares under the alternative hypothesis of CES production function, RSS_1 the total (constrained) residual sum of squares under the null hypothesis of Cobb-Douglas production function, m is the number of additional parameters estimated in the unconstrained form, n is the sample size, and k is the number of estimated parameters in the unconstrained form. F is distributed with m and n-k degrees of freedom.

The estimated production functions for total manufacturing are:

Cobb Douglas: $log\ Q/L = 0.510 + 0.261 log\ K/L + 0.060 log\ L$ $r = 0.358$
(6.623)   (1.524)

CES: $log\ Q/L = 0.380 + 0.240 log\ K/L + 0.067 log\ L + 0.067[logK/L]^2$
(6.623)   (3.086)   (3.086)

$r = 0.387$

Table 7.6: A Test of the σ=1 Hypothesis

Description	Residual sum of Squares	Degrees of Freedom	Test Statistic	Critical Value of F
Cobb-Douglas	302.779	372		
CES	295.199	371		
$RSS_1 - RSS_0$	7.580	1	9.526	F(1,371)
				=
				3.84 (5%)
				6.63 (1%)

Table 7.6 presents the results of the test. We observe from the inspection of the Table that the null hypothesis is rejected at any reasonable level of significance. This implies that though some factor substitution exists in manufacturing, the elasticity of substitution is significantly different from unity. The elasticity of substitution lies between zero and unity.

Hypothesis IV: Industry Effects

In addition to the independent variables in the equations, representing factor costs, industry dummies representing industry groupings were also introduced into some of the regressions to test for the effects of industry differences. The establishments were grouped into 16 groups. The differential effects of the 16 industries were held constant by using 15 industry variables in addition to the intercept term in a multiple regression. This is called an analysis of covariance model (ACOV). The regression coefficients of the 15 dummy variables (denoted by α_{φ}, for j = 1,2, . . ., 15) measure the positive, zero, or negative differential effect each industry has relative to the intercept term (which measures the 16th industry). The dummy variable for establishment i is denoted by D_{ij} in the analysis of covariance model shown in the equation (20).

(20) $X_i = \alpha_0 + \Sigma \alpha j Dij + Relative\ factor\ cost$

where, D_{ij} = 0 or 1   i= 1, 2, . . . ,375

X_i = Q/L, KFASSET/L, KPME/L, and ENERGY/L

Table 7.7 presents the results of estimating equation (20). The substantial increase in R for ACOV model over the models in Table 7.5 indicates the great significance of the industry dummies. A test of the overall contribution of the industry dummies was undertaken. The testing procedure is identical to that used in Hypothesis III. The residual sum of squares was computed for both an unconstrained form (the ACOV model) and a constrained form (with the dummies), RSS_2 and RSS_3 respectively and form the test statistic:

$$[(RSS_3 - RSS_2)/m]/[RSS_2 / (n-k)]$$

which is distributed as F(m, n-k) under the null hypothesis

$$\alpha_1 = \alpha_2 = \ldots = \alpha_{15} = 0.$$

The results of the test are reported in Table 7.7 as F_1.

The industry effect is accepted for the Q/L and ENERGY/L models, while it is rejected for the KPME/L model. For the KFASSET/L model, no clear cut decision is readily apparent. At the 5 percent significance level the no industry effect hypothesis is rejected. But at the 1 percent level the hypothesis cannot be rejected. Overall, the joint contribution of the industry dummies can be considered as having significant effect on factor use. In addition, the t-ratios for several dummies are large so that one may say that the dummies are not only significant as a group, but are individually significant especially for the Q/L and ENERGY/L models. There is a tendency for the estimated elasticities of substitution to fall when industry dummies are introduced.

Given the significant joint influence of the dummies, an attempt was made to apply the system of equations (15), (17), (18), (19) and the ACMS model to the 15 industries individually. The results are set out in Table 7.8, which shows the elasticity of substitution estimates. The "miscellaneous" category was left out because it is a conglomerate of unrelated industries. The elasticities are generally positive and less than unity. The most interesting finding is the effect of disaggregation of the labour input on the elasticity estimates. For, using the t-test we note that only 6 out of the 15 estimates were significant at least at the 10 percent level for the ACMS model, 8 for the generalized model (equation 15). $\sigma_{LUS/K}$ and $\sigma_{LS/K}$ were significant in 8 and 9 industries respectively. $\sigma_{LUS/LS}$ was significant in 11 out of

Table 7.7: Regression Equations for Total Manufacturing with Industry Dummy Variables

	ACMS Q/L	t-Statistic	KFASSET/L	t-Statistic	ENERGY/L	t-Statistic	KPME/L	Statistic
Constant	1.328		0.540		-2.432		-0.516	
Factor price ratio	0.558	7.052	0.269*	7.658	0.083*	2.541	0.205*	4.904
Industries with dummy variables								
311/12 Food	-0.190	0.900	0.008	0.030	0.837*	3.127	0.311	0.935
313 Beverages	0.188	0.681	-0.107	0.290	0.057	0.167	-0.052	0.119
321 Textiles	-0.374	1.586	0.207	0.670	0.133	0.448	0.416	1.130
332 Clothung	-0.500*	2.239	-0.585*	2.004	-0.622*	2.221	-0.136	0.391
323 Leather	-0.675*	2.417	-0.738*	2.012	-0.995*	2.830	-0.175	0.400
324 Footwear	-0.468*	1.499	-0.480	1.158	-0.737*	1.857	-0.037	0.075
331 Wood	-0.367*	1.855	-0.186	0.719	0.937	3.768	-0.329	1.067
332 Furniture	-0.711*	3.023	0.626*	2.040	-0.594*	2.021	-0.341	0.934
341/42 Paper, printing and publishing	-0.559*	2.499	-0.460	1.567	-0.486*	1.727	0.167	0.477
351/52 Chemicals	-0.212	0.963	-0.057	0.195	-0.115	0.410	0.209	0.602
355/56 Rubber and plastics	-0.120	0.452	0.205	0.583	0.081	0.241	0.608	1.454
36 Non-metalic minerals	-0.652*	2.580	0.297	0.888	0.202	0.628	-0.251	0.630
Fabricated metals	-0.176	0.768	-0.012	0.039	0.022	0.076	-0.060	0.165
Electrical machinery	0.348	1.159	-0.168	0.420	0.379	0.990	0.374	0.788
Transport	0.026*	2.488	0.026*	1.862	0.006	0.418	0.032	1.952*
R^2	0.279		0.208		0.248		0.114	
F	8.633		5.875		7.390		2.877	
	(16,358)		(16,358)		(16,358)		(16,358)	
F_1	2.861		1.789		7.328		1.376	
	(15,358)		(15,358)		(15,358)		(15,358)	

Notes.   *Statistically significant at least at 0.10 probability level, two-tailed test

Table 7.8 : Elasticities of Substitution Estimates for
Manufacturing Subsectors

	ACMS (1)	K/L (2)	K/LUS (3)	K/LS (4)	LS/LUS (5)
311/12	0.984[a]	0.359[a]	0.378[a]	0.303[a]	0.371[c]
	(4.605)	(3.330)	(3.516)	(2.442)	(1.643)
313	1.646[a]	0.624[c]	0.540	0.482[c]	0.439[b]
	(5.029)	(1.906)	(1.664)	(1.802)	(2.161)
321	0.356	0.239[c]	0.237[c]	0.279[b]	0.805[a]
	(1.122)	(2.012)	(1.894)	(2.319)	(3.773)
322	1.026[a]	0.430[a]	0.374[a]	0.600[a]	0.653[a]
	(2.836)	(3.663)	(3.115)	(4.096)	(2.841)
323	0.623	0.315[b]	0.297[c]	0.256[b]	0.222
	(1.104)	(2.510)	(2.132)	(2.183)	(1.047)
324	0.362	0.122	0.090	0.280	1.039[c]
	(0.839)	(0.730)	(0.486)	(1.528)	(1.946)
331	0.213	0.345[a]	0.387[a]	0.311[a]	0.367[a]
	(1.085)	(4.293)	(4.445)	(3.620)	(2.909)
332	0.157	0.171	0.137	0.300[b]	0.334
	(0.561)	(1.479)	(1.210)	(2.385)	(1.663)
341/42	0.544[c]	0.489[a]	0.497[a]	0.579[a]	0.405[b]
	(1.933)	(4.287)	(4.130)	(4.471)	(2.056)
351/52	0.673[a]	0.145	0.180[c]	0.156	0.354[c]
	(2.712)	(1.533)	(1.790)	(1.453)	(1.670)
355/56	0.322	0.163	0.263	0.240	0.479[c]
	(0.840)	(0.787)	(1.506)	(0.846)	(1.998)
36	0.570[a]	0.016	0.162	0.072	0.467
	(2.875)	(0.094)	(0.877)	(0.301)	(2.342)
381	0.497	0.357[a]	0.335[b]	0.444[a]	0.441[a]
	(1.614)	(2.526)	(2.383)	(2.924)	(2.661)
383	−1.068	0.192	0.235	0.149	0.714
	(1.178)	(1.001)	(1.022)	(0.566)	(1.546)
384	0.320	−0.074	−0.099	−0.108	−0.374
	(0.681)	(0.446)	(0.672)	(0.614)	(1.638)

Notes to Table 7.8: The figures in parantheses indicate the t-statistics
of the coefficients above them.
[a] indicates significance at 0.01 probability level.
[b] indicates significance at 0.05 probability level.
[c] indicates significance at 0.10 probability level.

the 15 industries, indicating some degree of substitutability between unskilled and skilled labour. None of the estimates for electrical (383) and transport equipment (384) industries was significant indicating that within the equipment industries substitution possibilities do not exist and inputs are used in fixed proportions.

How do we explain the non-significance of most of the estimates derived from the ACMS model? The most plausible explanation lies in the conditions under which the regression was estimated. It means that there are specification errors in using the ACMS model in an environment of non constant returns to scale and imperfections in factor and product markets. Another reason may be the 2-input framework used. A further explanation is more statistical, and suggests small differences in inter-establishment wage levels.

Conclusion

Combining the results on the shelf of techniques with the statistical estimation of elasticity of substitution, the main conclusions that can be derived are the following; (i) the study has contributed to the empirical literature on the choice of techniques and assuming all relevant assumptions hold there is some possibility of substitution between capital and labour, which suggests that producers are responsive to variations in factor costs ratios; (ii) the fact, that in a majority of cases the elasticity of substitution estimate is significantly different from unity suggests that the characterization of the production technology for Ghanaian manufacturing industries by Cobb Douglas may not be a correct practice; (iii) a methodology for estimating elasticity of substitution which is not sensitive to the nature of returns to scale or variation in market imperfection is more appropriate; (iv) a framework of estimation which disaggregates the factor inputs gives better results.

NOTES

1. The data was collected in 1977 from files of industrial establishments kept at the Central Bureau of Statistics.
2. The following criteria for selection were used to discard some of the establishment : establishments with (i) incomplete data; (ii) number of persons less than 4; (iii) book value of plant, machinery and equipment ≤ 0; (iv) payments to capital factor obtained as the difference between value added and total labour cost ≤ 0; (v) value added ≤ 0.

3. R. Islam (1977), evidence from selected plants from selected countries based on UNIDO *Profile of Manufacturing Establishments* Vols. I , II, and III provide data on alternatives available in the world and cast doubt about the hypothesis that opportunity for capital-labour substitution in many industries is very limited.

4. The classification of technology can be done in a number of ways, and the classification we have used is obviously arbitrary. As a proxy for technology we have used KINT2 (fixed assets per employee).

5. The wage cost levels were calculated on the basis of average price earnings ratio. The survey information gave data on wage bills for the various skill categories. The wage cost level in skill category j

$$W_{ij} = \sum_{j=1}^{n} WB_{ij} \, / \, \Sigma L_{ij} \qquad\qquad i = 1 \ldots z$$

WB_{ij} is the wage bill of establishment i, L_{ij} is labour input of establishment i in skill category j.

6. See for example, Katz (1969), pp. 73–75, Moroney (1970), Kmenta (1971), pp. 391-4-5, Girgis (1974), for a discussion of effects of specification errors on elasticity of substitution estimates.

REFERENCES

Central Bureau of Statistics, *Industrial Statistics*, Accra Periodical Series.

Girgis, Maurice (1974) "Aggregation and Misspecification of Biases in Estimates of Factor Elasticity of substitution: The Case of Egypt", *Weltwirschaflliches Archiv*, Bond 110, Heft 1, pp. 114–147.

Griliches, Z. and V. Ringstad (1971) *Economies of Scale and the Form of the Production Function*, North Holland Publishing Co., Amsterdam, London.

Islam, Rizwanul (1977) "Some Constraints on the choice of Technology," *The Bangladesh Development Studies*, Vol. 5, No. 3 July, pp. 255–79.

Katz, J. (1969) *Production Functions, Foreign Investments and Growth*, North Holland Publishing Co.

Kmenta (1971) *Elements of Econometrics*, Macmillan Publishing Co. Inc., New York.

Moroney, J. R. (1970) "Identification and Specification Analysis of Alternative Equations for Estimating the Elasticity of Substitution," *The Southern Economic Journal*, Vol. XXXVI, No. 3, January, pp. 287–299.

Roemer, Michael (1975) "The Neoclassical Employment Model Applied to Ghanaian Manufacturing," *Journal of Development Studies*, Vol. 11, No. 2, January, pp. 75–92.

Steel, William F. (1977) *Small-scale Employment and Production in Developing Countries: Evidence from Ghana* (Praeger Publishers, New York, London).

CHAPTER 8

Departures from the Frontier: An Analysis of Firm Level X-Inefficiency

Introduction

Attempts have been made to quantify the magnitude of x- or technical inefficiency among firms and farms in both the developed and developing economies.[1] Leibenstein (1966) has argued that losses from x-inefficiency may be more important than losses from allocative inefficiency. Recently, Page Jr. (1980) has explored the relationship between choice of technique, technical efficiency and economic performance in three industries in Ghana, logging, sawmilling and furniture manufacturing. The results of his estimates of technical efficiency revealed relatively high levels of average efficiency, which he explains reflect both the age and the structure of the individual industries.

In this chapter, x-inefficiency levels are measured for establishments of 16 manufacturing industries as departures from an efficiency frontier based on Farell's (1957) seminal paper on the measurement of productive efficiency using firm level data of Ghanaian manufacturing industries. The estimates permit measurements of relative performance of establishments within an industry and thereby give a picture of the structure of industry. A technique of production is technically efficient if it uses a smaller input combination for a given amount of a product.

We also in this chapter examine the relationship between competition and x-efficiency. Competition in the domestic product market and also the subjection of home producers to foreign competition tend to improve factor efficiency. The process of competition tends to eliminate producers with high costs, and the market enjoyed by the firms allow them to remain in business, even though they might be inefficient producers. Secondly, the process of competition by mounting pressures on firms profits tends to make management more disciplined and employees tend to utilize inputs more effectively than in the case where competition is absent. Thus, imperfect competition is a necessary condition for the existence of much of x-inefficiency.

In Ghana, the post-independence attempts to industrialize led to the creation of oligopolistic-monopolistic market structures and minimal competition. A wide range of industries were established, each dominated by a few firms. The degree of competition in product markets is related to the number and size distribution of competing units. The smaller the number of competing units and the more skewed their size distribution the lower is the probability that there will be aggressively competition.

The monopolists and oligopolists created continue to enjoy their power and created inefficiencies because of substantial barriers to entry into the various industries both at the production and marketing stages. Three barriers are usually identified, Bain (1956):(i) economies of scale, (ii) control of scarce factors, and (iii) absolute capital requirements. A fourth barrier more relevant to developing economies emphasized by White (1947a,b) is the conglomeration of tariffs, licences and sometimes outright bans on competing imports. Most of these categories of barriers have been created by government policies. Over-valued exchange rates prevail with consequent foreign exchange licensing and rationing; capital goods spare parts and raw materials are available to holders of scarce import licences at favourable exchange rates and low or zero tariffs. At the same time, consumption goods are imported at unfavourable exchange rates and high tariffs. Thus, those who have access to import licences have highly profitable markets for which they can produce. The tariffs, quotas and complete bans on finished goods provide a marketing barrier and the licences create a scarce resource barrier. The effect of this imperfect market structure is that entrepreneurs are able to trade off some of the potential benefits from cost minimization for inefficiency.

THE EFFICIENCY FRONTIER

Efficiency measures are often based on unit requirements of inputs, that is, production is transformed from the factor space into a space of input coefficients, $\varepsilon = (\varepsilon_1, \varepsilon_2 \dots \varepsilon_n)$.

$$X = f((v/x)x) = f(\varepsilon_x)$$

where X is output, and V is a vector $(V_1, \dots, V_n)$ of inputs. The

efficiency frontier can then be defined as the set of points where the
input coefficients $(\varepsilon_1, \ldots, \varepsilon_n)$ obtain their minimum values along rays
from the origin. Technical or X-inefficiency relates to an individual
firm's failure to produce on the efficiency frontier.

Let us illustrate the methodology with two inputs V_1 and V_2 for
product X. For this product, we calculate a unit isoquant which shows
the technique currently in use for producing this product. For each
establishment producing X, we calculate V_1 and V_2 per unit of output.
These points are plotted in Figure 8.1. There are twelve establishments
producing X, and thus, twelve points on the graph. There are five
efficient points — that is, points where combination of V_1 and V_2 is
such that reducing the amount of one input requires an increase in
the amount of the other input. Joining these efficient point traces out
an isoquant made up of the most efficient establishments. The
efficiency frontier EE represents a point of reference for measuring
relative inefficiency of the rest of the industry. It does not represent
the optimum factor combination but instead is an approximation to
the best practice techniques in actual use. This approach permits the

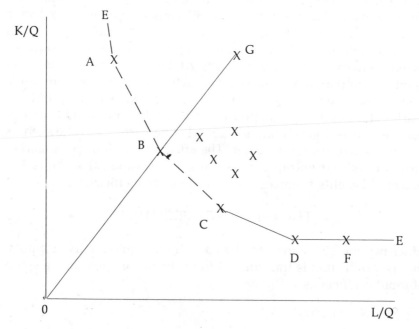

Fig 8.1: **Efficiency Frontier**

comparison of actual performance of establishments with the best practices actually existing in the economy, instead of using as a point of reference ideal combinations of inputs, which might not be feasible. F represents the most efficient labour-intensive establishment within the industry. If all establishments were as efficient as F, considerable benefits (in terms of output and employment) would accrue to the economy. Some advantages, which may be attributed to this approach, include the following: (i) it is not necessary to specify a functional form for the underlying production function; (ii) it can handle establishments using heterogeneous techniques; (iii) individual observation (for example, establishment) specific measures of technical efficiency can be computed.

The methodology is also beset with a number of deficiencies. The methodology is sensitive to extreme observations and measurement error; under-utilization of capacity may also introduce biases in estimating the real frontier; the results are relative in nature and also the number of observations included in the efficiency frontier is small regardless of the number of observations in the sample. To be able to identify genuine efficiency frontiers, we assume away the following factors: (i) that the output of each industry is fairly homogeneous enough, otherwise the more technically efficient establishments may be producing different products; (ii) that there is constant returns to scale; and (iii) that the sample of establishments in fact throws up examples which are good estimates of the technical efficient frontier.

MEASUREMENT OF FACTOR EFFICIENCY

The Measures

Two different measures of factor efficiency denoted by XF_1 and XF_2 are calculated for each establishment to measure the deviation of establishments from the most efficient technology. The XF_1 measure is obtained by comparing an observed input coefficient point for an establishment with an input coefficient on the efficiency frontier along a given ray from the origin. Thus, technical efficiency XF_1 of an establishment with observed input coefficient represented by G in Figure 8.1 is measured by the OB/OG. As the ratio approaches 1.00, maximum technical efficiency for the establishment is approached. Establishment G is using more of both inputs for the same level of output and is thus, technically inefficient. This deviation is reflected for example, in poor management skills, work stoppages, material bottlenecks and low employee effort. If these inefficiencies could be eliminated, the establishment could produce on the frontier.

Another measure, XF_2 measures the deviation of each establishment in a given industry in its choice of technology of the most labour-intensive establishment in the industry, which is also technically efficient:

$$XF_2 = \frac{\text{actual (K/L) in establishment i}}{\substack{\text{(K/L) of most efficient labour} \\ \text{intensive establishment in industry}}}$$

If XF_2 is greater than unity the establishment employed an excessively capital-intensive technology, and therefore there are potential employment gains from other establishments approximating this efficient labour-intensive technology.

The Evidence on X-Efficiency

The data employed has been drawn from unpublished surveys of establishments conducted by the Central Bureau of Statistics. The data and sample characteristics have been discussed in Chapter 6. The analysis is thus based on data for 375 manufacturing establishments grouped into sixteen 3-digit ISIC groups.

Output is measured by value added (cedis). Capital is measured by book value of fixed assets. The book value which is the written down value of fixed assets does not reflect the productive capacity of the assets because of the following factors:

(a) the prices of capital goods have increased over time, while the reported figures are not adjusted for the increase in the price of capital stock. Thus, identical plants may differ in book values merely because of different price levels at the time of purchase;

(b) the reported figures on fixed assets are arrived at by applying the depreciation rates allowed by the government, often tempered with differential incentives considerations, rather than the actual pattern of depreciation which differ from the accelerated depreciation rates;

(c) machines of different vintages are not of the same quality; machine of recent vintages embody more advanced technology and may thus have higher productive efficiency.

Labour input used is the total persons engaged which is the sum of the various skill groups provided by the questionnaire. This is the unweighted sum of unskilled production labour, skilled production labour, professional, managerial and administrative labour, technical, clerical and office workers, working proprietors, and other miscellaneous labour. The labour input used assumes that all types of labour are equally productive. The use of homogeneous labour may hide inter-establishment variability and may lead to differences in technical efficiency.

Using value added, capital and input data, the Farell efficiency frontier is derived for each of the sixteen 3-digit manufacturing industry groups. The frontiers are generated by plotting the labour-value added and capital-value added ratios and constructing a unit isoquant.

Efficiency indices XF_1 and XF_2 were calculated for each establishment from the efficiency frontier estimates. Bearing in mind the empirical qualifications expressed above about the construction of Farell's efficiency frontier, Table 8.1 illustrates the wide range of relative technical efficiency among the industrial establishments in Ghana. The results have been condensed at the industry level for the industry groups, and they show widespread X-inefficiency that exists in the manufacturing sector.

We observe that 37.9% of the industrial establishments have a relative X-efficiency less than one quarter and 64.6% less than one-half to that achieved by the establishments located on the efficiency frontiers. Differences in the degree of inefficiency show across industries. For example, in an industry such as textiles (321), 80% of the establishments have a relative degree of efficiency less than one-half, while in others such as beverages (313) only 35.7% of the establishments have a relative efficiency degree under one-half. Fourteen out of the sixteen industry groups have 50% or more of their establishments with relative X-efficiency under 0.5. The results of substantial X-inefficiency in Ghana manufacturing are consistent with Meller (1976) findings for Chilean firms and for plastic and steel industries in Brazil as found by Tyler (1979).

The results for XF_2 index of efficiency are also reported in Table 8.1. This index uses the capital-intensity of the most efficient labour-

Table 8.1: Relative Efficiency in Ghanaian Manufacturing 1974

ISIC Code	Industry	No. of establishments	No. of establishments on frontier	Range of efficiency (XF_1) Coefficients				No. of establishment with XF_2 less than unity
				1.00 0.75	0.74 0.50	0.49 0.25	0.24 0.00	
311/12	Food	39	6	6	2	10	21	3
313	Beverages	14	8	8	1	4	1	0
321	Textiles	25	3	3	2	7	13	0
322	Clothing	32	6	6	3	6	17	17
323	Leather	14	3	4	2	6	2	2
324	Footwear	10	4	4	-	4	2	0
331	Wood	55	11	13	8	16	18	1
332	Furniture	24	5	5	2	9	8	0
341/342	Paper, printing publishing	31	8	8	2	10	11	1
351/52	Chemicals	32	7	8	3	10	11	0
355/356	Rubber and plastics	16	5	5	1	3	7	2
36	Non-metal minerals	19	4	6	2	3	8	2
381	Fabricated metal products	27	7	11	3	5	8	0
383	Electrical machinery	11	3	3	-	1	7	1
384	Transport equipment	14	6	6	-	2	6	3
39	Other manufacturing[a]	12	5	5	1	4	2	0
3	All firms	375		101	32	100	142	32
	Relative percentages			(26.9)	(8.5)	(26.7)	(37.9)	

Sources and Notes: The estimates were derived from the efficiency frontiers.

(a) include establishments from industry groups tobacco (314) and steel (371) and non-electrical Machinery (382) and professional and scientific instruments (385).

intensive establishments as the base. Out of a sample of 375 establishments, only 32 used more labour-intensive technology than the most efficient labour-intensive establishments. The clothing industry dominated this category of labour-intensive establishments.

Our results indicate that a large number of establishments using very inefficient production techniques survive in Ghana. It seems market forces do not punish inefficiency. This suggests that there are imperfectly competitive product and factor markets in Ghana which allow inefficient firms to operate and survive. This could be attributed to the various government policies which prevented foreign imports to compete with domestic firms.

In the next section, we shall explore the determinants of the levels of relative efficiency with the emphasis on the effects of the non-competitive environment.

SOURCES OF DIFFERENCES IN EFFICIENCY AMONG MANUFACTURING ESTABLISHMENTS

This section seeks to examine the determinants of X-efficiency. Since we have examined competition as the main theoretical cause of X-inefficiency, we set up a general regression model, which uses the computed efficiency indices as the dependent variable and various aspects of market structure as the independent variables. For the analysis we have to quantify the indicators of competition. However, there is no agreed measure of competition. Eight different measures are used: concentration ratio, relative establishment size, absolute establishment size, effective protection, export ratio, import competing ratio, foreign raw material ratio, and absolute capital requirements.

The concentration ratio is the most generally used measure of the competitive structure of an industry; the assumption in the use of concentration ratio is that the higher the degree of sellers concentration, the lower is the degree of competition. The concentration term is expected to have a negative effect on X- or technical efficiency. In this study the concentration measure used is based on sales of the reporting establishments.

CR_2 the share in 3-digit industries'
Sales of the two largest establishments.

CR_4 the share in 3-digit industries'
Sales of the four largest establishments.

The individual establishments were adjoined to the respective 3-digit industry. It is true that the 3-digit classification cannot be considered to depict markets in an economically meaningful sense. It can, however, be presumed that a certain degree of 3-digit concentration implies a similar degree of concentration in higher digit industries making up a particular 3-digit industry. We expect CR_2 to be a more relevant variable than CR_4 for two reasons. Firstly, the normal pattern in most developing economies industry groups is that one or two firms dominate the market and this warrants the use of an indicator of concentration of the top-1 or top-2 firms. Secondly, where industry groups have only three or four firms, the 2-firm measure can take into account the distributional difference within the top four firms.

A second measure of competition is the establishment's relative and absolute size. Size may be taken as an index of an establishment's capacity to exercise dominance in its industry:

RELATSIZE   the ratio of establishment's
Sales to total 3-digit industry sales

SIZE   indicating absolute size as measured
by number of persons engaged

Size should exert a negative effect on technical efficiency. Size was also introduced as a dummy variable. The establishments were categorized into three size groups: less than 30 persons engaged, 30–100 persons, and greater than 100 persons engaged.

DSIZE 1   a dummy = 1 for establishments with persons engaged < 30, and = 0 otherwise

DSIZE 2   a dummy = 1 for establishments with persons engaged >100, and = 0 otherwise

The excluded category is 30–100 size group.

The third dimension of monopolistic competition and barriers to competition included in our tests is the degree of foreign competition which provides a transmission mechanism for efficiency occurring in the world market and injects into the domestic market a set of competitors not counted in our conventional measures of concentration. The degree of foreign competition was represented by three variables — import competing (IMCOMP), export ratio (DEXPT) and effective protection (EFFEPROTECT).

>IMPCOMP   value of competing imports from other countries as percentage of domestic supply (production plus imports minus exports)

The variable IMPCOMP measures the stringency of the import licensing system; by increasing the competitiveness of a market, imports should tend to reduce the tacit collusion among domestic sellers. Effective protection rates (EFFEPROTECT) are introduced to define more precisely the oligopolistic environment in which domestic establishments operate. If effective protection rates are low, then domestic establishments will find themselves more exposed to foreign competition. Thus, effective protection should be negatively related to efficiency.

The extent of involvement of an establishment in the export market is measured by:

>DEXPT   a dummy variable = 1 if an establishment export 10% or more of its sales produce and = 0 otherwise.

The variable DEXPT should have a positive relation to efficiency. Several scarce resources are rationed by the government — capital credit and foreign exchange. Unfortunately, as one might expect, it is difficult to find out who gets what.

The extent of resource barrier is measured by using a surrogate variable:

>RMATFRATIO   the ratio of foreign materials to total material inputs.

Establishments which use a high proportion of imported raw materials, are presumed to be the ones which get the scarce foreign exchange and thus, their monopolistic-oligopolistic powers are accentuated. Thus, these establishments should be expected to be more technically inefficient. In a survey conducted by Steel (1977), he found out that cost of entry into business was rising rapidly, and was a threat to the growth of new small businesses. Fixed capital costs had risen very rapidly. Some of the entrepreneurs interviewed pointed out that the cost of starting a new business had approximately doubled since they bought their assets. In this chapter we attempted to measure the absolute capital requirements as a barrier to entry using (ABSKREQS):

ABSKREQS   book value of total fixed capital per employee

One would expect an establishment with absolute capital requirements barrier to be less efficient.

In order to examine the effects of the non-competitive environment of factor usage it is necessary to consider other explanatory variables as well. Some of the factors which we wish to consider capture differences in the characteristics of the product; others deal with characteristics of the establishment and the internal organization or management practices. The following managerial and organizational variables were considered: nationality of ownership, non-owner managed versus owner-managed, private versus state-control.

There appears to be a controversy over the effects of nationality of ownership on technology in developing economies, but the conventional wisdom is that foreign firms use more capital-intensive technology than domestically-owned firms, because of limited search behaviour and desire to use technology nearer to their domain of competence. With respect to efficiency, the contention is that foreign firms do possess greater levels of technical efficiency and utilize capacity more intensively. We introduced nationality into the model by incorporating two variables:

DNATI   a dummy = 1 if the establishment is wholly foreign owned and
= 0 otherwise

DNAT2   a dummy = 1 if the establishment is jointly-owned by foreigners domestic businessmen and = 0 otherwise

The excluded category is the wholly domestically-owned establishments.

A hypothesis attributed to McCain (1975) with respect to the effect of ownership-management type on efficiency was also tested. McCain refers to self-employed individuals as operating with perfect X-efficiency. A variable to represent the ownership-management type was included.

> DMANAG a dummy variable = 1 if the establishment is
> owner-managed
> And = 0 if non-owner managed

State-owned and controlled establishments it is contended, are less efficient than their private counterparts [Leibenstein, 1978, pp. 171–78]. To capture this a dummy variable (DOWN) is used.

> DOWN a dummy variable = 1 if the establishment is
> privately-owned
> and = 0 if it is state-owned.

A variable (DPROCESS) was employed to indicate whether an industry was chemical or process related; these kinds of industries might be more rigid in their capital-labour requirements and less susceptible to labour substitution, and tend to be more efficient.

> DPROCESS   a dummy variable = 1 if the establishment is a
> chemical or process
> related industry
> and = 0 otherwise.

DENDUSE was included specifically to capture inter-industry differences in the nature of production. The use to which the product is put, whether consumer, intermediate or producer good is represented by

> DENDUSE 1 a dummy variable = 1 if the establishment
> belongs to an intermediate
> goods industry
> and = 0 otherwise

> DENDUSE 2 a dummy variable = 1 if the establishment
> belongs to a producer
> goods industry
> and = 0 otherwise.

The excluded category is the consumer goods industry.

An attempt was made to analyze the effects of the relative experience — learning by doing — of establishments. An increase in the volume of output is expected to lead to declines in the use of inputs, especially labour inputs or raw materials, which is different from economies of scale. As a proxy for a direct measure of learning-by-doing, the age of the establishment was employed. Age was introduced in two different forms:

AGE 1   the age of the establishment as of 1975

DAGE 2 a dummy variable = 1 for establishments established
in or after 1966
and = 0 for establishments before 1966.

The older establishments are expected to be more efficient. To investigate regional differences, we introduced

DREGION   a dummy variable = 1 for establishments in
Greater Accra and = 0 otherwise.

Establishments in Greater Accra are expected to be less efficient than those in the other regions.

In summary, the regression model estimated is of the form:

$$XFij = \beta_0 + \sum \beta_i X_i + \sum \gamma_k Y_k + U$$

where XFij are the efficiency indices (j = 1,2) for establishments (i = 1, . . . ,375,) β_0 is a constant, β_i denotes the coefficients of X_i (i=1, . . . ,m) describing the competitive environment, γ_k denotes the coefficients of Y_k variable (1, . . . ,n) describing the other independent variables; and U is the error term. All the dependent variables were transformed into logs, as well as all the independent variables with the exception of the dummy variables and RMATFRATIO, EFFEPROTECT 1, and EFFEPROTECT 2. We have resorted to additive formulations of all the competitive variables because of the unavailability of a single index to describe the competitive environments. Table 8.2 displays a summary of the definitions of the variables used in the regression analysis as well as their means and standard deviations in parentheses respectively. The regression analysis proceeded in two stages. To demonstrate the significance of each of the explanatory variables from

Table 8.2, the relationship between XFij and each regressor is undertaken by means of simple regression. In the second stage, the regressors whose coefficients are equal to or greater than their standard errors (t – ratios >1) are used in further investigation in a multiple regression analysis.

Table 8.2: Regressors Employed in the Empirical Analysis with Means and Standard Deviation in Parentheses

Variable Name	Variable Description
CR2	The share in 3-digit industries' sales of the two largest establishments (49.960, 19.194).
CR4	The share in 3-digit industries' sales of the four largest establishments (70.004, 17.630).
RELATESIZE	The ratio of establishment's sales to total 3-digit industry sales (5.8521, 12.790).
SIZE	Absolute size measured by number of persons engaged (152.9, 315.2)
DSIZE1	= 1 for establishments with labour engaged less than 30 persons (0.2560, 0.4370)
DSIZE2	= 1 for establishments with labour engaged greater than 100 persons (0.3093, 0.4628) and 0 otherwise.
IMPCOMP	Value of competing imports as a percentage of domestic supply (29.862, 24.941).
EFFEPROTECT1	Effective rates of protection on the basis of quota restrictions (QRS) (437.3, 9833.9)
EFFEPROTECT2	Effective rates of protection on the basis of the tariff systems (1374.3, 9833.9)
DEXPT	= 1 if and establishment exports 10% or more of its sales produce (0.0933, 0.2913) and = 0 otherwise.
RMATFRATIO	The ratio of foreign material imports to total material input (0.5868, 0.5162)
ABSKREQS	Absolute capital requirements measured by book value of total fixed assets per employee (2.7049, 3.603)
DNAT1	=1 if the establishment is wholly foreign-owned (0.3360, 0.4730) and = 0 otherwise.
DNAT2	= 1 if establishment is jointly-owned by foreigners and Ghanaians (0.1867, 0.3902) and = otherwise.
DMANAG	=1 if establishment is owner-managed and = 0 if non-owner-managed (0.5440, 0.4987)

Table 8.2 *(cont'd.)*

Variable Name	Variable Description
DOWN	=1 if establishment is private-owned and = 0 if it is state-owned (0.8773, 0.3902) and = 0 otherwise.
DPROCESS	=1 if an establishment is a chemical or process related industry (0.2053, 0.4045) and 0 otherwise.
AGE1	The age of the establishment as at 1975 (12.440, 8.9676).
DAGE2	=1 for establishments established in or after 1966 (0.5227, 0.5002) and = 0 for establishments before 1966.
DREGION	=1 for establishments in Greater Accra Region (0.6213, 0.4857) and = 0 otherwise

All the data used in the analysis with the exception of IMPCOMP and EFFEPROTECT have been obtained from the Central Bureau of Statistics (CBS) annual survey described in Section IV (b), and are for individual establishments. The data for IMPCOMP are derived from CBS, *Economic Surveys, Industrial Statistics and External Trade Statistics*, and are for 3-or 4-digit industry groups. EFFEPROTECT was taken from Leith (1974) and refer to the 1968 period. Concentration data is taken from Baah-Nuakoh (1997).

We first consider the statistical results for the efficiency index XF_r. The complete set of results for the simple regressions are presented in Table 8.3. The results show that six different indices of market imperfection – RELATSIZE, ABSKREQS, IMPCOMP, DEXPT, CR2 (CR4) and RMATFRATIO and seven other variables – DPROCESS, DAGE2, DNAT1, DNAT2, D MANAG, DENDUSE 1 and DENDUSE 2 satisfy the criterion that the regression coefficients are at least as large as the standard errors. Some of these variables showed wrong signs. Regressing XF_2 on the various independent variables, we obtained the results in Table 8.4. The results show that RELATSIZE, DEXPT, CR2, RMATFRATIO, DSIZE 1 and DSIZE 2 meet our criteria among the competition variables, while DPROCESS, DENDUSE2 and AGE1, DOWN DMANAG, and DNAT2 among the other group of variables also satisfy the criterion. All these variables with the exception of concentration and DEXPT variables are of the correct sign.

Table 8.3: Regression of XF$_1$ on Various Independent Variables

Expected Effect	Independent Variables	Constant Term	Regression Coefficient	t-Statistic	Multiple Correlation Coefficient
-	CR2	-0.6223	-0.1181	1.198	0.062
-	CR4	-0.3941	-0.1615	1.067	0.055
-	RELATESIZE	-1.1052	0.1237	5.493	0.274
-	SIZE	1.1785	0.0293	0.763	0.125
+	DSIZE1 ⎫	-1.0516	-0.1364	1.272	0.089
-	DSIZE2 ⎭		0.0600	0.592	
+	IMPCOMP	-1.9667	-0.0409	1.541	0.080
-	EFFEPROTECT1	-1.0802	0.0430*	0.968	0.050
-	EFFEPROTECT2	-1.1000	0.0430*	0.975	0.052
+	DEXPT	-1.0898	0.1693	1.136	0.059
-	RMATFRATIO	-1.1849	0.1890	2.259	0.116
-	ABSKREQS	-1.0436	-0.0893	2.527	0.130
+	DNAT1 ⎫	-1.1740	0.1563	1.607	0.121
+	DNAT2 ⎭		0.2546	2.160	0.055
+	DMANAG	-1.0240	-0.0920	1.057	
+	DOWN	-1.0985	0.0176	0.133	0.007
?	DENDUSE1 ⎫	-1.1870	0.2027	2.160	0.128
?	DENDUSE2 ⎭		0.2399	1.859	
+	DPROCESS	-1.1105	0.1071	1.657	0.085
+	AGE1	-1.1864	0.0483	0.704	0.036
-	DAGE2	-1.0215	-0.1005	1.158	0.060
-	DREGION	-1.0576	-0.0508	0.568	0.029

Notes. All variables in logs except dummies, RMATFRATIO, EFFEPROTECT 1, EFFEPROTECT 2.
 * The coefficient has been multiplied by 10^{-4}.

The results of the simple regression analysis have to be treated cautiously since they have not allowed for interactions among explanatory variables, and thus do not show whether the variables have independent influences once the variables are included simultaneously. An attempt was made to use multiple regression analysis, which would enable the effects of a few important variables to be considered simultaneously.

As expected, multicollinearity presented problems, tending to provide insignificant results and also change the signs of some coefficients when the independent variables are included in a single equation. As usual little could be done to get around the problem. Deleting some of the collinear variables would change the model and the empirical work would not serve the prime function of being

Table 8.4: Regression of XF$_2$ on Various Independent Variables

Expected Effect	Independent Variables	Constant Term	Regression Coefficient	t-Statistic	Multiple Correlation Coefficient
+	CR2	3.5937	−0.4327	2.515	0.129
+	CR4	3.0129	−0.2550	0.960	0.059
+	RELATESIZE	1.8999	0.1550	3.845	0.195
+	SIZE	0.8046	0.2721	4.108	0.224
−	DSIZE1 ⎤	1.9821	−0.4967	2.679	0.196
+	DSIZE2 ⎦		0.2718	1.552	
−	IMPCOMP	2.0513	−0.0428	0.917	0.047
+	EFFEPROTECT1	1.9365	0.0170*	0.222	0.011
+	EFFEPROTECT2	1.9364	0.0180*	0.237	0.012
−	DEXPT	1.9039	0.3763	1.439	0.074
+	RMATFRATIO	1.6296	0.5272	3.626	0.185
+	DNAT1 ⎤	1.9091	−0.0816	0.476	0.093
+	DNAT2 ⎦		0.3066	1.477	
−	DMANAG	2.0248	−0.1577	1.031	0.053
−	DOWN	2.3909	−0.5151	2.231	0.115
+	DENDUSE1 ⎤	1.8205	0.1591	0.961	0.091
+	DENDUSE2 ⎦		0.3916	1.721	
+	DPROCESS	1.7935	0.7085	3.826	0.194
−	AGE1	2.8318	0.3838	3.226	0.165
+	DAGE2	1.6753	0.5098	3.390	0.173
+	DREGION	1.8960	0.0692	0.440	0.023

Notes. Same as for Table 8.3.

a test of the theories. This cautionary comment is included prior to a presentation of the empirical results. A fuller idea of the multi-collinearity problems is given by the correlation matrix of the competitive variables given in the Table 8.5. The first column of the table shows the correlation between two-firm concentration and the other competing variables. The table shows significant correlation between concentration, import competing, relative size and DEXPT. The two concentration variables are highly correlated.

The RELATSIZE and SIZE variables are also correlated; however, their relationship with concentration is puzzling. The fact that SIZE is insignificant and RELATSIZE strongly related to concentration may be spurious. The entry barriers RMATFRATIO and ABSKREQS are significantly correlated. With all these relationships in mind, we examine the results of the multiple regression analysis. Tables 8.6 and 8.7 set out some of the results obtained. The overall explanatory power of our model is low but not extra-ordinary for a cross section analysis. There are obviously some measurement errors in our data base, and these have the effect of lowering both R^2s and t-values.

On the whole, the regressions show that the variables designating product market imperfection are significant factors in explaining the variations across establishments in efficiency. The findings suggest that large establishments tended to get closer to the efficiency frontier than the small establishments but deviate more significantly from the optimal technology, that is using technology which is inappropriate to the country's factor endowment. A question that might arise is whether the greater closeness of larger establishments to the efficiency frontier reflects genuine efficiency considerations or a stochastic error in measurement.

The RELATSIZE indicator measured by an establishment's share in total industry sales can be used as an indicator of market share. The regression results imply that the more efficient establishments tend to possess larger market shares of total market than the less efficient establishments.

Establishments with higher RMATFRATIO tend to be more technically efficient. Were these the establishments with ABSKREQS as barrier to entry? Establishments enjoying absolute capital requirements barrier tend to be less technically efficient.

Concentration is insignificant in the XF_1 regressions, and in the XF_2 regressions where it is significant it has a positive sign which

Table 8.5: Matrix of Simple Correlation Coefficients among the Competition Variables

	CR2	CR4	EFFE-PROTECT	EFFE-PROTECT2	DEXPT	RELATE-SIZE	SIZE	IMP COMP	ABSQ REQS	RMATF RATIO
CR2	1.000									
CR4	0.936*	1.000								
EFFEPROTECT1	0.129	0.089	1.000							
EFFEPROTECT2	0.127	0.086	0.996*	1.000						
DEXPT	-0.325*	-0.398	0.027	0.029	1.000					
RELATESIZE	0.289*	0.261*	0.052	0.051	0.012	1.000				
SIZE	-0.112	-0.034	0.036	0.037	0.099	0.381*	1.000			
IMPCOMP	0.391*	0.478*	0.176*	0.183*	-0.248*	0.152*	-0.101	1.00		
ABSKREQ	0.023	0.061	-0.028	-0.026	0.023	0.186*	0.081	0.09	1.00	
RMATFRATIO	0.179*	0.226*	0.038	0.039	-0.109	0.112	0.059	0.29	0.23	1.00

* Coefficients significantly different from zero at 5% or higher level.

Table 8.6: Estimated Equations for XF$_1$ (t-Statistic in Parethesis)

Independent Variable	(1)	(2)	(3)
CR2	–0.1118 (0.9431)	–0.0750 (0.630)	–0.029 (0.202)
RELATESIZE	0.1474 (6.2714)*	0.146 (6.247)*	0.136 (5.695)*
IMPCOMP	–0.0411 (1.2737)*	–0.070 (2.001)*	–0.083 (2.193)*
DEXPT	–0.0473 (0.2981)	–0.063 (0.398)	–0.077 (0.475)
RMATFRATIO			0.176 (2.027)
ABSKREQS	–0.1509 (4.3190)*	–0.154 (4.424)*	–0.159 (4.577)*
DNAT1	0.0850 (0.9075)	0.059 (0.625)	0.055 (0.580)
DNAT2	0.1951 (1.6913)*	0.158 (1.359)	0.156 (1.341)
DENDUSE1			0.097 (0.922)
DENDUSE2			0.107 (0.627)
DPROCESS		0.238 (2.106)*	0.145 (1.134)
CONSTANT	–0.5850	–0.680	–0.938
R^2	0.1370	0.1473	0.1594
F	8.3195* (7, 367)	7.9020* (8, 366)	6.2583* (11, 363)

implies that an establishment in a more concentrated industry tends to be less efficient in the sense that its capital-intensity tends to deviate from the optimal.

The foreign trade variables (IMPCOMP and DEXPT) fail to reach significance in most of the regressions. Nationality of ownership does not seem to be a significant determinant of X-efficiency in Ghanaian manufacturing.

Table 8.7: Estimated Equations for XF_2 (t-Statistic in Parentheses

Independent Variables	(1)	(2)	(3)	(4)	(5)
CR2	−0.541	−0.566	−0.596	−0.599	−0.693
	(2.537)*	(2.657)*	(2.936)*	(2.786)*	(2.725)*
RELATESIZE	0.165	0.151	0.166	0.166	0.153
	(4.045)*	(3.643)*	(4.012)*	(3.984)*	(3.553)*
IMPCOMP	0.022	0.023	0.030	0.029	-0.090
	(0.381)	(0.393)	(0.524)	(0.489)	(1.285)
DEXPT	0.040	0.065		−0.021	0.094
	(0.141)	(0.229)		(0.074)	(0.331)
RMATFRATIO					0.472
					(3.129)*
DNAT1			-0.231	-0.231	-0.271
			(1.355)*	(1.355)*	(1.634)*
DNAT2			0.156	0.158	0.005
			(0.755)	(0.758)	(0.023)
DOWN		-0.431			
		(1.868)*			
DMANAG					0.051
					(0.320)
DENDUSE1					-0.345
					(1.889)*
DENDUSE2					-0.553
					(1.860)*
DPROCESS					0.923
					(4.146)*
DAGE2					0.536
					(3.634)*
CONSTANT	3.905	4.378	4.146	4.163	4.308
R2	0.0609	0.0697	0.0697	0.0700	0.1726
F	5.9933	5.5250	5.5480	4.6120	0.1726
	(4, 370)	(5, 369)	(5, 368)	(6, 368)	(12, 362)

Our results do not support the contention that foreignowned firms choose less appropriate technology and are more efficient than domestically-owned firms. Foreignness does not significantly influence x-efficiency, although the jointly-owned establishments seem to be more technically efficient than solely domestically-owned establishments.

Contrary to the prediction of McCain (1975), the DMANAG variable was not significant in the X-efficiency regression and thus the null hypothesis that there is no difference between X-efficiency of owner-managed and non-owner-managed establishments cannot be rejected. Thus McCain's reference to the self-employed as operating with perfect x-efficiency is not supported by the data.

The question of the relative x-efficiency of public enterprises is tested by the DOWN variable. It is usually argued that public enterprises are inefficient operators due to lack of market discipline and government interference. We cannot reject the null hypothesis that there is no difference in the x-efficiency of public enterprises and private enterprises. What seems clear is that the deviation of technology of public enterprises from the optimal technology exceeds the deviation from the privately-owned enterprises.

DENDUSE variables are not significant in the XF_1 regressions but are negatively and strongly related to XE. DAGE2 shows a positive association with XF_2. Thus newer establishments deviate from labour-intensive and efficient technology. This finding conflicts with the hypothesis that older establishments should be more capital intensive, because of their easier access to capital and import licences.

Conclusion

This chapter has attempted to derive efficiency frontiers for Ghanaian manufacturing industries, and has developed and tested a variety of hypotheses about the effects of imperfect market structure on efficiency. Estimates of x-efficiency indicate that there exist a large number of inefficient establishments.

The prevalence of x-inefficient behaviour among Ghanaian establishments may be attributed to the following factors:

(i) problems of raw materials for establishments which depend on imported inputs and thus tend to create inefficiencies;

(ii) smallness is a problem with respect to inefficiency; for

larger establishments tend to be closer to the efficiency
frontiers;

(iii)   establishments which enjoy absolute capital advantages tend
        to be less technically efficient;

(iv)   establishments in concentrated industries tend to use
        technologies which deviate from optimal efficient labour-
        intensive technologies.

NOTES

1. See, for example, Timmer (1970), Shapiro and Muller (1977) Page Jr. (1980).
2. The non-competitive market structures have been discussed in Baah-Nuakoh
   (1982).
3. For each industry, two efficiency frontiers were constructed. Each point on
   the graph represents a different establishment within the industry, and all
   the establishments are producing the same quantity of value added. The
   first frontier derived represents the theoretical definition of efficiency frontier
   for establishments that may be considered as reasonably efficient; this is
   constructed to minimize biases due to measurement problems. Some of the
   industries such as footwear, electrical machinery, with only 10 observations
   may not give reasonable estimates; the miscellaneous category is a
   combination of unrelated industry groups; we may also note that, some of
   the industry groups such as ISIC 341/342 are not completely homogeneous.
4. To compute the efficiency indices, I have used an efficiency zone and not an
   efficiency frontier as a point of reference, that is, a thick isoquant which
   covers the area between efficiency frontiers 1 and 2. Then an efficiency
   index XF_1 for an establishment is obtained by comparing the distance from
   the origin with that of a hypothetical establishment on the frontier which is
   located on the same ray from the origin.
5. The use of CR4 did not improve the results and in most cases was statistically insignificant.

REFERENCES

Baah-Nuakoh, A. (1982), Elements of Ghanaian Industrial Market Structure, *Legon
      Economic Studies*, No. 8201, April.
Bain, Joe S. (1956). *Barriers to New Competition*, Cambridge, Harvard University
      Press.
Central Bureau of Statistics. *External Trade Statistics*, December, 1974.
Farrell, M. J. (1957). The Measurement of Productive Efficiency, *Journal of the Royal
      Statistical Society* (Series A), Vol. 120, Part 3, pp. 253–281.
Leibenstein, H. (1973). "Competition and Ex-Efficiency: Reply, " *Journal of Political
      Economy*, Vol. 81, May/June, No. 3, pp. 265–277.

Leibenstein, H. (1966) Allocative Efficiency vrs. X-Efficiency, *American Economic Review*, Vol. 56, June , pp. 392–415.

—— (1978) *General Ex-Efficiency Theory and Economic Development*, Oxford University Press, London.

Leith, J. C. (1974). *Foreign Trade Regimes and Economic Development*, National Bureau of Economic Research, New York.

McCain, R. A. (1975) Competition, Information, Redundancy, Ex-efficiency and the Cybernertics of the Firm, *Kyklos*, Vol. 28, No. 2, pp. 286–308.

Meller, P. (1976) "Efficiency Frontiers for Industrial Establishments of Different Sizes," *Explorations in Economic Research*, Vol. 3, No. 3 Summer, pp. 379–407.

Page, John M. Jr. (1980) "Technical Efficiency and Economic performance: Some Evidence from Ghana," *Oxford Economic Papers*, July, pp. 319–339.

Steel William F. (1977) *Small-Scale Employment and Production in Developing Countries: Evidence from Ghana*, Praeger Publishers, New York, London.

Tyler, William G. (1979) Technical Efficiency in Production in a Developing Country: An Empirical Examination of the Brazilian Plastics and Steel Industries, *Oxford Economic Papers*, Vol. 31 No. 3, November, pp. 477–4495.

White, L. J. (1974a) The General Problem of Industrial Concentration and Industrial Economic Power in less Developed Countries, *The Bangladesh Economic Review*, Vol. 11, No. 2, April, 19974, pp. 633–46.

—— (1974b) *Industrial Concentration and Economic Power in Pakistan*, Princeton, New Jersey, Princeton University Press.

—— (1976) Appropriate Technology X-Efficiency and a Competitive Environment: Some Evidence from Pakistan, *Quarterly Journal of Economics*, Vol. 90, November, pp.575.

Technology Choice in an Imperfect Competitive Framework: A Micro Cross-Section Analysis of Manufacturing Establishments

Introduction

This chapter attempts to test hypotheses which seek to identify the sources of inter-establishment differences in technology choice, specifically the role of imperfectly competitive environment. Empirical studies on technology choice in several developing economies have relied to a large extent on data aggregated to the industry level. While there may be advantages in using aggregated data, most of the decision-making on the type of technology to adopt and its operation are taken at the micro level; thus the possibility of biases associated with grouping of establishments into aggregated units suggests some disadvantages. Thus, a study based on micro data has a "comparative advantage" over that based on aggregate data.

An attempt is made here to analyse technology choice in Ghanaian manufacturing using individual establishment data belonging to 25 3-digit 1264 industries obtained through a survey conducted by the Central Bureau of Statistics and combined with other sources of information. The data pertains to the year 1974 and involves altogether 375 establishments discussed in Chapter 6.

This chapter takes the view that the problem of technology choice in developing economies is a structural disequilibrium problem emanating from the distortions in the product markets. During the post-independence industrialization period, the import substitution process in Ghana led to the creation of oligopolistic-monopolistic market structures and minimal competition. A wide range of industries were established, each dominated by a few firms.

The lack of competitive pressures creates inefficiency. If one of the pressures of monopoly is the "quiet life", the monopolist might not attain the technologically feasible minimum costs that competition might otherwise force on him (Leibenstein, 1966). With the quiet life the monopolist-oligopolist with market power may choose capital-intensive technologies that are inappropriate for a developing economy. Freed from the rigours of competition and cost minimization, a monopolist-oligopolist may include other variables in his objective function and choose a technology of high capital intensity.[1] To the foreign firm, this capital-intensive production technique may be closer to his domain of competence, and this could minimize his search costs for a more appropriate labour-intensive technology, and also freeing him from the difficulties of managing a large number of workers. To the indigenous firms, he may be defending an image of cultural competence in using high technology.[2]

The monopolist-oligopolists in developing economies continue to enjoy their power and create inefficiencies because of barriers to entry into various industries at the production and marketing stages. Four barriers are usually identified (Bain, 1956): (a) economies of scale; (b) control of scarce factors; (c) absolute capital requirements; and (d) product differentiation. Another barrier more relevant to developing economies emphasized by White (1974a, b) is the conglomeration of tariffs, licences, and sometimes outright bans on competing imports found in many developing countries. Most of these categories of barriers have been created by government policies: overvalued exchange rates with consequent foreign exchange licensing and rationing; capital goods, spare parts and raw materials being available to holders of scarce import licences at favourable exchange rates and low or zero tariffs. At the same time consumption goods are imported at unfavourable exchange rates and high tariffs. Thus, those who have had access to import licences have had highly profitable markets for which they could produce. The tariffs, quota and complete bans on finished goods provide a marketing barrier while licences create a scarce resource barrier.

It is argued in this chapter that entrepreneurs because of the oligopolistic-monopolistic positions and power that they enjoy are able to trade-off some of the potential benefits from cost minimization for inefficiency by adopting techniques of production which are capital-intensive. Both indigenous and foreign firms will operate in the capital-intensive set if they enjoy monopolistic-oligopolistic positions. The argument that foreign firms tend to use more capital-intensive

techniques in LDCs arise because they are more frequently in the
position of having oligopolistic power. Foreign firms generally prefer
to operate in industries which are more concentrated and where the
necessity to import technical know-how is relatively greater.

Attempts to relate competition in the product market to the
technology choice of firms in Ghana are not available. For developing economies in general only two major attempts [White (1976),
Lecraw (1979)] have been make formally to test the relationship between technology choice and the competitive environment. White in
a cross-section data for a sample of 31 industries found that greater
competition in Pakistani products forced industrialists to adopt more
labour-intensive methods relative to the United States "deal", and
industrialists in less competitive markets were freer to pursue their
engineering goals.

White set out specifically to test the hypothesis that entrepreneurs in more competitive environments are more likely to choose
more labour-intensive modes of production. He proposed the following function and estimated it in log-linear form:

$$P_{KL} = f [US_{KL}, PCON, EXPORT, PROCESS]$$

where P_{KL} represents the capital-labour ratio of Pakistan; PCON the
four-firm concentration ratio; EXPORT a dichotomous variable which
takes the value of unity if exports took 10 percent or more of any
industry's output in 1967/68, and zero otherwise, and this measures
the extent of involvement in international trade; US_{KL} the capital-
labour ratio in U.S. industries and PROCESS a dichotomous variable
to indicate whether an industry was a chemical or process related
industry. US_{KL} and PROCESS are "technology" variables while PCON
and EXPORT measure the competitive structure of Pakistani
industries. White found statistically significant relationships between
technology and combinations of the "technology" and "competitive
environment" variables.

Lecraw on the other hand, uses firm level data, and this is for
400 firms in light manufacturing sector of Thailand in an attempt to
offer a picture of factors that motivate firms in the same industry to
choose one technology over another using what he terms a "non-
neoclassical approach". Choice of technology by each firm was
measured from the production frontier, for each industry. Three
indices to measure the efficiency with which firm choose their
technology relative to the production isoquants and their factor prices

were constructed. The analysis relaxes the usual assumptions of profit maximization, risk neutrality and perfect information and considers the characteristics of the firms (management, ownership, experience, education, and projected profits from investment) and characteristics of industry (the number of firms) as the factors influencing the choice of technology. Competition variables in Lecraw's analysis include the number of firms within an industry, projected profits, and a dichotomous variable which takes the value of zero if the firm is market-oriented, that is, if the firm followed a strategy of product differentiation, branding, and had high advertising and selling costs, and the value of unity if the firm is production-oriented. The competition variables were found to influence the choice of technology significantly, and support the observation that lack of competitive pressure allows firms to choose inappropriate technology.

Other studies have also indicated the influence of the non-competitive environment on technology choice in developing economies. These include Meller (1976), Tyler (1979), Bergsman (1974) and Morley and Smith (1977). These studies have not analyzed in detail the nature of the market structure and power which gives rise to the inappropriateness of technology. This empirical gap on the nature of market structure and power may reflect the general nature of the neglect of the question of market structure in LDCs and the rudimentary state of industrial organization analyses. This neglect was emphasized by Leff (1979) who attributed this to the often held belief that in LDCs the emphasis should be on growth of output and not on market distortions.

We set up a general model to explain variations in technology choice between manufacturing establishments. Using multivariate regression analysis the effects of the non-competitive environment and other variable on technology choice are tested.

VARIABLES IN THE ANALYSIS

In this section the dependent variables and the factors that influence technology choice are briefly defined.

Technology Variables

For each establishment two different variables are employed to describe technology, which involve the use of book value of fixed assets and an energy measure per persons engaged.

Factors Explaining the Variance of Capital-Intensity

Our estimated equations include combinations of several independent variables. In addition to the variables representing the non-competitive environment, other factors which have some influence on technology choice are also considered. In the following sections we give a brief description of these variables, their *a priori* expectations and actual operationalizing in the empirical tests. The variables are grouped into oligopolistic and barriers to competition variables, managerial and organizational variable, technological variables and miscellaneous variables.

Variables indicating monopolistic-oligopolistic behaviour and barriers to competition

In order to implement quantitative tests with respect to these variables we had to quantify the indicators of non-competitive environment. However, there is generally no acceptable measure of competition or monopoly power. Thus, we had to rely on several complementary measures, bearing in mind the constraints on data availability – concentration ratio, relative and absolute firm size, effective protection, export ratio, import competing ratio, foreign raw material ratio.

    The first indicator that we consider is seller concentration which is the most generally used measure of the competitive structure of an industry and can be considered as shorthand expression, though an incomplete one, for the number and size distribution of suppliers. The assumption in the use of concentration is that the higher the degree of sellers' concentration, the lower is the degree of competition. The concentration term is expected to have a significantly positive effect on capital-intensity.

    In this study the concentration measure used is based on sales of the reporting establishments.

        CR2   the share in 3-digit industries sales
                  of the two largest establishments.

        CR3   the share in 3-digit industries sales
                  of the four largest establishments.

The individual establishments were adjoined to the respective 3-digit industry. It is true that the 3-digit classification cannot be considered to depict markets in an economically meaningful sense.

A second measure of competition is the establishment's relative and absolute size. Size may be taken as an index of an establishment's capacity to exercise dominance in its industry.

RELATSIZE   the ratio of establishment's sales to total 3-digit industry sales.

SIZE   the ratio of establishment's sales to total 3-digit industry sales.

Size should exert a positive influence on capital-intensity. Size was also introduced as dummy variables.

DSIZE 1 a dummy = 1 for establishments with persons engaged < 30, and= 0 otherwise.

DSIZE2 a dummy =1 for establishments with persons engaged >100, and= 0 otherwise.

The excluded category is 30–100 persons engaged size group.

The third dimension of monopolistic-oligopolistic power and barriers to competition included in our tests is the degree of foreign competition which provides a transmission mechanism for efficiency occurring in the world market and injects into the domestic market a set of competitors not counted in our conventional measures of concentration. In cases where industries face significant import competition, export a large portion of their output to markets which differ substantially from the domestic one, purely domestic elements of market structure will give an incomplete picture of competitive conditions in an industry. The degree of foreign competition was represented by three variables imports competition (IMPCOMP), effective protection (EFFEPROTECT), and export ratio (DEXPT).

IMPCOMP   value of competing imports from other countries as percentage of domestic supply (production plus imports minus exports).

The variable IMPCOMP measures the stringency of the import licensing system; by measuring the competitiveness of a market, imports should tend to reduce the completeness of tacit collusion among domestic sellers. Where there are competing imports capital-intensity may be low.

Effective protection rates (EFFEPROTECT) are introduced to define more precisely the oligopolistic environment in which domestic establishments operate. If effective protection rates are low, then domestic establishments will find themselves more exposed to foreign competition. Thus, there should be a positive relationship between capital-intensity and effective protection.

The extent of involvement of an establishment in the export market is measured by

DEXPT a dummy variable = 1 if an establishment exports
10% or more of its sales produce
and = 0 otherwise.

The variable DEXPT should have a negative relation to capital-intensity. Several scarce resources are rationed by the governments, resources such as capital, credit and foreign exchange. It is unfortunate, as one might expect, that the difficulty of finding out who gets what is immense. The practice for which it was possible to obtain data from the CBS survey was the importance of imported inputs in total material inputs. Thus, the extent of resource barrier is measured by using a surrogate variables:

RMATFRATIO the ratio of foreign materials to total material inputs.

Establishments which use a high proportion of imported raw materials are presumed to be the ones which get the scarce foreign exchange and thus, their monopolistic-oligopolistic powers are accentuated. Thus, these establishments should be expected to use more capital-intensive production methods.

Managerial and organizational variables

In order to examine the effects of the non-competitive environment on technology choice it is necessary to consider other explanatory variables as well. Some of the factors which we wish to consider capture differences in the characteristics of the product, others deal with the characteristics of the establishments and the internal organization or management practices.

Variables in this group describe the effects of differences in organization and management conditions in establishments which are related to technology choice. The following variables were considered: nationality of ownership, owner-management versus non-owner management, private versus state control.

There appears to be a controversy over the effects on nationality of ownership on technology in developing economies, but the conventional wisdom is that foreign firms use more capital-intensive technology than domestically-owned firms because of limited search behaviour and desire to use technology nearer to their domain of competence. We introduce nationality into the model by incorporating two variable:

> DNAT1   a dummy = 1 if the establishment is wholly foreign-
> owned
> and = 0 otherwise

> DNAT 2 a dummy = 1 if the establishment is jointly-owned
> by foreigners and domestic businessmen
> and =   0 otherwise

The excluded category is the wholly domestically-owned establishments. The effect of ownership-management was also tested. The owner-managed establishments should be less capital-intensive than non-owner-managed establishments. A variable to represent the ownership-management type was included:

> DMANAG a dummy variable = 1 if the establishment is
> owner managed
> and = 0 non-owner-managed

State-owned and controlled establishment, it is contended, are more capital-intensive than their private counterparts. This hypothesis was tested by incorporating:

> DOWN   a dummy variable = 1 if the establishment is
> privately-owned
> and = 0 if it is state-owned.

Technological variables

Three variables were included in the model designed more specifically to capture the inter-industry differences in the nature of production and the learning-by-doing effects. The use to which the product is put, whether consumer good, intermediate or producer goods is represented by

DENDUSE 1   a dummy variable = 1 if the establishment belongs to an intermediate goods industry
and = 0 otherwise

DENDUSE 2   a dummy variable = 1 if the establishment belongs to a producer goods industry
and = 0 otherwise.

The excluded category is the consumer goods industry. Consumption goods establishments are held to use less capital-intensive technology, though conflicting evidence has been found.[4]
A variable was employed to indicate whether an establishment was a chemical or process related; these kinds of establishments might be more rigid in their capital-labour requirements and less susceptible to labour substitution. This variable was introduced as:

DPROCESS   a dummy variable = 1 if the establishment is in a chemical or process related industry
and = 0 otherwise

An attempt was made to analyze the effects of the relative experience of establishments. As a proxy for a direct measure of learning-by-doing, the age of the establishment was employed. Age was introduced in two different forms:

AGE 1   the age of the establishment as of 1975

DAGE 2   a dummy variable = 1 for establishments established in/after 1966
and = 0 for establishments before 1966.

The older establishments are expected to be less capital-intensive. On the other hand, one may argue that the older establishments, with their contacts with the import licensing authorities could also obtain the scarce foreign exchange to expand capacity.

Miscellaneous variable

DREGION   a dummy variable = 1 for establishments in Greater
Accra Region
and = 0 otherwise

was introduced to investigate regional differences in capital-intensity. Establishments in Greater Accra should be more capital-intensive.

STATISTICAL TESTS AND RESULTS

Having discussed the independent variables that go into the specification of our model, the empirical form of the hypothesis is specified. The theory states that technology choice, represented by capital-intensity ($KINT_{ij}$) will be a function of market imperfection (competition) variables, organizational and managerial variables, technology variables, and miscellaneous variables. Both the linear and log-linear functional forms were assumed for empirical purposes. The log-linear transformation was used to reduce heteroscedasticity by compressing the scales in which the variables were expressed[5] We shall report the results for the log-linear form since they performed better than the linear regressions. The basic structural model is the following:

$$KINT_{ij} = \alpha_o + \Sigma\alpha_p X_p + \Sigma\phi_t T_t + \Sigma\beta_k Y_k + \psi MIS + U$$

where

α_o is a constant,

$\alpha_{p'}$ denotes the estimated coefficients of X_p variables (p = 1, . . . m) describing imperfect market structure

$\phi_{t'}$ coefficients of the T_t variables t = 1, . . . r) describing technological variables;

$\beta_{k'}$ coefficients of Y_k variables k = 1, . . . n) describing managerial and organizational variables;

ψ, the coefficient of the miscellaneous variable (*MIS*); and $KINT_{j'}$ technology measure type (j = 1, 2).

u error term

The equation forms the basic set of hypotheses concerning technology choice. We have resorted to additive formulation of all the competitive variables because of the unavailability of a single index to describe the imperfect market structure.

Our main statistical procedure was to employ ordinary least squares regression of the $KINT_j$ on the independent variables for a sample of 1974 cross-section data of 375 manufacturing establishments in Ghana. The analysis proceeded in two stages. To begin with, to demonstrate the significance of each member of the alternative set of hypotheses, the relationship between $KINT_j$ and each regression is undertaken by means of simple regression. In the second stage, the regressors whose coefficients are equal to or larger than its standard error (t-ratios ≥ 1) are accepted for further investigation in a multiple regression analysis.

Before reporting the results of our estimation some data problems must be pointed out. All the data used in the analysis with the exception of I COMP and EFFEPROTECT have been obtained from the CBS survey and for individual establishments. The data for IMPCOM and EFFEPROTECT had to be computed or taken from other sources and were for 3 or 4-digit industry categories. The establishments were then assigned to these 3 or 4-digit industries or industry groups.

Concentration series are based on the 1974 survey data and refer to 3-digit classification. It is true that the 3-digit category cannot be considered to depict markets in an economically meaningful sense. It can, however, be presumed that a certain degree of 3-digit concentration implies a similar degree of concentration in most higher digit industries making up a particular 3-digit industry. It must, however, be admitted that some degree of inaccuracy is introduced by using the 3-digit classification. Notwithstanding these problems, our results are of considerable interest and this is what we turn to next.

The complete set of results for the simple regressions are presented in Tables 9.1 and 9.2 which use total fixed assets per labour engaged and energy consumed per labour engaged as measures of capital-intensity respectively. The results show the importance of the market imperfection variables. For the KINT 1 regressions (Table 9.1), RELATSIZE, SIZE, IMPCOMP, and RMATRATIO seem to be the only variables among the competition variables which satisfy our criterion. Neither of our two measures of concentration seem to reveal any significance. The energy measure of capital per worker (Table 9.2) revealed that except for the protection measures all the competition variables are significant. The organizational variables as well as the technological variables met our criterion.

The results of the simple regression analysis have to be treated cautiously since they have not allowed for interactions among the explanatory variables, and thus do not show whether the variables have independent influences once the variables are included simultaneously. An attempt was made using multiple regression analysis which would enable the effects of a few important variables to be considered simultaneously.

Table 9.1: Regression of Kint1 (Fixed Assets per employee) Various Independent Variable

Expected Effect	Independent Variables	Constant term	Regression Coefficient	t-Statistic	Multiple Correlation Coefficient
+	CR2	0.3852	−0.0117	0.0816	0.0042
+	CR4	−0.3141	0.1554	0.7065	0.0366
+	RELATSIZE	0.2984	0.1669	5.0739	0.2541
+	SIZE	−0.7393	0.2603	4.7812	0.2493
−	DSIZE1	0.4451	−0.5133	3.3475	0.1986
+	DSIZE2		−0.0862	0.5972	
-	IMPCOMP	0.1693	0.0652	1.6920	0.0873
+	EFFEPROTECT	10.3378	0.018[a]	0.2760	0.0143
+	EFFEPROTECT2	0.3375	0.021[a]	0.3289	0.0170
−	EXPT	1.3227	0.8737	0.1893	0.0452
+	RMATFRATIO	0.1344	0.3511	2.9008	0.1485
+	DNAT1	0.1788	0.1790	1.2757	0.1636
+	DNAT2		0.5433	3.1933	
−	DMANAG	0.5039	−0.3006	2.3908	0.1636
-	DOWN	0.9162	−0.6564	3.4673	0.1767
+	DENDUSE1	0.2148	0.1792	1.3119	0.1170
+	DENDUSE2		0.3868	2.0567	
+	DPROCESS	0.2695	0.3455	2.2267	0.1145
?	AGE1	1.4152	−0.4620	4.7679	0.2397
?	DAGE2	0.0752	0.5073	4.1060	0.2080
+	DREGION	0.1366	0.3280	2.5436	0.1306

Notes: All variables in logs except dummies, RMATFRATIO, EFFEPROTECT 1, EFFEPROTECT 2.
[a]The coefficient has been multiplied by 10^4.

**Table 9.2: Regression of KINT1 (Fixed Assets per employee)
Various Independent Variables**

Expected Effect	Independent Variables	Constant term	Regression Coefficient	t- Statistic	Multiple Correlation Coefficient
+	CR2	−0.1194	−0.5880	4.261	0.215
+	CR4	1.2914	−0.8689	4.100	0.208
+	RELATSIZE	2.3893	−0.0858	2.586	0.208
+	SIZE	−3.2606	0.2131	3.953	0.225
−	DSIZE1	−2.4250	−0.2020	1.333	0.177
+	DSIZE2		0.3524	2.463	
−	IMPCOMP	−2.0626	−0.1163	3.094	0.158
+	EFFEPROTECT1	−2.3713	0.025[a]	0.395	0.020
+	EFFEPROTECT2	−2.3719	0.030[a]	0.480	0.025
−	DEXPT	−2.4804	1.2079	5.918	0.293
+	RMATFRATIO	−2.2563	−0.1899	1.582	0.082
+	DNAT1	0.6260	0.4709	3.451	0.224
+	DNAT2		−2.6428	3.784	
−	DMANAG	−2.0838	−0.5220	4.289	0.217
−	DOWN	−1.9779	−0.4443	2.365	0.122
+	DENDUSE1	−2.5440	0.3576	2.669	0.141
+	DENDUSE2		0.2656	1.442	
+	DPROCESS	−2.3645	0.0155	0.101	0.005
?	1 AGE	−2.0000	−0.1580	1.614	0.083
?	DAGE2	−2.4276	−0.1145	0.048	0.922
+	DREGION	−2.2191	0.2391	−1.877	0.097

Notes: Same as Table 9.1.

As expected, multicollinearity presented a serious problem, tending to provide insignificant results and also change the sign of some coefficients when the independent variables are included in a single equation.

Little could be done to get around the problem. Deleting some of the collinear problems would change the model and the empirical work would not serve the prime function of being a test of the theories. Thus, cautionary comment is included prior to a presentation of the empirical results. The results are given in Tables 9.3 and 9.4.

Although many of the empirical findings are significant and consistent with our theoretical predictions, the overall explanatory power of our model is obviously low but not extraordinary for a

Table 9.3: Estimated Equations for Capital-Intensity (Fixed Assets Measure of capital)

Independent Variables	Dependent Variables	
	KINTI	
	(1)	(2)
CR2	-0.2361	-0.2799
	(1.3478)	(1.3051)
RELATSIZE	0.1599	0.115
	(4.7775)*	(3.156)*
IMPCOMP	0.0930	0.0334
	(1.9412)*	(0.5620)
DEXPT	0.1885	0.2130
	(0.8011)	(0.892)
RMATFRATIO		0.224
		(1.789)*
GNAT1		0.120
		(0.840)
GNAT2		0.177
		(1.026)
DMANAG		-0.021
		(0.149)
DENDUSE1		0.122
		(0.877)
DENDUSE2		-0.103
		(0.434)
AGE1		-0.391
		(4.050)*
DOWN		-0.748
		(2.322)*
DREGIION		0.260
		(1.731)*
Constant	0.9412	2.218
R_2	0.075	0.159
F	7.5154	5.262
	(4, 370)	(13, 361)

Table 9.4: Estimated Equation for Capital-Intensity (Energy Measure of Capital)

Independent Variables	Dependent Variable (KINT 4)				
	(1)	(2)	(3)	(4)	(5)
CR2	-0.389*	-0.369*	-0.361	-0.375*	-0.311
	(2.306)	(2.206)	(2.155)	(2.215)	(1.500)
RELATSIZE	0.084*	0.063*	0.055*	0.063*	0.026
	(2.605)	(1.922)	(1.704)	(1.921)	(0.733)
IMPCOMP	0.001	0.003	-0.014	0.007	-0.014
	(0.023)	(0.062)	(0.300)	(0.144)	(0.248)
DEXPT	0.949*	0.906*	0.909*	0.909*	3.903*
	(4.191)	(4.042)	(4.051)	(4.044)	(3.903)
RMATFRATIO		-0.160		-0.155	-0.150
		(1.328)		(1.268)	(1.244)
DENDUSE1					0.081
					(0.601)
DENDUSE2					0.015
					(0.067
DOWN					-0.459*
					(2.309)
DMANAG					-0.241*
					(1.766)
DNAT1		0.472*	0.432*	0.432*	0.513*
		(3.224)	(3.253)	(3.222)	(3.722)
DNAT2		0.529*	0.527*	0.536*	0.380*
		(3.265)	(3.249)	(3.258)	(2.280)
AGE1					-0.168*
					(1.780)
DREGION					0.014
					(0.096)
DPROCESS					-0.040
					(0.243)
Constant	-0.993	-1.213	-1.296	-1.200	-0.506
R_2	0.115	0.155	0.151	0.155	0.190
F	12.040*	9.962*	10.920*	8.141*	6.548*
	(4, 370)	(7, 367)	(6, 368)	(7, 367)	(13, 361)

cross section analysis. Notwithstanding any assurances that may be given about the quality of the data, there are obviously some measurement errors in our data base, and these have the effect of lowering both R^2s and t-values.

It should be noted that industrial organization theory is primarily concerned with explaining differences in the behaviour among industries; thus, these studies use average data for all firms in an industry. Since our analysis uses data at the establishment level, the level of statistical significance would probably be lower than had industry data been used. Another interpretation problem concerns incomplete specification. The omitted dimensions of the cost vector (e.g., cost of labour) has the effect of imparting a positive bias to coefficients, that is, of biasing them towards zero. Thus, there are reasons to believe that our empirical results understate both the explanatory power of the model and the significance of the variables. However, we are consoled somewhat by the observation that the problems we have noted tend to bias our coefficients towards zero, thus increasing our confidence in the non-zero coefficients obtained. Finally, we should also note that our use of data on individual establishments helps us to avoid the biases that have affected cross-section studies that use industry aggregates as the units of observation.

On the whole, the regression show that competition variables are significant factors explaining the variations across establishments in technology choice RELATSIZE and RMATFRATIO are significant in most of the regressions.

The findings suggest that larger establishments are more capital-intensive than smaller establishments confirming Steel's [1977] finding for 1973. Our RELATSIZE indicator measured by an establishment's share in total industry sales can also be used as an indicator of market share. The regression results imply that the more capital-intensive establishments tend to possess larger shares of total market than the less capital-intensive establishments. RMATFRATIO shows a significantly positive relationship indicating that establishments, which had access to the scarce foreign exchange, chose to install capital-intensive technology, because import licence allocation was related to installed capacity. Thus there was an incentive to create excess capacity.

Concentration turns out to be significant but of the wrong sign. In general, concentration does not seem to be a successful indicator of market power in Ghana. A positive association is revealed[6]. The interpretation of this is that in a small open economy like Ghana the concentrations may not reflect the degree of market power exercised by the largest firms/establishments, but economies of scale and specialization, and the variable should be abandoned in its present form. For in Ghana open collusion was hardly forbidden and in the brewery industries, co-ordination for price setting was permitted through the Prices and Incomes Board. Thus, we should look at other variables to represent competition, especially import licensing data.

The foreign trade variables (IMPCOMP and DEXPORT) fail to reach significance in most of the regressions or are of the wrong sign. For example, DEXPORT is significant only in the energy measures of capital-intensity and are positively signed. The export industries tend to be capital-intensive, utilizing energy more intensively. A typical example is VALCO consuming about 65 percent of Akosombo Dam's power capacity. Because of cheap electricity input, at below world market price, VALCO could compete in international markets by using a less appropriate technology.

Nationality of ownership does not seem to be a significant determinant of technology choice in Ghanaian manufacturing. Our results do not support the contention that foreign-owned firms choose less appropriate technology than domestically-owned firms. It is in the energy measure of technology regressions that DNAT 1 and DNAT 2 seem to suggest some importance for nationality, that is, both the foreign-owned firms and the jointly-owned firms use more capital intensive production methods than solely-domestically-owned firms. The different results revealed by the fixed assets measure of capital-intensity and energy measure with respect to their relationship with ownership structure may reflect utilization of capacity by the different ownership categories, implying that foreign-owned establishment utilize their capacity more intensively than indigenous establishments. Another explanation may be that the foreign establishments are concentrated in industries, which use energy more intensively.

Owner-managed establishments are found to be less capital-intensive than non-owner-managed establishments. The DOWN variable tests the relative capital-intensiveness of public enterprises. Public enterprises, from our analysis, do appear to be more capital-intensive than privately-owned enterprises.

An important variable in our analysis is AGE. As the establishments increase in age, they become less capital-intensive. The newer establishments are more capital-intensive and thus, the results go contrary to the hypothesis that older establishments should be more capital-intensive because of their earlier access to capital and import licences. Our finding might be spurious and may be due to the fact that the book values of capital of the older establishments do not reflect the true value of capital in use, capital value being under-estimated because of accelerated depreciation policies.

Conclusion

This chapter has sought to analyze technology choice in an imper-fectly competitive environment. The analysis is conducted through the specification and testing of a generalized model which incorpo-rates various indicators of market structure drawing on the work from industrial organizations, and other important determinants of technology choice.

Due to econometric difficulties, the individual magnitudes of the impact of the variables considered should be viewed with caution. In spite of the difficulties and limitations of the analysis some of the variables proposed to capture the product market imperfection proved correctly signed and significant but the null hypothesis was accepted in certain cases. Concentration which is usually used to measure market power does not seem to have the anticipated effects. The hypothesis that there is a positive relationship between concentration and capital-intensity is not supported by our data. Thus, in the Ghanaian situation, concentration might not reflect market power. Barriers to entry, such as size and scarce resources of foreign exchange seem to be the most effective indicators of market power.

Given the importance of the non-competitive product market as well as factor market structure in the determination of technology choice, policies should not only be limited to relieving factor price distortion but instead general policies which will affect the factor and product market structures should be considered.

NOTES

1. See, for example, Wells (1973). White (1974a, b, 19776, 1978).
2. The effects of distorted input prices on the costs and opportunities for indulging in non-economic preference has been pointed out recently in

Winston [1979] which describes the way a group of Nigerian firms choose production techniques.
3. Effective protection was introduced in two ways: EFFEPROTECT 1 based on quota restrictions, and EFFEPROTECT 2 based on the tariff.
4. For example, see Sutton (1976) for British industry and Mabro and Radwan (1976) for Egyptian industry.
5. The only exceptions were EFFEPROTECT variables and RMATFRATIO because some of the establishments had negative or zero values for these variables.
6. The use of CR4 did not improve the results and in most cases was statistically insignificant.

REFERENCES

Bain, Joe S. (1956) *Barriers to New Competition*, Cambridge: Harvard University Press.

Bergsman, J. (1974) "Commercial Policy, Allocative Efficiency and X-Efficiency," *Quarterly Journal of Economics*, Vol. 88, August, pp. 409–433.

Lecraw, Donald J. (1979) "Choice of Technology in Low-Wage Countries: A Non-Neoclassical Approach," *The Quarterly Journal of Economics*, Vol. XCIII, No. 4, November, pp. 631–54.

Leff, Nathaniel H. (1978) "Industrial organization and Entrepreneurship; in the Developing Countries: the Economic Groups," *Economic Development and Cultural Change*, Vol. 26, July, No. 4, pp. 66–676.

—— (1979) "Monopoly Capitalism and Public Policy in Developing Countries," *Kyklos* Vol. 32 Fasc. 4, pp. 718–38.

Leibenstein, H. (1966) "Allocative Efficiency vrs. X-Efficiency," *American Economic Review*, Vol. 56, June, pp. 392–415.

Mabro, R. and Samir Radwan (1976) *The Industrialization of Egypt, 1939–1973: Policy and Performance*, Oxford University Press, London.

McCain, R. A. (1975) "Competition, Information, Redundancy, X-Efficiency and the Cybernetics of the Firm," *Kyklos*, Vol. 28, pp. 286–308.

Meller, P. (1976) "Efficiency Frontiers for Industrial Establishments of Different Sizes," *Explorations in Economic Research*, Vol. 3, No. 3, summer, pp. 379–407.

Morley, S. A. and G. Smith (1977) "Search and the Technological Choices of Multinational Firms in Brazil," *Quarterly Journal of Economics*, Vol. XCI, No. 2, May, pp. 263–87.

Sutton, J. (1976) "The Relative Factor Intensities of Investment and Consumer Goods Industries: A Note," *Econometrica*, Vol. 44, No. 4, July, pp. 819–21.

Tyler, William G. (1979) "Technical Efficiency in Production in a Developing Country: An Empirical Examination of the Brazillian Plastics and Steel Industries," *Oxford Economic Papers*, Vol. 31, No. 3, November, pp. 477–495.

Wells, Jr. Louis T. (1973) "Economic Man and Engineering Man: Choice and Technology in a Low-Wage Country," *Public Policy*, Vol. 21, Summer, pp. 319–42.

White, L. J. (1974a) "The General Problem of Industrial Concentration and Industrial Economic Power in Less Developed Countries," *The Bangladesh Economic Review*, Vol. 11, No. 2, April 1974, pp. 633–46.

—— (1976) *Industrial Concentration and Economic Power in Pakistan*, Princeton, New Jersey, Princeton University Press.

—— (1976) "Appropriate Technology, X-Inefficiency and a Competitive Environment: Some Evidence from Pakistan," *Quarterly Journal of Economics*, Vol. 90, November, pp. 575–85.

—— (1978) "The Evidence on Appropriate Factor Proportions for Manufacturing in Less Developed Countries: A Survey," *Economic Development and Cultural Change*, Vol. 27, No. 1, October, pp. 27–60.

Winston, Gordon C. (1979) "The Appeal of Inappropriate Technologies: Self-Inflicted Wages, Ethnic Pride and Corruption," *World Development*, Vol. 7, No. 8/9, August-September, pp. 835–46.